FINITE

FOODIE

THE FINITE FOODIE COOKBOOK

A Practical Guide for Aspiring Cooks
with Limited Resources and No Experience

Bobbi Mullins with Rebecca Huron and Gregory Ellson

HME PUBLISHING   RALEIGH, NC

Requests for permission to make copies of any part of the work should be submitted to the publisher at www.finitefoodie.com.

Design and production by Julie Allred, BW&A Books

ISBN: 978-0-9997428-0-8

Library of Congress Control Number: 2018903972

First printing, August 2018

Printed in the United States of America

CONTENTS

PREFACE

If you had told us ten years ago that we would be coming together as a family to write a cookbook, we would not have believed you. It still sounds crazy! The journey has been long and challenging, but also exhilarating. Together, we have eaten a great deal of delicious food. We have pushed ourselves in new ways and have grown closer as a family because of it.

Healthy, wholesome foods have always been important for our family. This emphasis began during my childhood in Texas. Fruit and pecan trees dotted our property, blackberry bushes lined the fence, grapes dangled from my grandmother's arbor, and a vegetable patch provided fresh seasonal produce. As a child, my snacks did not come out of a box, but were picked fresh off the vine or tree.

Once I had children, these memories inspired me to focus on nutrition with my own family. As the kids got older, they too began to develop a greater interest in good food. Rebecca enjoyed cooking at an early age, and she continued to enhance her culinary skills throughout her high school years. At the age of sixteen, she planned and prepared a three-course meal for fifty people at a church fundraiser. It was so successful that she was asked to do a repeat performance the following year. She was even hired by a guest at one of the dinners to cater an engagement party for seventy-five people! Greg, on the other hand, had always been content to eat, rather than prepare meals. Why cook if you have a mother and sister who would do it for you? Fortunately, he was never a picky eater, and he enthusiastically ate any type of food we made—the more unusual the better.

When Rebecca and Greg went to their respective colleges, they weren't very impressed with the cafeterias. As soon as they were able, they moved off campus where they could have a kitchen of their own. Rebecca made the decision to follow a gluten-free and vegetarian diet, which was not easy to do on a tight budget. It required careful planning. Greg also recognized the value of preparing his own meals. In fact, he sparked the original idea by posting pictures of his culinary creations in a Facebook album called "College Kids Can Eat Well Too." As Rebecca and Greg began to cook for themselves, the phone calls started pouring in asking about recommendations for the most useful kitchen equipment to buy, creative ideas for using their limited resources, and inexpensive recipes to add to their repertoires.

Once Rebecca and Greg graduated from college, we decided it was the right time to begin compiling our long-discussed cookbook. The process was not easy and came with a number of challenges. My husband and I moved from New York to North Carolina. Rebecca got married, moved from California to Oklahoma, received an MBA, had a baby, and most recently moved to Philadelphia where her husband, Nick, is pursuing a PhD. Greg moved to Texas, obtained his PhD, then got a job in Boston. Throughout it all, we continued to plug away, and now after years of hard work, countless hours in the kitchen, and innumerable edits, we have completed our project at last!

Visit our website, finitefoodie.com, for more ideas and recipes that complement the cookbook.

Thank you for supporting us.

Bobbi Mullins with Rebecca Huron and Gregory Ellson

CHAPTER 1

INTRODUCTION

In today's world, with a seemingly infinite number of online recipes and a vast array of cookbooks, the whole idea of preparing your own meals can feel overwhelming. So what makes *The Finite Foodie Cookbook* unique? We believe that anyone can easily prepare healthful, nutritious food, even with very limited resources and little to no previous experience. Our cookbook will show you how.

What this book is:

It is a good starting point for beginners, but will also build a strong culinary foundation for accomplishing more advanced recipes. We provide clear steps for setting up your kitchen with the most useful items. Our recipes are simple, inexpensive, and focused on wholesome ingredients, perfect for everyday meals. Most recipes offer one or more variations to keep things interesting. We furnish tips for meal planning, shopping, and properly storing your food. This book also includes notes on healthy eating habits, definitions of cooking terminology, and explanations of key cooking techniques.

What this book is not:

It is not a collection of complicated, unrealistic recipes. Instructions do not assume you have a degree in the culinary arts. We do not provide recipes that are unhealthy or lacking in nutritional value. Our cookbook is not designed to sit on a coffee table. It should be a trusted friend in your kitchen—one that collects drips and stains, not dust.

In the upcoming chapters, we go through the primary components for getting started. While you may want to jump ahead to the recipes, we encourage you to spend some time reviewing the chapters first. They will equip you with the expertise and tools needed to create mouthwatering meals with ease, and avoid many mistakes that sometimes discourage beginners. Even if you feel your kitchen and culinary experience are adequate, we believe our cookbook will help you become even more successful.

Now that you know what to expect, let's begin!

CHAPTER 2

FOOD IS YOUR FRIEND

It is never too early to begin eating a healthful diet. Wholesome, natural foods provide thousands of nutrients in complicated combinations that are not yet fully understood. However, we do know that a diet consisting primarily of processed food (like chips, sodas, and cookies) will not provide the full spectrum of health benefits that can be obtained from unprocessed foods. Supplements may fill in nutritional gaps, but they should only be used to *supplement* an already balanced diet. They do not work as a substitute!

Eating a nutritionally sound diet is not all that difficult, and the rewards are great. Just remember that adjusting your eating habits is a process. We will try to gently nudge you in the right direction, not push you unwillingly to the peak of nutritional perfection. Make changes gradually until your diet is made up of 75% to 95% wholesome foods. You can eat the occasional comfort food or dessert and still enjoy special family gatherings when your diet is primarily healthful to begin with.

Think of it this way—your health is like a bank account. What you put into your body makes a difference. When you make contributions to your health—like proper nutrition, exercise, rest, and sleep—your account is full. However, if you neglect these contributions, or withdraw more than you deposit, you will begin to drain the account. Illness will eventually result. If you stay in debt for a long period of time, it can take many years to get back to zero, much less have a surplus. And a surplus is what you'll need in order to be healthy now <u>and</u> as you age.

Eating healthful food and practicing good lifestyle choices can help you:

- Maintain a healthy weight
- Feel more energetic
- Enjoy balanced hormones and moods
- Sleep well
- Have a strong immune system
- Boast clear skin and shiny hair

Unhealthful food and habits can be a factor in these conditions:

- Asthma/allergies
- Autoimmune disease
- Cancer
- Diabetes
- Heart disease
- Obesity

How to make the right deposits into your body's bank account:

- Choose food in a form that is as close to nature as possible.
- Obtain adequate amounts of the three macronutrients: proteins, carbohydrates, and fats. Research varies on the exact ratios, but the USDA recommends obtaining 45% to 65% of calories from carbohydrates, about 30% from fats, and the rest in protein (usually about 1 gram of protein for every kilo or 2.2 pounds of body weight).
- Include high-quality proteins, like beans, nuts, dairy, eggs, fish, poultry, and meat. Look for local, grass-fed, organic, or at least antibiotic and hormone-free animal products. Most vegetables also contain small amounts of protein.
- Choose a wide variety of colorful fruits and vegetables as the main source of carbohydrates. Fill about three-quarters of your plate with them. (You can obtain all of the carbohydrates you need from fruits and vegetables.)
- Select whole grains, if you eat any at all.
- Include "good" fats like nuts, avocados, and olive oil.
- Eat plenty of high-fiber foods, which are vital for proper digestion and elimination. (Protein and fat do not contain fiber—but vegetables, fruit, whole grains, nuts, and seeds do.)
- Drink plenty of water (about 8 cups) every day.
- Get around 8 hours of sleep every night.
- Exercise regularly.

How to limit withdrawals from your body's bank account:

- Although protein is important, most American diets contain too much, and the quality is questionable. Buy the freshest and highest quality you can afford, which is easier to do when you eat less of it.
- Avoid—as much as possible—processed carbohydrates like white flour and white sugar. Processing removes nutrients and fiber, leaving mostly empty calories.
- Eliminate packaged foods that contain additives and artificial ingredients. Our bodies need whole food, not chemicals.
- Limit sugar in general, including artificial sweeteners. Use honey, maple syrup, molasses, and unrefined sugars sparingly.

- Avoid "bad" and damaged fats, like trans fats (hydrolyzed or otherwise chemically altered), rancid fats, fried foods, excessive animal fat, or overly heated fats.
- Shun highly processed meats like salami, bologna, and hot dogs.
- Know your body, and avoid foods that cause uncomfortable reactions. (Common allergens include gluten, dairy, soy, corn, eggs, fructose, and peanuts; but can be just about anything.)
- Limit alcohol consumption.

The easiest way to accomplish all of this is to prepare most of your meals at home. When you eat a wide variety of wholesome foods, you will obtain the nutrients your body needs, and you will soon learn to appreciate the taste much more than that of processed food. Furthermore, you'll feel great!

CHAPTER 3

EQUIP THE KITCHEN

With the right kitchen tools, you'll be able to cook just about anything. Our list reflects the actual types and sizes of equipment that we used to develop our recipes, but similar-size items can be substituted. See NOTES below for more details.

 TOP COOKWARE ESSENTIALS

Saucepans
- Large (4-quart) – most important
- Small (1-quart)
- Steamer insert (or use colander)

Skillets
- Large (10-inch) – most important
- Small (8-inch)

Ovenware
- Rimmed baking sheet (10×15-inch)
- Baking dish (8×8-inch)

Blender

Thermometers
- Meat thermometer
- Oven thermometer

Knives
- 8-inch chef's knife
- Honing steel or rod

Cutting boards (2 recommended)
- Cutting board for vegetables
- Cutting board for raw meat

Mixing bowls
- Medium and large (or a set)

Measuring utensils
- Measuring cups (for dry and liquid)
- Measuring spoons

Colander
- Fine metal mesh

TOP SMALL GADGET ESSENTIALS

Can opener with bottle opener

Food turner
- Sturdy stainless-steel

Grater
- 4-sided (box) grater

Ladle

Large kitchen spoon(s)
- Wood, stainless-steel, or plastic

Large kitchen spoon, slotted

Masher
- Sturdy stainless-steel

Tongs
- 10-inch, stainless-steel

Vegetable peeler

Whisk(s)
- One or more

NOTES:

Saucepans A 4-quart saucepan works for all of our recipes. Although it is sometimes called a medium saucepan, for the purposes of this cookbook it is the largest one required. A 5-quart saucepan is acceptable (although cumbersome) and will give you the flexibility to double many of the recipes. A 1-quart (or 2-quart) saucepan is optional and comes in handy from time to time. Add a steamer insert that can fit in the 4-quart saucepan, or use your metal colander as an insert for steaming vegetables.

Skillets A 10-inch skillet will work with all of our recipes, but any size between 10 and 12 inches is acceptable, preferably with a lid. A smaller (8-inch) skillet is optional and nice to have for making individual omelets (make sure the sides are slanted) and other small dishes.

Ovenware A rimmed metal baking sheet is sometimes called a cookie sheet, jelly roll pan, or half sheet pan. There are some minor differences, but as long as the pan has sides, it will work. We use a 10×15-inch (medium-size) baking sheet, and a few of our recipes require that size. An 8×8-inch glass baking dish (e.g., Pyrex®) is extremely versatile and shows up in many of our recipes.

Blender Start with an inexpensive blender for smoothies and puréed soups. Some blenders also come with a small food processor attachment. A hand-held immersion blender that is placed directly into a pot of soup or a container of smoothie ingredients is another handy option. If using a blender often, we recommend purchasing a high-powered version like Vitamix® or Ninja® whenever you can afford one.

Thermometers A meat thermometer ensures that chicken, beef, and pork have been heated enough to kill bacteria. Choose a design that works for both thick and thin foods. An oven thermometer verifies that the oven temperature is correct and properly preheated.

Knives and cutting boards See Chapter 6, Safe Food Handling and Knife Skills, for choosing the best knives and boards.

Mixing bowls Glass or ceramic bowls that are microwave-safe are recommended because of their versatility. *Note:* Plastics can release chemicals (hormone disruptors) into food when scratched and/or heated in a microwave. Choose at least two sizes (about 8-inch and 10-inch), or buy a set of three or more.

Measuring utensils Buy a set of metal or plastic measuring cups for "dry" ingredients (like flour), with at least four sizes: 1 cup, 1/2 cup, 1/3 cup, and 1/4 cup. A 2-cup (16-ounce) liquid measuring cup made with microwave-safe glass (e.g., Pyrex®) is also recommended. Choose a set of measuring spoons with at least four sizes: 1 tablespoon, 1 teaspoon, 1/2 teaspoon, and 1/4 teaspoon. (Sets that also include 1/2 tablespoon, 1/8 teaspoon, and a pinch are very useful.)

Colander A colander made with fine mesh is best for rinsing all foods, even grains as small as quinoa. When made of stainless steel rather than plastic, the colander can also be placed in a large saucepan to use as a steamer insert. Sets of two or three sizes are available as well.

Small gadgets Many of these kitchen utensils come in sets, along with a convenient holder. It may be more economical to pick up such a set and purchase the missing items individually.

CHAPTER 4

STOCK THE KITCHEN WITH STAPLES

Our recipes rely primarily on the following staples. Buy fresh foods and specialty items as needed for specific recipes. All lists are in alphabetical order and are followed by more details to help you shop wisely and store food correctly.

 TOP DRIED HERBS AND SPICES

Store in an airtight container away from sunlight, in a dry, cool location like a cabinet or drawer, preferably away from the oven.

1. **Allspice** (ground)
2. **Bay leaves**
3. **Cardamom** (ground)
4. **Chili powder**
5. **Chinese 5-spice blend**
6. **Cinnamon** (ground)
7. **Cloves** (ground)
8. **Coriander** (ground)
9. **Cumin** (ground)
10. **Curry powder**
11. **Dill** (leaves, not seeds)
12. **Ginger** (ground)
13. **Nutmeg** (ground)
14. **Oregano** (leaves, not ground)
15. **Paprika** (regular or smoked)
16. **Pepper**
17. **Red pepper flakes**
18. **Rosemary** (leaves, not ground)
19. **Salt**
20. **Thyme** (leaves, not ground)

TOP PANTRY STAPLES

Keep in pantry. Some can be refrigerated if desired. (See NOTES below.)

1. Baking powder
2. Baking soda
3. Beans (canned or dried)
4. Broth (canned or boxed)
5. Coconut milk (canned)
6. Garlic (fresh or jarred)
7. Grains (rice, quinoa, millet, kasha)
8. Oats
9. Oil for high-heat cooking
10. Oil for salads
11. Oil spray
12. Onions (fresh)
13. Pasta
14. Potatoes (fresh)
15. Sugar and other sweeteners
16. Tomatoes (canned, jarred, or boxed)
17. Tomato paste
18. Tuna/salmon (canned)
19. Vinegar(s)
20. White flour

TOP PERISHABLE STAPLES

Store in refrigerator or freezer, as indicated. A general rule of thumb for frozen food is to use within 6 to 12 months unless otherwise noted. (Some of these items come in shelf-stable containers that can be stored in the pantry until open.)

1. Bread
2. Butter
3. Capers
4. Cheese
5. Chipotle peppers in adobo
6. Eggs
7. Frozen fruit
8. Frozen meats
9. Frozen seafood
10. Frozen vegetables
11. Hot pepper sauce
12. Lemons/limes (and/or juice)
13. Mayonnaise
14. Milk (dairy or non-dairy)
15. Mustard
16. Nut butters
17. Pesto
18. Soy sauce
19. Tortillas
20. Whole grain flours and meals

NOTES:

Top Dried Herbs and Spices

Why these? When it comes to herbs and spices, taste preferences vary, making it difficult to decide on 20 (not as many as you might think). We all had a vote, so this list reflects our favorites. Rebecca prefers herbs used frequently in Mediterranean and Mexican cuisines, so her choices are oregano, thyme, rosemary, bay leaves, dill, cumin, and chili powder. Greg's top choices include spices and blends found in Asian and African food like Chinese 5-spice, curry powder, coriander, ginger, and red pepper flakes. Bobbi enjoys baking, so her additions are cinnamon, cardamom, allspice, nutmeg, and cloves. And of course, everyone needs salt (see our website post, *What's the Deal with Salt?*), pepper, and paprika. These are the only dried herbs and spices we use in our recipes, but they provide great versatility in various combinations.

Where to begin? Start with salt and pepper then pick out some recipes you want to try. Purchase the spices needed and continue adding as you expand your repertoire. Buy herbs and spices in the smallest jars available, or from the bulk section if your grocery store has one. As you open them, write the date on the jar. A general rule is to replace them after 1 year, although we have used some for 2 years with good results.

What about fresh herbs? Fresh herbs are a fantastic option, so feel free to substitute them for the dried herb whenever feasible. Generally speaking, use two to three times the amount of fresh herbs for dried. In other words, substitute 2 to 3 teaspoons fresh herb for 1 teaspoon dried. Basil, parsley, cilantro, tarragon, and mint lose much of their flavor when dried so we use the fresh herb. Cut herbs keep well in a vase of water on the counter or in the refrigerator. *Note:* Fresh basil should always be kept at room temperature.

Top Pantry Staples

1. Baking powder This is a chemical leavening agent used for baking. In other words, it makes baked goods rise. It contains baking soda and other ingredients, but is NOT a substitute for baking soda. Look for an aluminum-free baking powder. Buy a small container and mark the date when opened, since baking powder will lose its effectiveness over time. Serious bakers replace it every 3 to 6 months, but it should be fine for up to 1 year.

2. Baking soda This leavening agent is sodium bicarbonate (or bicarbonate of soda). It's a base (alkaline) that reacts with acidic ingredients in a recipe and causes the batter to rise. Like baking powder, it loses its effectiveness over time. After it's been open about 6 months, place the box in the refrigerator or freezer to absorb odors for a few more months. Old baking soda can also be used for scrubbing pans, oven interiors, and the kitchen sink. Wash it down the drain or disposal to freshen up pipes.

3. Beans (canned or dried) Look for BPA-free linings in canned beans. Dried beans are a less expensive option, but require more time to cook. For easy instructions on how to cook dried beans, visit our website.

4. Broth/stock (canned or boxed) Liquid broth (or stock) is recommended rather than bouillon cubes and powders, which are simply a blend of seasonings and "flavorings." Some liquid broths are actually made from reconstituted powder, so read the labels carefully to avoid artificial ingredients and added sugar. Broth pastes are a new option, which could be an acceptable alternative.

5. Coconut milk (canned) Regular coconut milk (not low-fat) provides the best results. It comes in medium (15-ounce) and small (6-ounce) cans.

6. Garlic Store fresh garlic in a dry, dark, ventilated place like a pantry, cabinet, or closet, away from potatoes. Keep uncovered, or in a jar designed for garlic. Use before cloves produce sprouts, which can be bitter. Buy chopped or roasted garlic in a jar to use when you're short on time, then store in refrigerator after opening.

7. Grains Recipes in this cookbook use brown rice, quinoa, millet, and buckwheat—all gluten-free grains. Together with beans, they provide an inexpensive, complete protein.

8. Oats Although oats are actually a grain, we place them in a separate category. Oats can be used for breakfast, baking, as a thickening agent, and as a filler in dishes like meatballs.

9. Oil for high-heat cooking Purchase one oil that is safe for high-heat cooking (above 375°F). Each type has a different smoke point, at which it becomes damaged and releases free radicals. Those compounds can damage human body cells over time. The topic of which oil is best for high-heat cooking is continually debated, with each having pros and cons. Popular choices include olive oil, coconut oil, avocado oil, canola oil, peanut oil, and sunflower oil. Buy small quantities that will be replaced frequently, and keep in a dark, cool place (not next to the oven), or refrigerate after opening if recommended.

10. Oil for salads If possible, purchase a small container of high-quality extra virgin olive oil for salads, low-heat cooking (below 375°F), and to toss with pasta. Extra virgin olive oil provides many health benefits and tastes wonderful. Other healthful options for salads (but not cooking) are walnut oil, macadamia nut oil, pumpkin seed oil, and flaxseed oil. Most should be stored in the refrigerator after opening.

11. Oil spray High-heat spray oil is convenient and reduces the amount of oil required for cooking.

12. Onions Select onions that are firm, heavy, and mold-free. They should not have a potent odor. Store in a mesh bag, bowl, or bin with good air circulation, and use within a few weeks. Keep away from potatoes.

13. Pasta Whole wheat pasta contains more nutrients than semolina (a refined flour). There are also gluten-free options like rice and soba noodles. Pasta is a great way to stretch out more expensive ingredients and serve a crowd on a shoestring.

14. Potatoes Both white and sweet potatoes should be firm, with no sprouts. They should not be stored in the refrigerator because the carbs will convert to simple sugars, changing the taste, texture, and nutritional makeup. Store potatoes in an open bin or paper bag in a cool, dark place. Light exposure causes a toxin to form, which produces a green tint under the skin. Remove the green portion before cooking. Keep potatoes away from onions and garlic, and use within a few weeks.

15. Sugar and other sweeteners When a recipe calls for "sugar," it is referring to granulated sugar. If possible, buy one made from unrefined evaporated cane juice, although it might cost a little more than regular white sugar. If not specified as cane sugar on the package, granulated sugar is probably made from genetically modified (GMO) sugar beets, which we try to avoid (like all GMO products). Sugars that are less refined—like Sucanat, turbinado, demerara, coconut sugar, and date sugar—can be substituted for granulated sugar in most recipes, but are more expensive. Other sweeteners specified in some of our recipes include brown sugar, molasses, honey, maple syrup, and confectioner's (or powdered) sugar. See *Talking About Sweets* on our website, for more information about these sweeteners.

16. Tomatoes Many recipes call for tomatoes—diced, crushed, whole, or in a sauce. They can be purchased in cans, jars, or shelf-stable (aseptic) boxes. To avoid exposure to Bisphenol-A (BPA), an endocrine disrupter that can leach into food (especially acidic ingredients), buy tomatoes in glass jars, aseptic boxes, or cans that have a BPA-free lining.

17. Tomato paste We give tomato paste its own separate listing as a flavor enhancer. It gives depth and sweetness to soups, sauces, salad dressings, and main dishes. Tomato paste can be purchased in cans, jars, and even tubes. It can also be mixed with water to make tomato sauce in a pinch—use 3 parts tomato paste and 4 parts water (or equal parts to simplify).

18. Tuna/salmon (canned or in pouches) Add to salads, soups, or pasta.

19. Vinegar Our favorites include raw apple cider vinegar (healthy choice), balsamic vinegar (bold choice), and rice wine vinegar (light choice). Other popular vinegars include, but are not limited to, red wine, white wine, champagne, and raspberry vinegars. *Note:* Distilled white vinegar is not appropriate for cooking, except to add to water for poaching eggs or fish. However, it is an inexpensive, non-toxic cleaner for floors and most surfaces in your kitchen, and we always have some around.

20. White flour Purchase a small amount of all-purpose, unbleached white flour for baking. Whole grain flours are generally recommended (see perishable staples), but there are times when white flour produces better results. Adding a little white flour to whole grain flour in baked goods will produce more lift and better texture. It can also be used in small amounts for dusting or breading foods, and for thickening light-colored sauces. Because it's refined, white flour can be stored in the pantry in an airtight container up to 1 year, unlike whole grain flours.

Top Perishable Staples (See eatbydate.com for more details on storage.)

1. Bread Whole grain breads are recommended. Read labels and look for the words, **100% whole wheat** (or other grain), since many whole grain breads contain only a small amount of whole grain flour. Also, be aware that "wheat flour" is just another name for white flour. Always refrigerate or freeze whole grain breads to prevent spoilage.

2. Butter Cook with butter, not margarine. If possible, buy organic. Conventional (non-organic) animal products, especially high-fat products like butter, can contain concentrated amounts of toxins. There are also some relatively good non-dairy blends available, but they do not work as a substitute in all recipes, especially baked goods. Keep butter in refrigerator up to 1 month, or in freezer up to 9 months after printed date.

3. Capers These tiny green flower buds from the caper bush (Capparis spinosa) are pickled in vinegar/brine, or salted and packaged dry. They're fairly expensive, but a little goes a long way. Store pickled capers in the refrigerator once open. Salted, dry-packed capers do not need refrigeration. Both types will easily last 1 year after opening.

4. Cheese Keep cheese on hand for cooking and snacking. Fresh Parmesan (shredded, grated, or whole) or other hard cheeses will last at least 6 weeks. Cheddar, Swiss, Monterey Jack, and other semi-soft cheeses are typically good for 1 month. To store, wrap hard and semi-soft cheeses loosely in parchment or wax paper, then place in a partially sealed plastic baggie. They can be frozen, but use within 6 months for best flavor. Fresh cheese like mozzarella, feta, and cottage cheese have a shorter shelf life. Keep them in their containers and eat within a week or so. Do not freeze fresh cheeses.

5. Chipotle peppers in adobo Chipotles are smoked jalapeño peppers, and adobo is a spiced, red sauce. They can be found in the Mexican food section at grocery stores in cans or jars, whole or minced.

6. Eggs Eggs are economical and highly nutritious. Hormone and antibiotic-free, pasture-raised, or organic eggs are the best choices. Fresh eggs straight from the farm (on location or at the farmers market) will last in the refrigerator about two months. Eggs from the grocery store will have a "sell by" date, just like dairy, and can be kept in the refrigerator about 3 to 4 weeks after that date. If you only use part of the egg (i.e., the yolk or egg white), store the remainder in a covered container and use within a few days. Store fresh eggs in the carton in which they were purchased to prolong freshness. *Note:* Hard-boiled eggs will keep in the refrigerator 5 to 7 days after they've been cooked.

7. Frozen fruit Frozen fruit is picked at its peak, when it has the highest nutritional value and flavor. It's often less expensive than fresh fruit. Add to smoothies and sauces, or serve with fresh cream or ice cream for a simple dessert.

8. Frozen meats Meats like chicken, beef, and pork can be purchased when on sale, and frozen until ready to use. To thaw, place in the refrigerator the day before needed.

9. Frozen seafood Fresh fish has a firmer texture than frozen, but it's not always available or affordable. Shrimp, cod, salmon, and halibut hold up well to freezing.

10. Frozen vegetables Certain vegetables do very well when frozen and thawed. They're economical, nutritious, and convenient to have on hand. Best options are chopped greens, peas, corn, bell peppers, and mushrooms. Other frozen vegetables that are acceptable, depending on their use, include broccoli, green beans, and vegetable mixtures.

11. Hot pepper sauce Hot pepper sauce (or hot sauce) can add complexity as well as heat. Our favorites include Tabasco, sriracha, Cholula, and Thai curry paste, but there are hundreds available, each with a different flavor profile. After opening, store in refrigerator for 3 to 5 years.

12. Lemons/limes Fresh lemons and limes are one of the most economical and effective ways to brighten up a dish. Store in the crisper drawer of refrigerator with other fruit, up to 1 month. For convenience, also keep a bottle of lemon and/or lime juice in refrigerator up to 1 or 2 years after opening.

13. Mayonnaise Look for mayonnaise made with simple, wholesome ingredients. As always, read the labels. Avoid imposters that may look like mayonnaise, but have ingredients like high fructose corn syrup, cornstarch, preservatives, and flavorings. Use mayonnaise on sandwiches and in salad dressings, egg salad, and potato salad. Store in refrigerator after opening, up to 3 months.

14. Milk All types of milk can be used in coffee, tea, cereal, and numerous recipes. Dairy and non-dairy milk are interchangeable in most instances, with some exceptions. Generally speaking, unopened dairy will last in the refrigerator 7 to 10 days after sell-by date. Once open, it's best to use the product within 5 to 7 days.

15. Mustard We prefer Dijon, a tangy French mustard that is extremely versatile. Other mustard choices (most are interchangeable) include yellow, brown, whole seed, etc. Use it in sandwiches, salad dressings, egg salad, deviled eggs, etc. Store in refrigerator after opening, up to 18 months.

16. Nut/seed butters Peanut butter is an economical protein. For those allergic to peanuts, but not other nuts or seeds, look for almond, cashew, and sunflower seed butters, as well as tahini (sesame paste). All-natural nut or seed butters with no added ingredients (except salt) are recommended, but they separate over time. Stir well to blend in the oil, then keep refrigerated. Natural nut butter in a jar will last up to 2 years unopened and 3 to 6 months in the refrigerator after opening. Fresh-ground nut butter should be stored in the refrigerator immediately.

17. Pesto Classic pesto is a sauce made from basil, olive oil, garlic, pine nuts, Parmesan cheese and salt. There are dairy-free and nut-free variations, as well as pesto made with other herbs. It can be purchased frozen or in a jar. Frozen pesto will keep up to 8 months in the freezer. Refrigerate jarred pesto once open, and use within 1 month.

18. Soy sauce Look for a naturally fermented soy sauce, like shōyu, tamari, or liquid aminos. Store in the pantry until open, then in the refrigerator several months. If it begins to smell "off" or develop mold, discard. Some types keep longer than others, so check the best-by date.

19. Tortillas Corn and wheat tortillas are convenient for use in Mexican dishes and as a sandwich wrap. Corn tortillas are gluten-free, making them a great choice for those with gluten intolerances. Try to buy organic or verified non-GMO corn tortillas, since most corn today is genetically modified. Keep refrigerated up to 8 weeks after best-by date, or 10 days after opening. Keep in freezer up to 8 months after the best-by date. We recommend whole wheat flour tortillas. Keep refrigerated and use within 4 weeks after best-by date if unopened. Otherwise, follow guidelines for corn tortillas.

20. Whole grain flour and meal White whole wheat flour is an extremely versatile whole grain flour. It resembles unbleached white flour because it's made from a type of wheat that is lighter in color than that used for regular whole wheat flour. White whole wheat flour can be used for baking, breading, and thickening. Whole wheat pastry flour, another option, produces slightly better results in baked goods and can also be used for the above-mentioned purposes, although it is a little darker in color. Gluten-free options include:

- One-to-One Gluten-Free Baking Flour by Bob's Red Mill: a gluten-free blend of flours, starches, and other ingredients, which is a direct substitute for regular flour in virtually any recipe.
- All-purpose gluten-free mixes: more nutritious than the previously mentioned flour, but cannot be used as a one-to-one replacement for regular flour in most instances.
- Almond meal/flour: a favorite for desserts, high in protein but relatively expensive.
- Cornmeal: an affordable gluten-free grain used in cornbread, breading, and some gluten-free recipes.

CHAPTER 5

PLAN, SHOP, STORE

Planning menus and creating shopping lists may sound boring, but it's the best way to save money and prepare great meals. You might even learn to enjoy it!

General Guidelines for Planning and Shopping

1. Stock the pantry and refrigerator/freezer with staples. See Chapter 4.

2. Keep a running shopping list. As you think of items needed, immediately write them down, or register on our website, finitefoodie.com, for access to meal planning and shopping lists with mobile capability.

3. Plan meals for 3 to 7 days. See our sample meal plan below to serve as a guide. Make up your own design, or use our website tool.

4. Check the pantry and refrigerator. Before leaving for the grocery store, add any last-minute items needed to prepare the meals you've planned and to replace staples.

5. Eat before shopping. Don't go to the grocery store when you're hungry, or you might buy more than you need.

6. Use your list, and shop methodically. Fresh foods are almost always located around the perimeter of the store, so focus your attention there. Check out the frozen section as well, but try to avoid the aisles with prepared foods, except to find necessary pantry staples on your list.

Sample Meal Plan

This is a 3-day sample meal plan with 3 meals daily, to use as a guide. You might prefer to do a 5- or 7-day plan, or plan for dinners only. Find what works best for you and don't forget to leave a few empty spots for eating leftovers or going out.

MONDAY	WEDNESDAY	FRIDAY
Breakfast: OVERNIGHT OATS (p. 53)	**Breakfast:** POACHED EGGS (p. 67); toast; grapefruit	**Breakfast:** SMOOTHIE (p. 58)
Lunch: HUMMUS (p. 36) wrap with greens, tomato and avocado; fresh fruit	**Lunch:** LENTIL SOUP (p. 139); green salad; fresh fruit	**Lunch:** FRITTATA (p. 63); carrot sticks; toast
Dinner: MIXED VEGETABLES AND RICE (p. 152)	**Dinner:** ROAST CHICKEN (p. 124); GREENS AND CARROTS (p. 203); sliced tomatoes	**Dinner:** Use leftover chicken in: CHICKEN FRIED BROWN RICE (p. 117)

How to Choose the Freshest Meat, Poultry, and Seafood

You'll save money and have the best results by selecting the freshest ingredients. Whether you're buying meat, poultry, or seafood, the biggest clue for freshness is the smell. Don't be embarrassed to sniff packaged meats or ask the butcher to smell the item before you decide to take it. Also, most stores will allow you to return a purchase on the same day if you notice that it has a bad odor when you open it at home.

Here are a few more clues for choosing fresh animal products:

1. Red meat (beef, bison, pork, lamb) These meats should be red or pink. If it has begun to turn brown, that's an indication that is has been sitting out (exposed to air) for some time. Brown does not necessarily mean the meat is bad, but it does suggest that the meat is not as fresh as it could be. This color test applies to any cut, even the mounds of ground beef at the butcher counter, which are often covered with fresh, pink meat to hide the fact that the center portion has turned brown. Buy ground beef or bison packaged in vacuum-sealed plastic to avoid this problem, but be sure to check the expiration date. Avoid packages with air pockets—they should be tightly sealed. Keep store-wrapped ground meat in the refrigerator up to 2 days. Vacuum-sealed packages should be used by the best-by date. Freeze ground meat and use within 4 months. When purchasing packaged steaks and roasts, give them a squeeze. Meat that contains too much muscle or gristle will be hard, but tender meat will feel soft. Whole cuts like steaks, chops, and roasts can be refrigerated up to 3 days, or frozen in airtight wrapping up to 1 year.

2. Poultry Poultry should be pink, and the skin should appear fresh. Avoid grayish-tinged poultry or any that simply looks or smells off. Vacuum-packed is a good option, as long as you check the expiration date and avoid those with air pockets. Keep poultry in refrigerator up to 2 days, or on ice in the refrigerator up to 3 days. Whole chickens can be frozen up to 1 year, and chicken pieces up to 9 months.

3. Seafood Ask to smell the item, unless you are very confident in the fish market. If the fish has a slightly bad odor, you could ask the person behind the counter to rinse it and allow you to sniff again. If the odor is gone, the fish should be good. Shop from a reputable dealer and buy local whenever possible. Fish should be shiny and moist, not dry and dull. If a fish fillet has dark or yellowish edges, it's very possibly old or has been sitting out too long. Shrimp should not have blackened edges or spots. Scallops should be creamy white. Shellfish like clams, oysters and mussels should clamp shut when tapped with a finger. If they don't close when touched, they're probably dead and must be discarded. Keep seafood in refrigerator up to 2 days, or on ice in the refrigerator up to 3 days. Flash-frozen packages of seafood can be stored in the freezer up to 1 year.

Storing Fresh Foods

It's very discouraging to spend hard-earned dollars at the grocery store, only to throw half of your purchases away. Chemical compounds released by fruit can cause vegetables to go bad more quickly, so always store them in separate refrigerator drawers. Generally speaking, frozen food is best eaten within 6 to 12 months, unless otherwise indicated. For more tips on extending the life of specific foods, use our simple guidelines on the following two pages.

ITEM	PANTRY	REFRIGERATOR	FREEZER
Fresh fruit (including tomatoes and avocados, but excluding berries, citrus, apples, and bananas)	Best left at room temperature to fully ripen. Eat right away or transfer to refrigerator.	Store ripe (or cut) fruit in refrigerator and eat within 3 to 5 days, depending on the fruit.	Freeze in airtight containers.
Apples	Can be left in the pantry or on the counter for 5 to 7 days, or in a cool, dark place (like a garage) for 3 to 4 months.	Keep apples in the refrigerator for 3 to 4 weeks.	Apples do not freeze well.
Bananas	Can be stored in the pantry or in a bowl on the counter, away from apples (unless you want them to ripen quickly).	Never store bananas in the refrigerator—they will turn brown.	Peel and freeze in baggies for smoothies and baked goods.
Berries	Do not leave at room temperature, as they deteriorate quickly.	Store in refrigerator right away and eat within a few days of purchasing.	Freeze in baggies and use in smoothies, pancakes, and sauces.
Dried fruit (raisins, cranberries, dates, etc.)	Keep in pantry up to 1 year past the printed date of a sealed package, and 3 to 6 months if opened or purchased in bulk.	Store in refrigerator, up to 2 years for sealed packages, or 6 to 12 months if opened.	Freeze indefinitely if sealed, or up to 1 year if opened or bulk.
Flaxseed, chia, and hemp seeds	Chia seeds keep up to 2 years in pantry. Whole flaxseeds up to 1 year. Unopened, vacuum-packed hemp up to 1 year.	Ground flaxseeds should be refrigerated and eaten in 3 to 4 months (or frozen). Keep hemp seeds in refrigerator up to 1 year.	Freeze any seed up to 1 year.
Ginger	Can be stored in pantry for 1 week, but not ideal.	Best stored in a resealable baggie (with all of the air pushed out) in the vegetable drawer of the refrigerator.	Can be frozen whole (unpeeled) in an airtight freezer bag or container, but wash and dry first. Break off what's needed and grate or chop—no need to thaw.

ITEM	PANTRY	REFRIGERATOR	FREEZER
Nuts	Store raw, whole nuts in pantry for a few months.	Always store chopped, ground, or roasted nuts in refrigerator. Can store all nuts in refrigerator up to 6 months.	Can store all nuts (except ground) in freezer up to 1 year.
Vegetables* (See Chapter 4 for storing garlic, onions, and potatoes)	Most winter squashes can be stored in a cool, dry place for 1 to 3 months, depending on the type.	Most vegetables should be stored in refrigerator, in a breathable bag or an open plastic bag. Amounts of time and specifics vary.	Most vegetables freeze well and last up to 12 months. Keep in airtight bags.

*Many vegetables that are fresh from the garden or farmers markets are best left unwashed until ready to use. If you wash them and only use a portion, wrap the remainder in a paper towel and place in an unsealed plastic bag that allows excess moisture to escape. This works especially well with lettuce, cabbage, and cucumbers.

CHAPTER 6

SAFE FOOD HANDLING
AND KNIFE SKILLS

Safe Food Handling

1. Be clean Always wash hands well before handling food, whether making dinner or just cutting a piece of fruit. It's especially important to wash hands thoroughly after handling raw meats. Use **soap and water** and scrub for 20 seconds. Anti-bacterial soap is not necessary.

2. Prepare clean Always keep raw meats separate from raw fruits and vegetables. Wash all vegetables with running water, even if you plan to peel them. Clean cutting boards, knives, counter tops, etc., with hot water and soap after preparing food, especially raw meat. We prefer to use dishcloths over sponges because dishcloths can be washed frequently. If you use sponges, disinfect by soaking them in a chlorine-water solution or heating them in a microwave for a few minutes. (To sterilize a sponge with a microwave, make sure the sponge is wet. Heat at full power 2 to 4 minutes. **Never put a sponge or scrubber in the microwave if it has metal in it.**) Replace sponges frequently. Wash dishcloths and microwave sponges every few days and after cleaning up areas that have been in contact with raw meat.

3. Cook and serve clean The best way to make sure meats have been cooked enough to kill bacteria is to use a food thermometer that indicates the proper internal temperature. For those who like rare beef or soft-cooked eggs, be sure they are fresh and from reputable vendors. Leftovers of any food should be used within three days and reheated thoroughly (to an internal temperature of 165°F). Bring soups and sauces to a boil. To microwave leftovers, cover the dish with a plate or plastic wrap (cut a few slits through the wrap). Cook, stir, and repeat until heated evenly.

4. Store clean Keeping food refrigerated is one of the best ways to avoid bacteria growth. Come straight home after grocery shopping or take an ice chest (with ice) for the foods that are frozen or need refrigeration. Once home, place most perishable food immediately in the refrigerator or freezer. (Some fruit and vegetables can be stored on the counter until ripe or cut.) It's best to thaw frozen food in the refrigerator. This could take an hour for a thin piece of fish or a few days for a large chicken or roast. Alternatively, thaw vacuum-sealed food in a bowl filled with lukewarm water, or in the microwave. Read your microwave instructions for best results. Don't leave cooked food out longer than 2 hours, or 1 hour if it's over 90°F outside. Set the refrigerator at 40°F and the freezer at 0°F.

5. Clean cutting boards It is important to clean and sanitize cutting boards regularly. Some boards can be washed in the dishwasher, but cleaning by hand with soap and hot water will remove most bacteria, according to America's Test Kitchen. We periodically clean our cutting boards designated for raw meat with diluted chlorine bleach. Fill a spray bottle with 2 cups water and 1 teaspoon bleach. Spray the cutting board thoroughly, then rinse it with running water. Finish with soap and water. Another option is to spray a 3% solution of hydrogen peroxide onto the board, leave a few minutes, then wash with soap and hot water. An environmentally friendly way to clean a cutting board is to wipe it down with white vinegar after washing with soap and hot water. This will kill most bacteria, but perhaps not quite as much as bleach. Bacteria love moisture, so air-dry cutting boards completely before storing. For more details, go to rodalesorganiclife.com.

Knife/Cutting Skills

For the purposes of this cookbook, we will assume you are starting out with one knife—an 8-inch chef's knife. But before using your knife, it's important to purchase a good cutting board.

1. How to Choose a Cutting Board A knife and cutting board go together. Do not cut on other surfaces unless you have no choice! A somewhat soft wood like maple is best for your knives if you chop hard or thick items frequently. (That's why chefs love them.) However, maple is expensive and bulky. Bamboo is a more economical alternative, but it's harder than maple, as are boards made from wood/resin fibers and hard plastics. Therefore, knives will become dull more quickly. Glass cutting boards are the worst and will definitely ruin knives, so don't use them. Flexible silicone cutting mats and boards are easy on knives and inexpensive, but will eventually need to be replaced since they will get cut marks that can make the board hard to sanitize. Try to have at least two cutting boards (or mats)—one for produce and one for meat, poultry, and fish. In a pinch use a wooden cutting board that has one side dedicated to meats and the flip side to vegetables. However, **do not** cut raw meat on one side and then turn it over and immediately cut up a salad on the other! Cut vegetables first, then meat. The best and easiest way to prevent cross-contamination is to have a separate board dedicated to raw meats, poultry, and fish. Some studies show that bacteria do not survive on washed wooden cutting boards for more than 3 minutes, but might survive on plastic in the small cuts on the surface. For more detailed information, see:

foodhandler.com/cutting-board-safety
kitchenknifeguru.com/cutting-boards/cutting-boards-bamboo-and-others

"I have a lightweight plastic set of four cutting mats with pictures to specify what to cut on each one. They're hanging on a hook in my kitchen for easy access." GREG

2. Cutting board maintenance Wood and bamboo boards need to be coated with oil whenever they begin to dry out or no longer repel water. Many companies recommend mineral oil, but we prefer products like Block Brothers Block Oil, which is non-toxic and not made from petroleum. According to some literature, coconut oil or walnut oil are acceptable alternatives that will not go rancid or become gummy. However, olive oil and other cooking oils are not recommended. Be sure the oil soaks in completely, then wipe off any excess.

3. How to Choose a Knife The first and most important knife to own is an 8-inch chef's knife, which can be used for just about anything as long as the blade is sharp. When you're able to add more knives to your collection, we suggest 1) a paring knife for peeling fruit and other smaller jobs, and 2) a serrated knife for cutting fragile food items like tomatoes and bread. Sets are usually more economical, but often contain knives of lesser quality. Buy the best knives you can afford—they're the most important kitchen tools you'll own.

4. How to Hold a Knife The correct way to hold a knife feels a little awkward at first, because most people are used to holding a dinner knife. Resist the urge to hold your chef's knife like a steak knife, with your index finger stretched over and resting on the top of the blade. Instead, pinch the blade with the thumb and index finger at the base where it joins the handle. Wrap the remaining three fingers around the handle. Alternatively, wrap all fingers and thumb around the handle.

5. How to Hold the Food Whenever possible, use a "claw" grip to hold the item to be cut. Keep the thumb and little finger tucked under the palm of the hand, out of the way, or to support the food behind the other three fingers. Steady the food with the tips of your first three fingers and push the knuckles slightly forward. Once the knife gets to the end of the food, the blade will rest against your knuckles. The cutting edge cannot nip a fingertip this way. It will be awkward at first and requires some practice.

6. How to Set Up for Slicing and Chopping Align the cutting board parallel to the edge of the counter. Turn the hip and torso (of the same side as the hand holding the knife) away from the counter at a 45° angle. Place the item to be sliced with a flat side down (if available) and parallel to the edge of the cutting board. Using a chef's knife, place the tip above the item to be cut and hold the handle up at a 45° angle to the surface. Keep part of the knife's edge in contact with the board at all times and come down in a seesaw motion, moving the blade forward and back slightly as you do. Use the inner 3 to 4 inches of the blade (closest to the handle) for cutting. To dice, take slices or julienne strips and cut across to form small cubes. To chop or mince, use the same seesaw motion, but rotate the base of the knife from right to left while keeping the tip of the knife in one place. To chop tougher items, place the palm of the other hand on top of the flat edge of the blade with fingers flexed up and out of the way as you chop.

RECIPES

UNDERSTANDING OUR RECIPES

You've stocked your kitchen, and now it's time to start cooking! We developed and tested these recipes in our own small kitchens, using the recommended kitchen tools. So, if we can do it, you can too! First, review these tips.

Read the Recipe

Always read through the entire recipe first, especially if it's new to you. You will understand the whole recipe better and become aware of anything that needs to be prepared ahead of time. Each recipe has easy step-by-step instructions that are written to save time, respect space constraints, and leave behind as few dirty dishes as possible.

In addition to the ingredient list and instructions, the recipes will indicate the following:

- **Yields:** Provides the approximate number of servings, or the total amount a recipe makes.
- **Difficulty:** Each recipe is rated Easy, Moderate, or Involved (as compared to each other). Since all of the recipes in this cookbook are meant for inexperienced cooks, none are truly difficult, so please don't let an Involved rating scare you.
- **Cost ($):** Recipes are rated $ for Inexpensive, $$ for Moderate, or $$$ for Expensive. Cost is relative to other recipes in the book, but can vary depending on what is available in your area and the time of year.
- **Prep, Passive, and Cook Times:** Estimates the approximate amount of time needed for prep work and cooking, as well as passive time (letting something soak, chill, or cool). Remember, everyone works at a different pace, and the first attempt at a recipe generally takes a little longer.
- **Tools and Special Supplies:** Lists the main kitchen tools required, as well as special supplies like parchment paper or foil.
- **Tips, Techniques, and Terminology:** Additional information highlighted in boxes throughout the recipe section. These are also listed in the index.
- **Serving Suggestions:** Our suggestions for serving the recipe and possible dishes to accompany it.
- **Variations:** Our favorite variations of the recipe.

FAQs: Answers to Frequent Questions

1. Butter *When the recipe calls for butter, does it make a difference if you use salted or unsalted?* Not usually, and if so, it should be indicated in the recipe. Typically, unsalted butter is best for baking, and by using it for all purposes you'll have the option to add as much or as little salt as desired.

2. Flour *How do you measure flour, especially for baking?* Fluff it up first with a spoon (scoop and lift a few spoonfuls). Next, scoop out the flour one spoonful at a time and gently place it in a measuring cup until overflowing. Use a straight edge (like the back edge of a knife) and scrape across the top to push away the excess and create a level top. Do not press down or tap the cup, as this will pack the flour. We primarily use white whole wheat flour or whole wheat pastry flour in our recipes, but occasionally incorporate a little all-purpose white flour for a lighter color and texture, even though white flour has less nutritional value. See our staples list for more information about these flours.

3. Hot pepper sauce *What type of hot sauce should I use?* Buy your favorite(s) and adjust amounts in recipes to taste. The amount of heat in a dash of hot sauce varies from brand to brand. Bobbi and Richard prefer Tabasco (intense, tangy, Cajun); Greg likes sriracha (sweet, smooth, Asian); and Rebecca and Nick favor Cholula (spicy, bright, Mexican). Even if you're not a big fan of spicy food, we still recommend using some sparingly to add more depth of flavor.

4. Red pepper flakes *Can I use ground cayenne or red pepper instead?* We had a hard time deciding between red pepper flakes and cayenne. We settled on the flakes, but feel free to purchase and use both. Cayenne is ground, so use less if you're substituting it for red pepper flakes.

5. Salt *Can I use all types of salt interchangeably?* We like unrefined sea salt (Celtic), Himalayan salt, or full-spectrum salt (like Real Salt®). Natural, unrefined salt has trace minerals, and therefore some nutritional value. Our ingredient lists will simply say "salt," and you can use whichever type you prefer, including plain old white salt. If you use Kosher salt, you might need to increase the amount. To learn more, see our website post, *What's the Deal with Salt?*

6. Sugar *When a recipe calls for sugar, what type does it mean?* Sugar is short for granulated sugar. Other types of dry, unrefined sugars (e.g., coconut nectar sugar, date sugar, Sucanat®, demerara, evaporated cane juice, and turbinado) might work as a substitute, although they are darker and could change the color and taste slightly. When a recipe specifies brown sugar, it is referring to the moist brown sugar labeled "light (or dark) brown sugar," which is a mixture of granulated sugar and molasses. Dark brown sugar has a little more molasses in it than light, but they're virtually interchangeable. You can even make your own brown sugar, per our chart at the end of the chapter. Powdered sugar is also called confectioner's sugar, and should not be substituted with any other kind. For more details, see our website post, *Talking About Sweets.*

Establish a Core Group of Go-To Recipes

After trying numerous recipes, decide which ones work best for you. We suggest having 5 to 7 go-to recipes in your core group. Prepare them frequently enough so you only need to glance at the recipe. Take notes of minor changes you've made (if any) that personalize the recipe to your taste preferences. However, don't get stuck in a rut—occasionally add a new recipe to your repertoire when you're ready.

A Word About Creativity

We've provided optional ingredients and substitutions in recipes when appropriate, but as you become more comfortable, you'll come up with your own tweaks. Try recipes once, as written. Adjust seasonings to suit your taste, then jot down notes for easy reference the next time you make it.

CHART OF COMMON SUBSTITUTIONS

ITEM	SUBSTITUTION	NOTES
Brown sugar (1 cup)	1 cup white sugar and 2 tablespoons molasses	Dark brown sugar has a little more molasses than light brown sugar, but they are mostly interchangeable
Butter	Oil	Mostly interchangeable in equal amounts
Butter or oil	Applesauce, in equal amounts	Lowers fat content in baked goods
Buttermilk	1 tablespoon lemon juice added to 1 to 2 cups milk (dairy or non-dairy)	Or mix 1 part plain yogurt to 3 parts milk
Egg	1/4 cup yogurt, 1/4 cup puréed fruit or baby food, or 1/4 cup applesauce	Don't use applesauce to substitute for both egg and fat in one recipe
Granulated sugar	1/2 cup honey or 2/3 cup maple syrup for 1 cup sugar (with additional changes in liquids and baking temperature possible)	Can use equal amount of other dry sugars (i.e., coconut or date sugar) in most cases
Milk (cow)	Dairy-free milk, juice, or water in equal amounts	Appropriateness depends on recipe
Tomato sauce	3 parts tomato paste and 4 parts water	Example: 3/4 cup tomato paste and 1 cup water

APPETIZERS AND PARTY FOOD

Appetizers should be simple, not stressful. These recipes come together quickly, but will still impress your friends. Garnish as indicated, and you'll have an instant masterpiece. Go ahead and have a party!

APPETIZER PLATTERS

Easy $ to $$$

Platters are one of the easiest ways to provide appetizers to any size crowd. We've provided general suggestions to use as inspiration, but make your platter as elaborate or simple as you wish. Artistically arrange items on plates, cutting boards, or in bowls, then **garnish*** *with fresh green herbs like parsley, rosemary, or sage. Serve with crackers, breadsticks, or artisanal bread, and provide toothpicks or other serving utensils as needed.*

Prep Time: 5 to 15 minutes
Tools: servings pieces (platter, bowls, spreaders, knives, cutting boards, etc.)
Special Supplies: decorative toothpicks (optional)

SIMPLE PLATTER

Olives
Nuts
Small cubes of cheese

BEER PARTY PLATTER

Mixed nuts
Pretzels
Vegetable chips
Cheddar cheese cubes

Pepper jack cheese cubes
Pickles
Beer mustard

SOUTHERN RELISH TRAY

Olives stuffed with pimentos
Pickled okra
Relish, or chowchow
Dill pickle slices

Baby sweet pickles
Pickled watermelon rinds
DEVILED EGGS (see recipe)
Pimento cheese

*Garnish – an item added to a dish to improve the appearance and sometimes to improve the flavor as well. The term can be used as a noun or a verb. Example: Garnish your dish with a garnish, like parsley.

*Peppadew peppers are round red peppers that are sweet and spicy. **Pepperoncini** are green pickled peppers that tend to be mild. These can be found along with bulk olives and marinated vegetables in many grocery stores.

CHEESE, FRUIT, AND NUT PLATTER

1 soft, mild cheese (Brie, goat cheese, fresh mozzarella)

1 medium-bodied cheese (Cheddar, Jarlsberg, Gouda, fontina)

1 hard or pungent cheese (Asiago, Gorgonzola, cheeses with seeds)

1 sweet cheese (made with fruit, honey, or wine)

Fruit (grapes, apples, pears, figs, clementines, berries)

Crackers and/or bread

Nuts (walnuts, almonds, pecans, pistachios)

ITALIAN VEGGIE PLATTER

Olives

Roasted bell peppers

Sun-dried tomatoes in olive oil, or fresh cherry tomatoes

Artichoke hearts

Peppadew peppers* (optional)

Pepperoncini* (optional)

ITALIAN MEAT AND CHEESE PLATTER

Mozzarella (marinated, or seasoned with salt, pepper, and basil)

1 medium-bodied cheese (Provolone, fontina)

1 hard cheese (Asiago, Romano, Parmesan)

Gorgonzola, or sweet cheese (made with fruit, honey, or wine)

Salami, prosciutto, pepperoni, and/or other cured meats (sliced)

Olives (optional)

BLACK BEAN DIP

1-1/2 cups   Easy $

"This is a spicy bean dip for both hummus lovers and haters. It's a change of pace from the ubiquitous tahini-based dips so popular today, and it appeals to Mexican food fanatics like myself!" REBECCA

Prep Time: 15 to 20 minutes

Tools: colander, knife and cutting board, blender, measuring cups and spoons

1 (15-ounce) can black beans

1 small garlic clove

1/2 cup cilantro leaves (loosely packed)

2 tablespoons lime juice

2 tablespoons oil (extra virgin olive oil recommended)

2 tablespoons water

1 teaspoon ground cumin

1 teaspoon chili powder, or smoked paprika

1 teaspoon minced **chipotle peppers in adobo*** (optional)

1-1/2 teaspoons salt

1/2 teaspoon dried thyme leaves

Garnish: (optional)

Lime slices, avocado slices, and/or sour cream

*TIP
We start with 1 teaspoon **minced chipotle in adobo**, then add more to taste. They can be quite hot, and vary from one brand to the next. For a milder version, leave chipotle out or use 2 tablespoons canned green chilies instead.

1. Drain and rinse beans in a colander.
2. Add garlic clove and cilantro leaves.
3. Add beans and all other ingredients. Blend until smooth. Add more water if needed for proper consistency. It should be soft enough to scoop with a chip or cracker, but not too runny. (The dip will thicken once chilled.)
4. Adjust seasonings, to taste. Garnish as desired.

SERVING SUGGESTIONS:
- Serve with fresh vegetables, tortilla chips, and crackers.
- For a Mexican-themed party, serve with salsa, guacamole, and tortilla chips.
- Make a sandwich by spreading dip on a tortilla or wrap. Add sprouts, avocado, roasted vegetables, salad greens, cheese, or grilled chicken.

CAPRESE KABOBS

24 kabobs   Easy $

"Caprese means 'from the island of Capri,' which is where this now-famous salad originated. It consists of basil, mozzarella, and tomatoes, representing the green, white, and red of the Italian flag. These cute little Caprese kabobs were served to me at my wedding shower, and I've been a fan ever since. We dip them in a tart balsamic vinaigrette, but you can simplify things further by simply drizzling oil and vinegar over them. We often have them as a snack or bring them to a cookout, since they're so easy to assemble. You can make different versions by using other ingredients or changing the presentation (see Variations). Dress them up with decorative toothpicks for fun." REBECCA

Prep Time: 5 to 10 minutes
Tools: knife and cutting board (optional), measuring cups and spoons, small bowl
Special Supplies: toothpicks or skewers

Kabobs:

24 cherry tomatoes
24 small **mozzarella balls*** (bocconcini)
24 basil leaves

Balsamic Vinaigrette:

1/4 cup + 1 tablespoon balsamic vinegar
2 teaspoons mayonnaise
1/2 teaspoon oregano (dried or fresh)
1/2 teaspoon salt
Pinch red pepper flakes
Pinch ground black pepper
1/4 cup olive oil (extra virgin recommended)

TIPS

- If you can't find small ***mozzarella balls**, cut 2 large balls into 24 (1-inch) cubes.

- If not using vinaigrette right away, cover with plastic and leave at room temperature. Beat again right before serving.

For kabobs:

1. Skewer a small ball (or cube) of mozzarella, a basil leaf, and a cherry tomato, in that order.

For vinaigrette:

1. Measure vinegar into a 1- or 2-cup liquid measuring cup (or small bowl).
2. Stir in all other ingredients except oil.
3. Slowly add oil while beating with a whisk (or fork) to emulsify.

SERVING SUGGESTION:

- Arrange kabobs on a platter. Vinaigrette should be in a bowl for dipping, or in a small pitcher. Serve with a sliced baguette, or other crusty bread.

VARIATIONS:

- Omit vinaigrette. Arrange kabobs on a platter, then drizzle extra virgin olive oil and balsamic vinegar over them. Sprinkle salt, pepper, and red pepper flakes on top.
- CAPRESE SALAD PLATTER – Use 1 large tomato and 1 large ball of mozzarella. Slice, then arrange on a platter alternating and overlapping the slices. Sprinkle chopped fresh basil on top, then drizzle vinaigrette (or oil and vinegar) over them. Incorporate slices of roasted red and yellow bell peppers and/or avocados if desired.
- CAPRESE MIXED SALAD – Chop and mix all ingredients and serve on a bed of arugula.
- WATERMELON FETA KABOBS – Make with a cherry tomato, basil leaf (or mint), cube of feta, and cube of watermelon. Serve with SWEET BALSAMIC REDUCTION.

CATALONIAN TOMATO BREAD

Easy $

"During a trip to Barcelona, we were introduced to this delicious tapa that was on every menu and served with most meals. It's simple, but wonderfully delicious! Make as many slices as you want, or set out all of the ingredients and let everyone make their own, the Catalonian way!" BOBBI

Prep Time: 5 minutes
Tools: knife and cutting board

Focaccia, or rustic country bread
Whole garlic cloves (peeled)
Campari tomatoes, or other small round
   tomatoes
Olive oil (extra virgin recommended)
Salt
Aioli* (optional)

> ***Aioli** is a paste traditionally made by smashing garlic and olive oil together until creamy. Most prepared aioli sold in grocery stores is made with mayonnaise. Use either type, or leave out altogether.

1. Slice bread. If using focaccia, slice lengthwise in half, then across to form 2-inch-wide strips. If using a round rustic loaf, cut across into 1/2-inch-thick slices. Toast.
2. Peel a clove of garlic and gently rub it across the toast.
3. Cut the small tomato in half across the middle (not stem end to bottom). Rub the cut side over the toast.
4. Drizzle olive oil and sprinkle salt over the toast.
5. Serve with a dollop of aioli if desired.

> ***A whole chicken wing is made up of two parts, a drumette and a flat.** If precut pieces are not available, buy whole wings and cut in half. To cut, turn over to the underside of the joint and slice through the skin and meat. Move the joint to see where the bones meet, then slice through the cartilage that holds the joint together. It should be easy to do. If not, you might be cutting through bone.

CHICKEN WINGS

5 to 6 (4-piece) servings   Moderate $

*Our wings are very simple to make, in spite of the moderate rating. We **parboil*** them to remove some of the fat, then roast them in the oven rather than frying. This way, they're less greasy than those you would typically purchase at restaurants. Ours are rather mild compared to the current trend of fire-hot wings, so feel free to double or triple the amount of hot sauce, or serve with extra hot sauce on the side. These can also be served as a dinner entrée for two.*

Prep Time: 15 minutes   **Passive Time:** 1 to 2 minutes   **Cook Time:** 20 to 25 minutes
Tools: knife and cutting board (if cutting wings in half), large (4-quart) saucepan, rimmed baking sheet, liquid measuring cup, measuring spoons, large bowl

20 to 24 pieces chicken **wings*** (10 to 12 whole wings, or about 2 pounds)

Water (for cooking)
2 teaspoons salt

Sauce:

3 tablespoons vinegar (apple cider vinegar recommended)

3 tablespoons soy sauce

1 tablespoon paprika (smoked recommended)

1 tablespoon hot pepper sauce, or to taste (Cholula recommended)

1/2 tablespoon honey

1 teaspoon ground black pepper

1/2 teaspoon salt

For wings:

1. Fill saucepan about half full of water, then add salt. Cover and bring to a boil over high heat. Using tongs (or a large spoon), gently lower wings into boiling water. Once it begins to boil gently, immediately turn to medium-low and simmer 5 more minutes.

2. Place two layers of paper towels inside a rimmed baking sheet. When the wings are done, remove from water with tongs and place on paper towels to drain. Discard water used for parboiling (or save for chicken stock). *Note:* Make ahead up to this point, then refrigerate until ready to cook if desired.

3. Preheat oven to 475°F. Spray or rub oil on baking sheet.

*Parboil – to partially precook meats or starchy foods in water before finishing them off on the grill, in the oven, or in a stir-fry. It is similar to "blanch," and the terms are sometimes confused. Each recipe will indicate the proper amount of time to parboil the item.

For sauce:

1. Combine all sauce ingredients in a liquid measuring cup. Mix well with a fork. *Note:* Hot pepper sauces have different levels of heat intensity, so adjust amount according to your taste preference.

To combine and cook:

1. Place wings back into the saucepan and drizzle <u>half</u> the sauce over them. Toss to coat.

2. Spray or rub oil onto a baking sheet. Alternatively, line with parchment paper. Use tongs to transfer wings to baking sheet, spreading so they don't touch each other. Discard any sauce left in the pan. Cook 10 minutes on one side, turn over, and cook 10 to 15 minutes on the other side. They should be browned, but not burned.

3. Cool 2 to 3 minutes, then place wings on a platter and drizzle remaining sauce over them, or place in a large bowl and toss with remaining sauce. If not ready to serve, return to baking sheet and place in warm oven.

4. Serve with extra hot sauce on the side if desired.

CLASSIC HUMMUS

1-1/2 cups   Easy $$

"I've been making hummus since the early 1980's, long before it became such a fad (albeit a good one). Hummus comes from the Arabic word for chickpeas, and is traditionally made with chickpeas and tahini (sesame paste). Although there are many flavors of hummus that use other ingredients, this classic version is still my favorite. It's great with carrot sticks, pita bread, in sandwiches, or on a salad. This recipe requires a blender or food processor." BOBBI

Prep Time: 5 to 10 minutes
Tools: colander, blender, measuring cups and spoons, knife and cutting board

1 (15-ounce) can of chickpeas
1 small garlic clove, or 1 tablespoon jarred, chopped garlic

*Tahini is a paste made from sesame seeds, similar to peanut butter. Most grocery stores carry it alongside other nut and seed butters.

Juice of 1 lemon
1/4 cup **tahini***
2 tablespoons olive oil (extra virgin recommended)
1 tablespoon soy sauce (optional)
1/2 tablespoon ground cumin
1/2 teaspoon salt
1/4 teaspoon smoked paprika (optional)
1/8 teaspoon hot pepper sauce
1/4 cup water

1. Drain and rinse chickpeas in a colander. Place in blender.
2. Add remaining ingredients, <u>except</u> water. Blend until fairly smooth.
3. While blender is running on a low speed, slowly add water and continue to blend until smooth and creamy. Use more or less water for desired consistency. It should be thicker than salad dressing but not as thick as mashed potatoes.
4. Adjust seasonings, to taste. *Note:* The flavor intensity of fresh garlic increases over time, so go easy if making it the day before.

TIP

Chopped garlic in a jar is very convenient, but it's not as strong as fresh garlic. Whenever you're substituting jarred for fresh, use more—and vice versa.

SERVING SUGGESTIONS:

- Transfer to a bowl and garnish with a sprinkling of paprika, a swirl of olive oil, chopped parsley, cilantro, toasted pine nuts, sesame seeds, chopped black olives, roasted bell peppers, sun-dried tomatoes, or a combination.
- Serve with wedges of pita bread, crackers, and raw vegetables (carrot and celery sticks are easy, inexpensive choices).

VARIATIONS:

- Endless! Make up your own variations by adding 1 to 2 tablespoons roasted red peppers, sun-dried tomatoes, roasted garlic, spinach, artichokes, etc., into the blender. Garnish with the added ingredient.

DEVILED EGGS

6 (2-piece) servings   Easy $

"Everyone in our family (from oldest to youngest) loves Deviled Eggs, which are thankfully one of the easiest and most economical appetizers you can make! Chopped pickles are optional, but we encourage you to use pickle juice for a fluffy texture. We prefer dill pickles and dill pickle juice, but feel free to substitute sweet pickles if you prefer. Be aware that Prep Time does not include the time required to boil the eggs, which can be done up to 24 hours in advance. This recipe is easy to double for a larger family gathering." BOBBI

Prep Time: 10 to 15 minutes

Tools: saucepan (for boiling eggs), knife and cutting board, medium bowl, measuring cups and spoons

6 hard-boiled eggs

1/4 cup mayonnaise

2 teaspoons Dijon mustard

2 teaspoons pickle juice

1/2 tablespoon dill (dried or fresh)

1/4 teaspoon salt

1/8 teaspoon ground black pepper

2 dashes hot pepper sauce

1 tablespoon finely chopped dill pickles (optional)

Garnish:

Paprika, dill, or sliced olives

1. Cook eggs according to our recipe for BOILED EGGS, up to one day in advance.
2. Peel eggs then cut in half from top (narrow end) to bottom. Place yolks in a medium bowl, and place whites onto a platter, cut-side up.
3. Add mayonnaise, mustard, pickle juice, dill, and seasonings to the yolks. Mash with a fork (or back of a spoon) until well blended. Add more pickle juice, mustard, or mayonnaise if needed. *Note:* Beat with an electric mixer for a fluffier filling.
4. Stir in chopped pickles if desired. Adjust seasonings, to taste.
5. Fill the center of each egg white with a scoop of the filling.
6. Garnish as desired.

VARIATIONS:

- NANA'S DEVILED EGGS – Include optional chopped pickles. Substitute 1 teaspoon yellow mustard for 1 teaspoon of the Dijon, and eliminate dill. Garnish with paprika, sliced pimento stuffed olive, or chopped pickles.
- PESTO DEVILED EGGS – Substitute 1 tablespoon basil pesto sauce for Dijon mustard, and eliminate dill, pickles, and salt. Garnish plate with sprigs of basil. Top with a small dot of pesto, or sliced black olives if desired.
- DEVILED EGG SALAD – Increase chopped pickles to 1/4 cup and double salt and pepper. Chop eggs, then mix everything together. (Great lunch option!)
- Substitute 2 or more tablespoons sour cream or Greek yogurt for the same amount of mayonnaise.
- Replace dill with 1 to 2 tablespoons chopped fresh herbs like parsley, cilantro, tarragon, basil, or chives.
- Add finely chopped shallot, red onion, or green onion tops, and garnish with more of the same.

MEDITERRANEAN MELTS

20 pieces   Moderate $

Impress your friends with these lovely melts that take less than 20 minutes to make, start to finish! These are a little fancier than simple bruschetta, but not much more difficult to throw together last-minute. Mushroom Melts (see Variations) take about 5 minutes longer because the topping is cooked first, but they still go together with ease and have been a crowd favorite at numerous gatherings. We sometimes use larger slices of bread and serve these as open-faced sandwiches for lunch.

Prep Time: 15 minutes   **Cook Time:** 3 minutes

Tools: knife and cutting board, medium bowl, measuring cups and spoons, baking sheet

1/4 cup finely chopped onion

1 large Roma tomato (about 1 cup chopped)

8 pitted Kalamata olives (optional)

1/2 cup crumbled feta cheese

2 tablespoons mayonnaise

1 teaspoon dried oregano leaves

1/8 teaspoon ground black pepper

1 long baguette (white, whole grain, or gluten-free)

1/4 cup grated Parmesan cheese

Garnish:

Chopped parsley, or sprig of fresh oregano

Preheat broiler about 5 to 10 minutes before ready to cook.

For topping:

1. Chop onion, tomato, and olives. Place in a medium bowl.

2. Add crumbled feta, mayonnaise, oregano, salt, and pepper. Blend well.

Note: Make ahead to this point if desired, then refrigerate until ready to assemble and cook.

To assemble and cook:

1. Slice half of the baguette into 1/2-inch-thick pieces, cutting straight across for smaller rounds, or on the diagonal for larger, oblong shapes.

2. Place slices on an ungreased baking sheet. Spread a spoonful of the tomato mixture on each slice. Sprinkle some Parmesan on top. Cut more of the baguette as needed to use all of the tomato mixture.

3. Broil about 3 minutes, or until cheese has melted and is lightly browned.

4. Garnish with fresh parsley, either by chopping and sprinkling some over the melts, or by placing sprigs around them. Serve immediately.

VARIATION:

- MUSHROOM MELTS –
    1. Melt 2 tablespoons butter in a large skillet over medium-low heat, then cook 1/4 cup chopped onion and 2 cups finely chopped mushrooms until soft. (Omit tomatoes and olives.)
    2. Remove from heat and stir in 1/2 cup grated Parmesan cheese, 2 tablespoons sour cream or Greek yogurt, 1 teaspoon Dijon mustard, 1/2 teaspoon rosemary leaves, 1/4 teaspoon salt, 1/8 teaspoon black pepper, and 1/8 teaspoon red pepper flakes.
    3. Place topping on baguette slices and cover with a piece of Swiss, Havarti, or Monterrey Jack cheese if desired. Broil 3 to 4 minutes. Garnish with parsley.

REBECCA'S CHUNKY GUACAMOLE

5 cups   Easy $$

"My friends and family always ask me to bring this to gatherings and parties. I cut the recipe in half and serve it with quesadillas for dinner at home." REBECCA

Prep Time: 10 to 15 minutes
Tools: knife and cutting board, measuring cups and spoons, large bowl

1 large Roma tomato (about 1 cup chopped)
1/2 cup chopped cilantro
1/4 cup thinly sliced scallions (green onions)
4 avocados (somewhat soft)

1/4 cup lime juice (2 to 3 limes)
1 teaspoon salt
1/2 small jalapeño pepper, or 1/2 teaspoon hot pepper sauce

1. Coarsely chop tomato and cilantro. Place in a large bowl.
2. Thinly slice scallions, using both green and white parts. Add to bowl.
3. Dice **avocados*** and scoop out into the bowl.
4. Add lime juice and salt.

*How to Slice and Dice Avocados – Cut avocado in half. Remove the pit (large seed) by jabbing it with a knife and pulling it out. Hold one half of the avocado in the palm of your hand with flesh-side up. With a knife, cut through the soft flesh (but not through the outer peel) from top, stem end to bottom into desired thickness for slices. To dice, slice across in the other direction. Scoop out the flesh with a spoon.

5. Cut jalapeño (if using) in half and remove seeds. Mince <u>one half</u> as finely as you can, then add to bowl (or add hot sauce) and stir well.

6. Adjust spices and seasonings, to taste, adding additional minced jalapeño if desired.

SERVING SUGGESTIONS:

- Serve with tortilla chips as a snack or appetizer.
- Place a scoop on top of grilled salmon, chicken, or omelet.
- Serve with any Mexican dish.

SALSA

2-1/2 to 3 cups   Easy $

"It was the end of the summer, and I had a bumper crop of tomatoes. Believe it or not, I had never made basic tomato salsa, so I thought it was about time to try. It was surprisingly easy, and tasted much fresher than jarred salsa. Once you've made this basic version, feel free to experiment and give it your own signature. I usually add cilantro as indicated, but sometimes I use whatever herbs are plentiful in my garden at the time (e.g., basil, chives, savory, tarragon, parsley)." BOBBI

Prep Time: 15 minutes

Tools: knife and cutting board, medium bowl, measuring cups and spoons, hand juicer (optional)

2 large tomatoes (about 2 cups chopped)

1/4 cup finely chopped onion

2 garlic cloves

1/4 cup chopped **cilantro***

1/2 small jalapeño (optional)

1 lime (about 1-1/2 tablespoons juice)

1/2 tablespoon oil (extra virgin olive oil recommended)

1 teaspoon salt

1/4 teaspoon ground cumin

1/8 teaspoon ground black pepper

Hot pepper sauce, to taste

*TIP
Cilantro stems are more flavorful than the leaves, in a good way. We usually remove only the larger stems (primarily for aesthetic reasons) and chop the smaller ones along with the leaves.

1. Cut tomatoes in halves or quarters. Scoop or squeeze out most of the center seeds and juices. Chop to the size you prefer. Place in a medium bowl.
2. Finely chop onion, garlic, and cilantro, then add to tomatoes.
3. Cut off stem end of the pepper and slice in half lengthwise. Remove and discard inner seeds and pith. Wear gloves if sensitive. Mince <u>one half</u> of the jalapeño and add to the tomato mixture.
4. Juice lime directly into salsa. Add oil and stir well.
5. Add salt, pepper, cumin, and hot sauce, to taste. Add more jalapeño if desired.

SERVING SUGGESTIONS:

- Serve with chips and guacamole.
- Serve on top of grilled chicken or salmon.
- Use in SALSA CHICKEN WITH SPINACH.

SWEET AND SALTY NUTS

3 cups   Easy $

This is a surprisingly delicious way to use Chinese 5-spice. Bring these to a Chinese New Year's dinner, and see if your friends can identify the secret ingredient!

Prep Time: 5 to 10 minutes   **Passive Time:** 10 minutes   **Cook Time:** 40 to 50 minutes
Tools: rimmed baking sheet, measuring cups and spoons, medium and large bowls

1/4 cup sugar
1/2 tablespoon Chinese 5-spice blend
1 egg white
2 cups raw peanuts (with or without skin)

1 cup raw cashews (whole cashews recommended)
Salt (kosher or coarse ground recommended)

Preheat oven to 275°F. Spray oil onto a rimmed baking sheet, or line with parchment paper.

1. Mix sugar and 5-spice in a large bowl. Set aside.
2. Place egg white in a medium bowl and beat with a whisk (or fork) until foamy.
3. Add nuts to the egg white and stir to coat.
4. Pour nuts into the sugar and spice mixture and stir well.
5. Spread evenly on baking sheet and sprinkle salt over them. Bake 40 to 50 minutes.
6. Cool slightly (about 10 minutes), then break apart and serve. Store in an airtight container after completely cooled.

BREAKFAST, BRUNCH, LUNCH

Whether you're eating a quick breakfast before dashing out the door, enjoying a lazy Sunday morning brunch, or packing a lunch-to-go, we offer a good selection of recipes. Also included are numerous variations to make sure you won't get bored. Although listed here, many of these dishes are perfect for a light dinner as well.

AÇAI BOWL

2 servings   Easy $$

"When I was in high school, my mom and I went to California to visit colleges. That's when we experienced Açai Bowls for the first time. From that point on, we were hooked. We set out to make our own at home, so we wouldn't have to wait for another trip to the West Coast. Now, we can enjoy this energy-boosting breakfast treat anytime. See Variations for more options, including a pitaya (aka dragon fruit) bowl." REBECCA

Prep Time: 10 minutes
Tools: blender, knife and cutting board, measuring cups and spoons

Purée mixture:
2 (100g) packets frozen unsweetened **açai*** purée, or 1-1/2 cups frozen blueberries
1 banana (frozen)
1/4 cup coconut milk, or almond milk
1 tablespoon honey
Juice from 1 lime

Toppings:
2/3 cup granola
1 banana
1 cup fresh berries (assorted)
2 tablespoons shredded or flaked coconut (optional)
2 tablespoons nuts, or seeds (optional)

*Açai is a South American super fruit that has high levels of antioxidants, vitamins A, B, C, and K, iron, calcium, magnesium, zinc, fiber, fatty acids, and amino acids. It has low levels of sugar and calories. Since the berries don't travel well, they can only be purchased in the U.S. as a frozen purée. Sambazon is a common brand that can be found in many grocery stores in the frozen fruit section.

For purée mixture:

1. Combine *purée* ingredients in a blender and blend until smooth. Adjust amounts as needed to reach the consistency of sorbet.

To assemble and serve:

1. Slice banana and fresh strawberries (if using).
2. Divide purée between two bowls.
3. Sprinkle 1/3 cup granola over each serving.
4. Arrange berries, banana slices, coconut, and nuts (and/or seeds) on top as desired.

VARIATIONS:

- If you can't find frozen açai purée, use frozen blueberries, blackberries, raspberries, or a mixture of berries. Another popular option is to combine half açai purée and half frozen berries.

- MEXICAN PITAYA BOWL – Substitute 2 cups frozen pitaya chunks for açai. *Note:* Some stores now carry frozen pitaya purée, but we usually chop our own chunks and freeze them. Increase coconut milk to 1/2 cup and honey to 2 tablespoons. Otherwise, follow recipe.

- HOT AND COLD AÇAI OR PITAYA BOWL – Cook oatmeal or quinoa according to package instructions, using half water and half coconut or almond milk. Prepare purée mixture per the recipe. Place a scoop of hot cereal in a bowl, then top with some of the açai or pitaya mixture. Add other toppings as desired.

BAKED FRENCH TOAST

12 pieces   Easy $

If you like French toast, but don't want to stand over the stove cooking batch after batch, try baking it in the oven on a baking sheet. We use whole wheat hamburger buns, which have a surprisingly nice texture for French toast. However, sliced bread—enough to fill the baking sheet—will also work. Toasted pecans and brown sugar add a sweet crunch, making maple syrup optional.

Prep Time: 15 minutes   **Passive Time:** 2 minutes   **Cook Time:** 25 minutes
Tools: rimmed (10×15-inch) baking sheet, large bowl, measuring cups and spoons

6 whole wheat hamburger buns
3 tablespoons butter
4 eggs
1-1/2 cups milk

1/2 teaspoon ground cinnamon
1/2 teaspoon ground cardamom
1/4 teaspoon ground nutmeg

Topping:

1/4 cup chopped pecans

1/4 cup brown sugar

Preheat oven to 375°F.

1. Place butter in rimmed baking sheet, and set in oven while it preheats. Watch carefully and remove from oven as soon as butter melts and before it turns brown. Cool slightly.

2. While butter melts, lightly beat eggs in a large bowl. Mix in milk and spices.

3. Open buns and rub cut side (inside of buns) in the melted butter. Flip over and arrange on baking sheet with cut-side up.

4. Pour egg mixture over the bread. Sprinkle pecans and brown sugar evenly on top. Let stand 5 minutes.

5. Turn buns over and press down to fit into baking sheet.

6. Bake (uncovered) 25 minutes.

7. Remove from baking sheet with a food turner, and serve with the cut-side up.

8. Serve with or without maple syrup.

BREAKFAST SPINACH BURRITOS

10 burritos   Easy $$

"Watch one episode of your favorite show on Netflix while you make these, and you'll have enough breakfast burritos for a week or two. Freeze them and thaw out in the microwave for a quick, hot breakfast. If I can do it, you can do it!" GREG

Prep Time: 30 to 45 minutes, start to finish
Tools: knife and cutting board, large (10-inch) skillet, measuring cups, grater
Special Supplies: aluminum foil

1 large onion

1 tablespoon high-heat cooking oil

1 large bell pepper (any color)

2 cups sliced mushrooms (fresh or frozen)

1 (10-ounce) package frozen chopped spinach

2 tablespoons butter, or high-heat cooking oil

1 dozen eggs

1/2 teaspoon salt

1/4 teaspoon ground black pepper

8 ounces sharp cheddar cheese (2 to 3 cups, grated)

Hot pepper sauce, to taste (sriracha recommended)

10 (8-inch) whole wheat or spinach tortillas/wraps

For vegetables:

1. Chop onion. Heat oil in a large skillet over medium-low heat, then add onion. Cook and stir occasionally while you continue.

2. Chop pepper and slice mushrooms (or thaw frozen mushrooms in the microwave), adding to the onions as you finish each one. Cook another few minutes, then add frozen spinach. Cook and stir until vegetables are soft and spinach is hot. Transfer to a colander and press down with the back of a spoon to remove all of the excess liquid and avoid soggy tortillas.

For eggs:

1. Clean the large skillet well, then place over medium heat. Once hot, add butter to melt. Add eggs, salt, and pepper. Stir with fork to scramble, but don't overcook (see SCRAMBLED EGGS recipe for more details).

2. Remove skillet from heat. Stir in vegetable mixture.

3. Grate cheese and set aside.

To assemble:

1. Make 10 squares out of aluminum foil, using the full width of the foil.

2. Place one tortilla on a foil square. Spread about 1/2 to 3/4 cup egg mixture in the center third. Sprinkle about 1/4 cup grated cheese over filling. Squeeze a line of hot sauce across it.

3. Fold top and bottom 1 inch of tortilla over filling, then fold sides. Wrap burrito in the foil.

4. Repeat until all are done. These will keep in the refrigerator up to two days. Freeze others by placing the wrapped tortillas into a plastic bag or container.

SERVING SUGGESTION:

- To reheat frozen burritos, do not thaw. Simply remove foil, wrap burrito in a damp paper towel, and microwave on medium heat about 3 to 5 minutes. Unwrap and enjoy!

CHALLAH FRENCH TOAST

10 slices   Easy $

Also called pain perdu, French toast is a great way to turn stale bread into an elegant breakfast. We buy bread and let it dry out on purpose, just to have an excuse to make this! Challah is an egg bread, similar to brioche. Both have a great texture and work well in this dish. Of course, French bread (or even whole wheat bread) can also be substituted. We make our batter with whole milk, but you can substitute half-and-half for a richer version, or almond milk for a dairy-free option. We usually serve this breakfast for holidays, or anytime we want to celebrate something special.

Prep and Cook Time: 30 minutes, start to finish

Tools: knife and cutting board, baking sheet, large bowl, measuring cups and spoons, large (10-inch) skillet

1 loaf challah bread

6 eggs

1-1/4 cups whole milk

1 tablespoon maple syrup, or other sweetener

1 teaspoon vanilla

1/2 teaspoon ground cinnamon

Pinch salt

Butter, or spray oil (for cooking)

Toppings:

Maple syrup, or powdered sugar

Fresh fruit (optional)

Preheat oven on lowest setting.

1. Cut bread into 1-inch-thick slices (or less) and set on a baking sheet. Place in oven to dry out slightly while you continue.

2. Break eggs into a large bowl. Whisk in milk, maple syrup, vanilla, cinnamon, and salt. Don't overbeat, but make sure the ingredients are well blended.

3. Remove bread from oven and transfer to a plate. Return empty baking sheet to oven to keep warm.

4. Place a large skillet over medium-low heat.

5. While skillet warms up, gently lower two or three slices of challah bread into the egg mixture. Turn over the bread after 10 to 15 seconds and soak another 5 to 10 seconds on the other side, or until they feel heavy (but not so wet that they fall apart).

6. Melt about 1 teaspoon butter in the hot skillet (or use spray oil). Gently place the soaked pieces in the skillet, and cook on the first side about 2 minutes, or until nicely browned. Flip over, and cook another 2 minutes, or until firm but still moist in the center.

7. When second side is almost done, place another two or three slices of bread in the egg mixture to begin soaking as previously described. Repeat until all slices have been cooked.

8. Place cooked slices on baking sheet and keep warm in oven until ready to eat.

9. Serve with maple syrup, or **dust*** with powdered sugar.

*TIP

To **dust** with powdered sugar, place a tablespoon of powdered sugar in a fine mesh colander or tea strainer, then tap on the side to release a fine layer of sugar.

SERVING SUGGESTION:

- Sprinkle fresh berries on the top, or serve on the side.

CHEESY GREEN RICE CASSEROLE

4 to 6 servings   Moderate $

"This recipe works for breakfast, lunch, or dinner, and it's one of my favorite dishes to bring to a potluck. Why? Because it's an economical, gluten-free meal-in-one! Start preparing the vegetables while rice is cooking, to save time. I like it with mild chilies, but Nick prefers the spicier version with chipotle peppers (see Variations). He even adds an extra chipotle on top of his serving, but that's not for the faint of heart!" REBECCA

Prep Time: 50 minutes   **Passive Time:** 10 minutes   **Cook Time:** 25 minutes
Tools: measuring cups and spoons, colander, large (4-quart) saucepan, 8×8-inch baking dish, knife and cutting board, grater, small bowl

Rice:

1 cup brown rice (dry, uncooked)

1-3/4 cups water

1 teaspoon salt

Casserole:

2 cups chopped frozen greens

2 tablespoons butter

1 **small onion,*** or shallot

4 garlic cloves

4 ounces grated Monterey Jack or
  Cheddar cheese (about 1-1/2 cups),
  <u>divided</u>

3 eggs

1 (4-ounce) can chopped mild green
  chilies

1 cup plain yogurt

1 teaspoon chili powder

1 teaspoon ground cumin

1 teaspoon paprika (smoked
  recommended)

TIP
Prep time includes preparing the rice,
but one way to save about half an hour is
to cook rice up to 24 hours in advance.

***A small onion** should be about 2-1/2 inches
in diameter. This is the size that usually
comes in a bag of onions at the grocery store.
Any onion 2-1/2 to 3 inches in diameter is
a medium size, and more than 3 inches is
considered a large onion. If the recipe calls
for a small onion, but yours is 3 inches or
larger, use half. It doesn't have to be exact
and depends on how much onion you want
in the dish.

For rice:

1. Rinse rice in a colander and drain. Bring water and salt to a boil in large saucepan
   over high heat.

2. Add rice, stir, then bring back to a boil. Turn heat down to low or medium-low. Cover
   and cook 35 minutes. Remove from heat and let stand 10 minutes. Fluff with a fork.

3. Once rice has been removed from the heat to stand, preheat oven to 375°F. Spray oil
   into baking dish, then place butter in it. Set in oven (while it preheats) to melt butter.
   Remove dish from oven.

For vegetables:

1. Measure frozen spinach in a 2-cup, glass measuring cup and thaw slightly at room
   temperature or in the microwave.

2. Finely chop onion and mince garlic. Add to melted butter in baking dish and return
   to oven to soften, stirring occasionally.

3. Grate cheese. Lightly beat eggs in a small bowl.

To assemble and bake:

1. When onion and garlic are soft and fragrant, remove baking dish from oven and stir
   in spinach, green chilies, yogurt, chili powder, cumin, and paprika. Add rice and stir
   again.

2. Mix in eggs, then stir in a little more than half of the cheese.

3. Smooth the top and sprinkle remaining cheese over the casserole.

4. Bake (uncovered) in preheated oven 25 minutes, or until bubbling and slightly browned. Let stand about 10 minutes before serving.

SERVING SUGGESTIONS:
- Serve with carrot sticks, CARROT APPLE SALAD, or fruit salad.

VARIATIONS:
- For a spicier version, substitute 1 tablespoon minced chipotle pepper in adobo for the mild green chilies.
- Substitute 1 (5-ounce) package fresh baby greens (like spinach or kale) for frozen greens, and chop coarsely.
- Add 1 cup chopped red bell pepper, fire roasted bell peppers, or mushrooms, along with the onion and garlic.

GRILLED CHEESE SANDWICH

1 sandwich   Easy $

Who doesn't love a grilled cheese sandwich? We make ours with plain old Cheddar cheese and whole wheat bread. For a creamier melted cheese texture, mix Cheddar and Monterrey Jack (or pepper jack). We add Dijon mustard for a little pizazz. Use a large skillet to cook two at a time. Take a look at our Variations, and enjoy a different grilled cheese sandwich every day of the week!

Prep Time: 5 minutes   **Cook Time:** 5 minutes
Tools: knife and cutting board, grater (optional), small (8-inch) skillet

2 to 3 slices Cheddar cheese, or 1/2 cup grated

1/4 cup grated Monterey Jack cheese (optional)

2 slices bread

Dijon mustard

1 to 2 teaspoons butter

1. Slice and/or grate cheese.

2. Lay bread on a plate and spread Dijon mustard on one or both slices.

3. Place cheese slices and/or grated cheese on one slice. Top with remaining slice of bread.

4. Heat skillet over medium heat. Add 1 teaspoon butter* and swirl the skillet to coat. Turn heat down to medium-low or low.

5. Place sandwich into skillet. Cook about 2 minutes on each side, or until bread has browned. (Add another teaspoon of butter before cooking other side if desired.) *Note:* If you have a lid, cover the pan to melt cheese more quickly. Check frequently, since it will also brown more quickly.

*TIP
Alternatively, use softened butter and spread it evenly on the outside of both pieces of bread before assembling. Heat skillet then place buttered sandwich directly into it.

SERVING SUGGESTION:

- You can't beat the classic meal of a grilled cheese sandwich with tomato soup!

VARIATIONS:

- Try Swiss, Gouda, Havarti, fontina, mozzarella, provolone, or a combination.
- TOMATO GRILLED CHEESE – Add sliced tomatoes on top of cheese, or in between cheeses.
- CAPRESE GRILLED CHEESE – Use mozzarella instead of Cheddar and 2 tablespoons grated Parmesan cheese instead of Monterey Jack. Add sliced tomato and substitute pesto for mustard.
- EASY CROQUE MONSIEUR – Add 1 to 2 slices ham, then sprinkle 1/4 cup grated Swiss cheese on top, omitting other cheeses.
- EASY CROQUE MADAME – Make a Croque Monsieur and when it's done, top sandwich with a fried or poached egg.
- VERMONTER – Use extra sharp white Cheddar and add thin slices of tart apple.
- GO DUTCH – Use rye bread, Gouda (or Edam) cheese and beer mustard. Add sliced ham if desired.

HOT CEREALS

Easy $

Hot cereal is an easy and satisfying breakfast. There are many options including oats, oat bran, cream of rice, cream of wheat, cream of buckwheat, and mixed grains. We always suggest following package instructions. However, if you buy various types of oats in the bulk section (without directions), follow this simple cooking guide. We use water, milk, or a combination of the two, as the liquid component.

Prep Time: 2 minutes   **Passive Time:** 2 to 5 minutes   **Cook Time:** varies
Tools: saucepan (size varies per number of servings), measuring cups

FOR ROLLED OATS:

2 parts liquid and 1 part rolled oats, using 1/2 cup oats per serving.
Cook 10 minutes.

FOR STEEL-CUT OATS:

3 parts liquid and 1 part steel-cut oats, using 1/2 cup oats per serving.
Cook 20 minutes.

FOR OAT BRAN:

1 cup liquid and 1/3 cup oat bran per serving.
Cook 2 minutes.

1. Combine liquid and salt in a saucepan and bring to a boil over medium-high heat.
2. Add oats and stir until boiling again.
3. Turn heat to low and cook according to above instructions.
4. Remove from heat. Cover and let stand a few minutes.

TIP
Add a pinch of salt to cooking water to bring out the flavor of the grains.

VARIATIONS:

- ALMOND DATE – Cook oats in almond milk. Top with sliced almonds and chopped dates.
- APPLE SPICE – Top with chopped apples, raisins (or currants), pecans, cinnamon, and brown sugar.
- CHOCOLATE CHERRY – Top with dark chocolate chunks and dried or fresh (pitted) cherries.
- CRANBERRY ALMOND – Top with cranberries, sliced almonds, cinnamon, nutmeg, cream, and honey.
- GINGER MAPLE WALNUT – Stir in ground ginger, cinnamon, and cardamom. Top with walnuts, maple syrup, and chopped candied ginger (optional).
- HONEY PEAR AND PINE NUTS – Top with chopped pear, honey, and toasted pine nuts.
- PISTACHIO POMEGRANATE – Top with pistachios, pomegranate arils (seeds), and honey.
- PUMPKIN COCONUT – Cook oats in half water and half coconut milk. When done, stir in 1 to 2 tablespoons pumpkin purée per serving, ground ginger, cinnamon, and nutmeg. Top with walnuts, shredded coconut, and maple syrup.
- SEEDY-NUTTY – Cook oats in coconut or almond milk. Top with your choice of nuts, ground flaxseeds, pumpkin seeds, shredded coconut, and hemp hearts. Add ground cinnamon and honey.
- SUGAR AND SPICE – Top with brown sugar and your choice of spices like cinnamon, ginger, nutmeg, allspice, cardamom, or cloves.

OVERNIGHT OATS

1 serving   Easy $ to $$

If you love oatmeal but don't want hot cereal in the summer, or if you don't have time to prepare breakfast in the morning, try overnight oats. The variations are endless, but we've included some of our favorites.

Prep Time: 5 minutes   **Passive Time:** overnight
Tools: measuring cups and spoons
Special Supplies: mason jar (or small bowl with lid)

Basic mixture:
1 cup almond milk, or similar
1/2 cup old-fashioned rolled oats
1 tablespoon nut butter
1 teaspoon honey, or other sweetener

TIP
If desired, wait to sweeten in the morning, after all extras have been added. You might not need any added sweeteners.

1. Pour milk into a mason jar (or small bowl). Add oats, nut butter, and honey if desired. Mix well with a spoon.

2. Stir in extras like dried fruit, chia or flaxseeds, and spices. Wait until the morning before adding items that will become soggy or discolored, like fresh fruit, nuts, or granola. Cover and refrigerate overnight.

3. In the morning, stir again. Add more spices or sweetener, to taste.

4. Sprinkle remaining add-ins on top.

VARIATIONS:

- Substitute a different grain, like buckwheat groats, quinoa, millet, or a combination for up to half of the oats.

- BOBBI'S BASIC – Add dried fruit, coconut, ground flaxseeds (or chia seeds), spices (cinnamon, ginger, cardamom, nutmeg, and/or cloves) to basic mixture. In the morning, garnish with nuts, seeds, granola, fruit, and/or yogurt.

- AMBROSIA – Substitute coconut milk for the almond milk. Add chopped dried apricots, shredded coconut, and allspice to basic mixture. In the morning garnish with pineapple (crushed or chopped), chopped pecans, and shredded coconut.

- APPLE PIE – Use maple syrup as sweetener. Add raisins (or currants), cinnamon, vanilla, and nutmeg to basic mixture. In the morning, garnish with chopped apple and walnuts (or pecans). *Note:* Substitute chopped dried apples for fresh, and add the night before.

- CHOCOLATE-COVERED CHERRY – Add dried cherries, cacao nibs (or dark chocolate chips), 1 tablespoon almond butter, and 1 teaspoon cacao powder to basic mixture. In the morning, garnish with pecans.

- PRALINE – Use brown sugar as sweetener in the basic mixture. In the morning, add cream and chopped pecans.
- TIN ROOF – Use peanut butter. In the morning, add about 1/2 tablespoon cacao nibs (or chocolate chips) and salted peanuts.
- TURKISH DELIGHT – Add 1 to 2 chopped dried figs, 1 tablespoon dried mulberries (or raisins), cinnamon, and cardamom to basic mixture. In the morning, garnish with walnuts.

PANCAKES

18 to 20 (3-inch) pancakes   Easy $

"Rebecca and Greg grew up eating these simple whole wheat pancakes almost every weekend, so they learned to appreciate the earthy flavor of whole wheat at an early age. We would top our pancakes with fresh fruit and nuts, and I felt comfortable knowing the kids were having a nutritious breakfast. If you don't like the heaviness of 100% whole wheat, substitute white flour for half of it. Using this recipe as a base, you can be very creative—see our Variations for ideas. If you make pancakes often, you might consider purchasing a cast iron griddle pan." BOBBI

Prep Time: 10 minutes   **Passive Time:** 10 minutes   **Cook Time:** 2 to 3 minutes, per batch
Tools: measuring cups and spoons, medium and large bowls, large (10-inch) skillet, food turner

Dry ingredients:

2 cups whole wheat flour (pastry flour recommended)
1 tablespoon granulated sugar
2-1/2 teaspoons baking powder
1 teaspoon baking soda
1 teaspoon ground cinnamon
1/2 teaspoon salt

Wet ingredients:

2 eggs
2 cups milk
1 tablespoon high-heat cooking oil

1. Combine dry ingredients in a large bowl and stir.
2. Lightly beat eggs in a medium bowl. Stir in milk and oil.
3. Make a well in the center of the dry ingredients and pour milk mixture into it. Stir gently with a whisk (or kitchen spoon) just until flour is incorporated. (Don't worry about small lumps.)
4. Let stand about 10 minutes to thicken. (This is a good time to clean up or cut fresh fruit.)

To cook pancakes:

1. **Heat*** a large skillet over medium heat. Once hot enough, spray lightly with oil, or add about 1/2 teaspoon of oil or butter.

2. *Optional step:* Heat oil a few seconds, then carefully wipe off the excess oil with a paper towel, leaving a thin film. This will help the pancakes brown evenly, with no dark splotches. Omit this step if using butter.

3. Return skillet to stovetop and turn heat to medium-low. Pour 1/4 cup batter per pancake into the skillet, to make three pancakes at a time.

4. When a few bubbles begin to pop on the top and the underside is golden brown (about 1 to 2 minutes), turn over with a food turner. Cook another 30 to 60 seconds on the other side. (Adjust heat as needed.)

5. Repeat until all pancakes are done, spraying skillet with oil and wiping us excess every two or three batches. Serve as they come out of the skillet, or **keep warm*** until ready to serve.

SERVING SUGGESTION:

- Add a dollop of butter on top and serve with real (not artificial) maple syrup. Sprinkle fresh fruit and/or chopped nuts over pancakes if desired.

---

*You can place cooked pancakes on a plate and simply cover the pancakes lightly with a piece of foil to **keep warm**, but they tend to become somewhat soggy. To prevent this, turn oven to low. If you have a cooling rack (used for cakes and cookies), set it on the oven rack and place the pancakes in one layer on top of it. If you don't have a cooling rack, place the pancakes directly onto the oven racks, but make sure the pancakes don't fall through. This keeps the pancakes from getting soggy on the bottom. To prevent drying out, don't overcook and turn the heat off once the oven is adequately warm. Serve pancakes as soon as possible.

---

*TIP

Always **heat** the empty skillet first, then add fat so it doesn't burn. To determine if the skillet is ready, sprinkle a drop of water onto the hot skillet. If it stays in a round shape and bounces, the pan is hot enough. If the drop of water explodes and splatters, remove skillet from heat and cool a few seconds.

VARIATIONS:

- APPLE – Finely chop half an apple. Place in a small bowl and toss with 1 tablespoon flour and 1 tablespoon brown sugar. Fold into batter. Chop other half of apple and toss with another tablespoon of brown sugar and 2 tablespoons chopped walnuts. Sprinkle this mixture on top of cooked pancakes.
- BLUEBERRY – Toss 1/2 cup blueberries (fresh or frozen) in 1 tablespoon flour, then fold into batter before cooking. Add grated zest of one lemon if desired.
- BUTTERMILK – Use buttermilk, or add 1 tablespoon lemon juice to milk and let stand until ready to mix into batter.
- CHOCOLATE CHIP – Add 1/4 cup tiny chocolate chips to batter, and sprinkle more on top.
- GINGERBREAD – Add 1 tablespoon ground ginger, 1/4 teaspoon ground nutmeg, and 1/8 teaspoon ground cloves to dry ingredients.
- MAPLE WALNUT – Stir 1/2 cup finely chopped walnuts into batter and top with extra walnuts and maple syrup.
- PUMPKIN SPICE – Substitute 1/3 cup pumpkin purée for one of the eggs. Add 1 teaspoon ground ginger, 1/4 teaspoon allspice, 1/4 teaspoon ground cardamom, and 1/8 teaspoon ground cloves.
- STRAWBERRY YOGURT – Use 1 cup milk and 1 cup plain yogurt. Substitute 1/2 teaspoon ground cardamom for cinnamon. Stir 1 cup chopped strawberries into batter. Top with additional strawberries and sugar. Add a dollop of whipped cream if desired.
- Apply any of these variations to your favorite pancake mix.

QUINOA BLACK BEAN CASSEROLE

4 to 6 servings   Moderate $$

"Quinoa is an absolute staple in our house, even though it's a little more expensive than rice or pasta. It's a high-protein, gluten-free grain that works with our vegetarian diet. We're always looking for creative ways to use quinoa, and this casserole is one of our favorites. (It's also a good way to use up some leftover quinoa from the night before.) Made with 1 tablespoon chipotles, the dish will be medium-spicy, so we suggest you start there. If you're like Nick and want it extra-spicy, use 2 tablespoons, or just serve extra on the side." REBECCA

Prep Time: 15 minutes   **Passive Time:** 10 minutes   **Cook Time:** 45 minutes
Tools: 8×8-inch baking dish, knife and cutting board, measuring cups and spoons, colander, grater, large bowl

2 cups <u>cooked</u> quinoa

1 (15-ounce) can black beans

6 eggs

1 small onion

1/2 cup chopped cilantro, or parsley

1 to 2 tablespoons minced chipotle peppers in adobo

1 (14.5-ounce) can diced tomatoes

1 teaspoon ground cumin

1/2 teaspoon salt

8 ounces Monterrey Jack cheese (2 to 3 cups grated), <u>divided in half</u>

Garnish: (optional)

1 avocado

Preheat oven to 375°F. Spray oil into baking dish.

1. Use leftover quinoa, or cook some now according to package instructions (or follow our recipe for BASIC QUINOA).

2. Drain and rinse beans in a colander.

3. Break eggs into a large bowl and beat lightly with a whisk (or fork).

4. **Finely chop*** onion and cilantro, then **mince*** chipotle pepper, adding each to the eggs as you finish.

5. Stir in quinoa, beans, tomatoes (with their juices), cumin, and salt.

6. Grate cheese and stir in <u>half</u>.

7. Pour mixture into baking dish. Sprinkle remaining cheese on top. Bake (uncovered) 45 minutes. Remove from heat and let stand at least 10 minutes.

8. Cut into four or six pieces. Garnish with avocado slices if desired.

VARIATIONS:

• Make with brown rice for a more economical version.

• For a milder version, substitute 1 (4-ounce) can chopped green chilies for chipotle pepper.

• Eliminate chipotle pepper and use pepper jack in place of plain Monterey Jack.

---

*What's the difference between the terms mince and finely chop?
It's all about the size.

• **Mince** – to cut into very tiny pieces, about 1/16 inch or smaller.

• **Chop** – to cut into small pieces, usually 1/2 inch or less, but not necessarily uniform. Other variations: **coarsely chop** – slightly bigger pieces; **finely chop** – smaller pieces, but larger than minced.

SMOOTHIES

2 cups   Easy $ to $$

Smoothies are a great way to start your day. Use our Basic Smoothie Guideline and create all sorts of combinations. Berries, frozen cherries, peaches, mango, papaya, and pineapple are among our favorites. We usually add a scoop of protein powder (whey or plant) and ground flaxseeds (or chia) to all of our smoothies, and sometimes a scoop of green powder, coconut oil, fish oil, nutritional yeast, bee pollen, etc. You can make these as nutrient-packed as you want! Also see our specific Variations.

Prep Time: 5 to 10 minutes (if cutting up fruit)
Tools: blender, measuring cups spoons, knife and cutting board (optional)

BASIC SMOOTHIE GUIDELINES
1 cup cold water, milk, non-dairy milk, or combination
1 cup fresh or frozen fruit
Ice cubes (if not using frozen fruit)

Add-ins: (optional)

2 tablespoons yogurt

1 scoop protein powder (whey or plant-based)

1 tablespoon ground flaxseeds, chia, or hemp seeds

1 tablespoon nut butter

1 tablespoon coconut

Sweetener (honey, sugar, stevia)

Superfoods (green powder, bee pollen, nutritional yeast, coconut oil, fish oil, etc.)

Spices, or herbs

1. Pour liquid into blender container.
2. Add fruit and optional ice cubes. Adjust amount for desired consistency.
3. Include any of the optional add-ins you choose.
4. Blend until smooth.

---

*Cacao powder is made from the cacao nut, and is minimally processed at a low temperature, preserving most of the fiber, nutrients, and antioxidants. It's more expensive, but also more healthful. Cocoa powder is also made from cacao, but is more processed, and at a higher temperature. Most cocoa powder is then alkalinized (Dutch-process) which makes for a smoother, but less rich flavor. Cocoa powder still contains a fair amount of the nutrients and is less expensive than cacao powder, so it has its advantages. Cacao nibs are broken up pieces of the roasted cacao bean.

VARIATIONS: (Add a scoop of whey or plant-based protein powder if desired.)

- ALMOND JOY – Blend 1 cup ice cubes, 1/2 cup almond or coconut milk, 1/2 frozen banana, 2 tablespoons coconut, 1 tablespoon unsweetened **cacao*** (or cocoa) powder, 1 tablespoon almond butter, and 1 teaspoon honey until smooth.

- AVOCADO – Follow Basic and simply add 1/4 to 1/2 ripe avocado.

- CHERRY AVOCADO – Follow Basic, use 1/2 cup frozen cherries and 1/2 frozen banana as the fruit. Add 1/4 ripe avocado, and 2 to 4 fresh basil leaves (optional).

- MELON – Substitute 1 cup cantaloupe, honeydew, or watermelon chunks for 1/2 cup of liquid, and use water for the remaining 1/2 cup. Add 1 cup fruit (mango, papaya, peach, and kiwi are good choices). Add ice cubes if not using frozen fruit.

- PAPAYA GINGER – Use papaya as the fruit. Add 1 teaspoon ground ginger (or 1 small piece fresh ginger if you have a powerful blender), juice from 1/2 lime, 2 fresh mint leaves (optional), and honey, to taste.

- PINEAPPLE COCONUT – Blend 1 cup ice cubes, 1/2 cup coconut milk (not canned), 1 cup pineapple chunks, 1/2 frozen banana, 1 tablespoon shredded coconut, 1 tablespoon cashew butter or tahini (optional), 1/8 teaspoon ground allspice (optional), and honey, to taste.

EGGS

BOILED EGGS (SOFT, MEDIUM, OR HARD)

Easy $

"Boiled eggs are very easy to make, but not so easy to cook perfectly every time. I ate a lot of boiled eggs trying to perfect these instructions! Unlike some people, I prefer to bring the water to a boil before placing the eggs in it. That way I can more accurately time how long they've been boiling. Other factors to take into consideration include the size of eggs and how many are in the pan. We used 4 to 6 large eggs, and cooked them in a 4-quart saucepan. We used our 1-quart saucepan for 1 to 3 eggs." BOBBI

Prep Time: 1 minute   **Passive Time:** varies   **Cook Time:** varies
Tools: saucepan

Eggs
Water (for cooking)
Pinch salt

1. Fill a saucepan with at least three inches of water and a pinch of salt.
2. Cover the pan and bring the water to a boil over high to medium-high heat. (It takes longer on a gas stovetop than an electric one.)
3. Once water is boiling, lower heat to medium. Place egg in a spoon, then gently lower into boiling water. Repeat with each egg. Water should cover the eggs, but not so close to the top of the pan that it will boil over.
4. Immediately set timer to 5 minutes. Bring to and maintain a gentle boil (uncovered). Lower heat as needed to keep water at a gentle boil.
5. After 5 minutes, remove pan from heat. (If water does not come to a boil within 5 minutes, add 1 minute to the standing times specified below for medium and hard-boiled eggs.)

TIP
Eggs are easier to peel shortly after rinsing and while still warm. If the shell does not come off easily, hold egg under a thin stream of water while peeling it.

6. Cover pan with lid and use the following guide to determine how long to leave eggs in the hot water, depending on what type of egg you want:
   - **Soft-boiled** *(white is cooked but yolk is runny):* Do not leave in water at all. Remove eggs right away and let stand 1 minute before rinsing.
   - **Medium-boiled** *(yolk is not quite done all the way through and is still dark yellow):* Leave eggs in hot water 4 to 5 minutes.
   - **Hard-boiled** *(yolk is cooked through, but there's no gray coating):* Leave eggs in hot water 10 to 11 minutes. (The gray coating on the outside of the yolk is fine to eat, just not pretty. It indicates the eggs were overcooked.)
7. When the appropriate time has passed, rinse with cold water for 30 seconds, or place in a bowl of ice-cold water.

CRUSTLESS QUICHE

4 to 6 servings   Moderate $$

Do you love quiche, but not the extra calories in a pie crust? Try this easy alternative that is much lighter on the calorie scale. There are many variations, but this is our original, from which all of the others were created. Once you get the hang of it, you can come up with your own versions. We use frozen chopped kale, but any type of leafy greens will work. Make your quiche with 6 to 8 eggs, depending on their size and your preference. Cheddar, Swiss, and Monterey Jack cheeses are our favorites, but feta, Brie, mozzarella, or mixtures are also nice. Pesto is the secret ingredient that adds another layer of flavor. The small amount of flour absorbs excess moisture and provides a thin, crust-like layer on the bottom.

Prep Time: 20 minutes   **Cook Time:** 35 minutes   **Passive Time:** 10 minutes
Tools: 8×8-inch baking dish (or a 9-inch pie plate), measuring cups and spoons, knife and cutting board, large (10-inch) skillet, grater

Vegetables:

1-1/2 cups frozen chopped kale, or other greens

1 small onion

1 tablespoon butter, or high-heat cooking oil

1 cup cherry tomatoes, or chopped tomatoes (fresh or canned)

4 garlic cloves

Egg Mixture:

6 to 8 eggs

2 tablespoons pesto (optional)

1/2 teaspoon salt

Pinch nutmeg

Pinch red pepper flakes

1 cup milk (2%, whole, half-and-half, or non-dairy)

3 tablespoons flour (wheat or gluten-free)

8 ounces cheese (about 2 cups grated), divided

Garnish: (optional) Ground nutmeg

Preheat oven to 375°F. Spray or rub oil into 8×8-inch baking dish.

For vegetables:

1. Place frozen kale in a microwave-safe measuring cup (or small bowl) and thaw in microwave on high 1 minute. (Alternatively add frozen kale to skillet as indicated below, but cook a little longer.)

2. Chop onion. Melt butter in a large skillet over medium-low heat, then add onion. Cook and stir while you continue. Lower heat if needed.

3. Slice cherry tomatoes into halves or quarters. (If using a large tomato, cut in halves or quarters then gently squeeze out some of the juices and scrape out most of the seeds before chopping.) Drain excess juices. Add tomatoes to skillet. Cook and stir while you continue.

4. Mince garlic and add to skillet. Cook another minute.

5. Stir in chopped kale and continue cooking until most of the moisture has evaporated, about 3 to 5 minutes. Remove from heat.

TIP

If using fresh (not frozen) kale or collards, be sure to **blanch*** them first to soften. Use the same amount of blanched greens as frozen. Tender greens like spinach and chard do not need to be blanched.

For egg mixture:

1. While vegetables cook, break eggs directly into baking dish (to save on dirty dishes). Add pesto, salt, nutmeg, and red pepper flakes, then beat lightly with a whisk (or fork).

2. Measure about 1/4 cup milk in a liquid measuring cup. Blend in flour until dissolved and smooth. Now, add more milk to reach the 1-cup mark.

3. Stir milk mixture into eggs.

To assemble and bake:

1. Grate cheese (or use pre-grated). Stir about 1-1/2 cups into the egg mixture.

2. Pour vegetables into egg mixture and spread out evenly.

3. Sprinkle remaining cheese on top. Dust with a little ground nutmeg if desired.

4. Bake (uncovered) 35 minutes, or until firm and lightly browned. Let stand about 10 minutes before cutting into 4 squares or 6 rectangles.

SERVING SUGGESTION:

• Serve with a salad, crudité, or fresh fruit.

*Blanch – to partially cook vegetables in order to soften, lock in color, or facilitate removal of the skin (e.g., tomatoes). To blanch tough greens like kale, remove the center stem, then cut leaves into small, bite-size pieces. Next, use one of the following techniques:

- Fill a large saucepan about half full of water. Add 1 teaspoon salt. Cover and bring to a boil over high heat. Add greens. Remove from heat after 1 minute. Immediately drain in a colander then rinse for a few minutes under cold water or submerge in ice-cold water. Drain thoroughly and/or pat dry with paper towels.

- To blanch in a microwave, place greens in a large microwave-safe bowl with 1 tablespoon water. Cover with plastic wrap and cut two slits in it for steam to escape (or cover with a plate) and cook on high for 2 minutes. Stir, then cook another 1 to 2 minutes until wilted and soft but still bright green. Drain off excess liquids and/or pat dry with paper towels.

VARIATIONS:
- Substitute 4 cups chopped fresh spinach or Swiss chard (lightly packed) for the kale. Add to tomato mixture and cook down slightly.
- Substitute 2 cups chopped broccoli, cauliflower, asparagus, or summer squash for the kale.
- Substitute 1 cup chopped bell peppers or sliced mushrooms for tomatoes.
- Add 1 cup chopped ham, with or without vegetables.
- DAIRY-FREE – Leave out the cheese and use almond milk. Add about 1 teaspoon salt.

FRITTATAS

4 to 8 servings   Easy $

"This is an easy and attractive way to serve eggs, but you will need a skillet with an oven-proof handle. The secret ingredient needed for a creamy frittata* is half-and-half (cream is a little heavy and milk is too light). Hot sauce provides a subtle complexity, but Nick likes it very spicy, so we add quite a bit more. Start with this basic cheesy frittata recipe, then check out some of our variations or make up your own!" REBECCA

Prep Time: 10 minutes   **Passive Time:** 5 to 10 minutes   **Cook Time:** 7 to 8 minutes
Tools: grater, large bowl, measuring cups and spoons, large (10-inch) skillet with ovenproof handle

*A **frittata** is an Italian egg dish. It is started on the stovetop in a skillet, but finished in the oven. Extra ingredients are mixed into the egg batter before it has thoroughly cooked. Frittatas are cut into wedges (like a pie).

1-1/2 cups grated cheese (e.g., Cheddar, Swiss, Havarti, Monterey Jack), divided
8 eggs
3 tablespoons half-and-half

1/2 teaspoon salt
1/8 teaspoon ground black pepper
Hot pepper sauce, to taste
1 tablespoon butter, or oil

Position top rack about 6 inches from the broiler. Preheat oven to 450°F.

*TIP
To prevent little bits of eggshell from getting into the frittata, lightly tap **eggs** on a flat surface like the counter instead of a sharp edge like the side of a bowl.

1. Grate cheese and set aside.

2. Combine **eggs,** * half-and-half, salt, pepper, and hot sauce in a large bowl. Using a whisk (or fork) beat until well blended, but don't overbeat. Stir in about 1 cup of grated cheese.

3. Heat empty skillet over medium heat about 30 seconds. Add butter (or oil) and swirl around to melt and coat bottom and sides of pan. *Note:* By adding fat once the skillet is hot, the eggs will not stick (a typical problem with stainless-steel skillets). Butter will possibly turn brown, but the pan is too hot if the butter burns and smokes—so start over!

4. Pour egg mixture into skillet. Gently stir until eggs begin to thicken, about 30 to 60 seconds. Sprinkle remaining cheese on top

5. Turn heat to medium-low and cook (uncovered) without stirring, until light brown on the bottom, about 2 minutes. (Check by lifting the edge with a fork—it should be lightly browned.)

6. Place skillet on the top rack (so the heat source is not too close) in preheated oven and cook 4 to 5 minutes. The frittata is ready when firm on the edges and somewhat jiggly in the center. (Eggs continue to cook and set after they've been removed from the oven.) If desired, turn heat to broil in the last minute of cooking to better brown the top.

7. Let stand for 5 to 10 minutes (while you clean up). Cut into wedges to serve.

VARIATIONS:

- MIXED CHEESE FRITTATA (Rebecca's favorite) – Use 1/2 cup each of extra sharp Cheddar, Gouda and Gruyère cheeses (or your favorite blend), for a total of 1-1/2 cups cheese. If you want to use crumbled cheese like feta or goat, reduce the total to 1 cup.

- HERBY FRITTATA (Bobbi's favorite) – Add 1 to 2 teaspoons dried herbs from your pantry (e.g., dill, thyme, oregano, rosemary), or about 2 to 4 tablespoons fresh herbs (e.g., tarragon, basil, cilantro, chives). Whisk into eggs before cooking.

- INDIVIDUAL FRITTATA – Use 2 to 3 eggs and 1/2 cup cheese. Cut everything else in half, and cook in a small (8-inch) skillet with an ovenproof handle. Bake 3 to 7 minutes.

- FRITTATA WITH VEGETABLES – If using a stainless-steel skillet for the frittata, cook 1 to 2 cups vegetables in 1 tablespoon butter (or oil) in a separate saucepan or skillet. (Add optional chopped ham or other cooked meat at this point.) Follow recipe instructions for preparing frittata on the stovetop, and sprinkle vegetable mixture evenly over it once eggs have just started to firm up, right before adding remaining cheese. Finish in oven per recipe. *Note:* If using a non-stick skillet, cook vegetables in the skillet and pour egg mixture over them, then continue following recipe.

OMELETS

1 serving   Easy $

*"When I lived with a family in France, the father was a chef. He showed me how to make an **omelet*** (although in France it's spelled, 'omelette'), and it's been a family favorite ever since. Later, I learned an optional trick from America's Test Kitchen—adding frozen chunks of butter to the eggs gives the omelet a better texture. My French family usually served their omelets plain, or with a few herbs. However, we like to pile vegetables and cheese on ours. See our Variations or make up your own creations."* BOBBI

Prep Time: 5 minutes   **Cook Time:** 5 minutes
Tools: small (8-inch) skillet (or omelet pan), small bowl

1 tablespoon butter
2 eggs
2 to 3 dashes hot sauce
Salt and pepper, to taste

1. *Optional step:* Cut 1 tablespoon butter into 4 small squares and set two in the freezer at least 5 minutes.

2. Break eggs into a small bowl. Add hot sauce, salt, and pepper. Beat with a whisk (or fork) until well blended, but do not **overbeat.***

*TIP
Overbeating eggs breaks down the proteins, resulting in tough, rubbery eggs.

*An **omelet** is a French egg dish cooked entirely on the stovetop. Any extra ingredients (except for herbs and sometimes cheese) are piled on top. Omelets are then folded in half or rolled up.

3. Place <u>empty</u> small skillet over medium heat until hot. Add remaining 2 squares (1/2 tablespoon) butter. *Note:* By adding fat once the skillet is hot, the eggs will not stick (a typical problem with stainless-steel skillets).

4. Pour eggs into skillet and cook 15 to 30 seconds, allowing them to set (firm up) just a little. With a fork, slowly begin pushing eggs from the sides of the skillet, into the center, all the way around, allowing uncooked eggs to run to outer edges and underneath. Go around twice.

5. Turn heat to low and cover with a lid (optional) to continue cooking until top is done to your preference, about 1 to 2 minutes.

6. To serve, use a food turner and fold over in half, then slide from pan. (Alternatively, slide from pan without folding over, and cool slightly. Roll up into a cylinder and slice across.)

VARIATIONS:

- FILLED OMELET – Sprinkle extra ingredients over half of the omelet, then fold empty half over the filling. Slide onto a plate, or pick up with a food turner. Vegetables that work well in an omelet include chopped broccoli, spinach, asparagus, tomatoes, onions, mushrooms, and peppers. *Note:* Be sure to cook most vegetables earlier, so they'll be ready when the eggs are. Tomatoes and tender greens like spinach can be used cooked or not.

- HERB OMELET – Mix chopped tarragon, chives, dill, thyme, oregano, cilantro, parsley, basil, or a combination into the egg batter and garnish with a sprig.

- MEXICAN OMELET – Fill with black beans, guacamole, and/or salsa.

- GREEK OMELET – Fill with feta cheese, black olives, and oregano.

PERFECT POACHED EGGS

1 serving   Easy $

"The texture of eggs can vary greatly, depending on how they're prepared. Poached eggs are full of flavor, but fragile. Even though they're simple to make, they're tricky to get just right. I like to practice my one-handed, egg-cracking skills and break the egg into a ladle that I'm holding upright with my other hand. If you need two hands, break the egg into a small cup or bowl. Poached eggs should have a soft yolk. If you want it cooked through, you might as well make a hard-boiled egg." GREG

Prep Time: 2 to 5 minutes   **Cook Time:** 3 to 4 minutes
Tools: large (4-quart) saucepan, small cup/bowl (or ladle), slotted spoon

Water (for cooking)
1/2 tablespoon **vinegar***
1 egg

1. Set egg out to warm to room temperature for best results.
2. Fill a large saucepan with at least 3 inches of water. Add vinegar.
3. Place saucepan over high heat until water is just beginning to boil, then reduce temperature to the point where the water is almost boiling (a few bubbles are coming up the sides).
4. Break an egg into a small cup, bowl, or ladle.
5. Softly stir water with a large kitchen spoon to get it spinning in a whirlpool. Pour egg into the center.
6. Set timer and cook 3 minutes for a very soft yolk or 4 minutes for a slightly thicker yolk.
7. Remove immediately with a slotted spoon and allow the water to drain, or place on a paper towel, or in a small bowl that can be tipped to drain.
8. Gently place egg on a plate or piece of toast.

*TIP
Although any **vinegar** will do, plain old white vinegar is best. Vinegar helps the egg white stay together as it cooks. Keep a big jug of distilled white vinegar around for poaching eggs—and for cleaning purposes. A little white vinegar in a spray bottle with water makes a great rinse for vegetables, as well as the perfect window cleaner. Add a few tablespoons to a bucket of warm water to mop the kitchen floor.

POACHED EGGS ON ARUGULA SALAD

2 servings   Easy $

"My mom and I first made this for lunch during a mom/daughter weekend. We both love a good salad and understand the importance of adding a little protein. This light and nutritious salad will fill you up, but not so much that you won't have room for dessert!" REBECCA

Prep Time: 10 minutes   **Cook Time:** 3 to 5 minutes

Tools: large (4-quart) saucepan, measuring cups and spoons, small cup (or bowl), slotted spoon, knife and cutting board, large bowl

Eggs:

Water (for cooking)

1/2 tablespoon vinegar

2 to 4 eggs

Dressing:

2 to 4 tablespoons oil, to taste (extra virgin olive oil recommended)

Juice of 1 lemon (about 3 tablespoons)

Salt and pepper, to taste

Salad:

4 cups arugula

1/4 cup grated Parmesan cheese

1 small avocado

For eggs:

1. Set eggs out at room temperature, then fill a large saucepan half full of water. Bring almost to a boil over medium-high heat.
2. Form a whirlpool and drop one egg at a time into the center. Poach 3 to 4 minutes. (See recipe for POACHED EGGS for more details.)

For dressing:

1. While waiting for water to boil, combine oil, lemon juice, salt, and pepper in a small bowl. Mix with a small whisk (or fork).

For salad:

1. Place arugula in a large bowl and pour some or all of the dressing on top. Toss well.
2. Add Parmesan and avocado, then toss again. Divide salad amongst two smaller bowls, one for each person.
3. Top each with 1 or 2 poached eggs.

VARIATIONS:

- Add raw or lightly steamed sugar snap peas.
- Add 1 to 2 tablespoons chopped shallot, red onion, or thinly sliced green tops of a scallion.

POACHED EGGS OVER SWEET POTATO FRIES

2 servings   Easy $

"In Spain, we were served an appetizer of fried matchstick potatoes, with fried eggs on top, and a generous drizzle of paprika-infused olive oil. I have to admit that it was delicious, even if it did have a million calories! This is our healthier take on that scrumptious dish. We like to eat it for lunch or a light supper, but feel free to toss everything together and serve in small portions as an appetizer for a small dinner party." BOBBI

Prep Time: 5 minutes   **Cook Time:** 15 to 20 minutes
Tools: baking sheet, large (4-quart) saucepan, measuring spoon, small cup (or bowl), slotted spoon

4 cups sweet potato fries (frozen—spicy or plain)

2 eggs

Water (for cooking)

1/2 tablespoon vinegar

Garnish:

1/2 tablespoon olive oil (extra virgin recommended)

Paprika (smoked recommended)

TIP
We use frozen sweet potato fries to save time, but you could roast sweet potato chunks instead, or make our recipe for ROASTED BUTTERNUT SQUASH STICKS.

1. Prepare fries according to package instructions.
2. Set eggs out at room temperature. Fill a large saucepan about half full of water and add vinegar.
3. When fries have about 10 minutes left to cook, bring water almost to a boil, then lower heat to keep at a gentle simmer. Form a whirlpool and drop one egg at a time into the center. Poach 3 to 4 minutes. (See recipe for POACHED EGGS for more details.)
4. Divide cooked fries between two shallow bowls or small plates. Place one poached egg on top of each.
5. Drizzle olive oil over the egg and sprinkle paprika on top.
6. To eat, cut across the egg several times and toss to coat fries with egg yolk.

VARIATIONS:

- For a more traditional Spanish version, use white potato fries and a fried egg.
- Serve poached egg in a baked sweet potato with olive oil and paprika.

SCRAMBLED EGGS

Easy $

There are two basic ways to scramble eggs, country-style and blended. Either way, use a small (8-inch) skillet for 2 to 4 eggs, and a large (10-inch) skillet for 5 or more. A few dashes of hot sauce add complexity of flavor. Herbs can be stirred into the eggs before, during, or after they've been cooked. Chives, dill, tarragon, parsley, and other delicate herbs complement eggs well.

Prep and Cook Time: 5 minutes, start to finish
Tools: large or small skillet, bowl (optional)

COUNTRY-STYLE:

Eggs
Salt and pepper

Hot pepper sauce (optional)
Butter, or oil (for cooking)

1. Heat empty skillet over medium heat. Add butter (or oil) to the skillet and swirl around to coat bottom of pan.
2. Break eggs directly into the skillet. Do not stir right away. Sprinkle salt, pepper, and hot sauce on top.
3. Once the egg whites begin to become opaque, turn heat down to medium-low and gently scramble with a whisk (or fork). You should see separate bits of egg white and yellow yolk throughout, which is the hallmark of country-style scrambled eggs.
4. Remove from heat just before eggs are done to your preference, since they'll continue to cook somewhat while they rest.

BLENDED:

Eggs
Half-and-half
Salt and pepper

Hot pepper sauce (optional)
Butter, or oil (for cooking)

1. Break eggs into a bowl. Add about 1 teaspoon half-and-half per egg, salt, pepper, and hot sauce, to taste.
2. Lightly beat with a whisk (or fork) until well blended, but do not overbeat.
3. Heat empty skillet over medium to medium-high heat. Add butter (or oil) to the skillet and swirl around to coat the bottom.
4. Immediately pour eggs into skillet and stir just until eggs begin to clump. Turn heat down to medium-low or low and continuing stirring until eggs have solidified, but are still moist.

VARIATIONS:

- CHEESY SPINACH SCRAMBLE – Melt 1 tablespoon butter in the skillet and cook 2 cups fresh baby spinach for 1 minute. Follow instructions for blended eggs using 4 eggs (for 2 servings). Add eggs to spinach and cook per recipe. Remove from heat and stir in 1/4 cup grated or crumbled cheese.

- HAM AND CHEESE SCRAMBLE – Chop desired amount of ham, then brown in skillet over medium heat. Remove and set aside. Grate cheese. Follow instructions for scrambled eggs. Stir in ham and cheese once eggs begin to set.

- HERBY SCRAMBLE – Add 1 to 2 tablespoons chopped fresh herbs when eggs are almost done. We recommend chives, tarragon, basil, dill, parsley, and cilantro.

- LEFTOVER VEGETABLE SCRAMBLE – Warm up leftover steamed, sautéed, or roasted vegetables in the microwave or oven. Follow instructions for country-style or blended eggs. Once eggs begin to set, stir vegetables into eggs and continue to follow recipe, adding cheese if desired.

- MUSHROOM ONION SCRAMBLE – Melt 1 tablespoon butter in the skillet and cook 2 tablespoons chopped onion and 1/4 cup sliced mushrooms until soft. Follow instructions for blended eggs using 4 eggs (for 2 servings). Add eggs and a pinch of dried oregano to mushroom mixture and cook per recipe.

DINNER ENTRÉES

Yes, you *can* cook dinner from scratch—without using expensive meal-in-a-box deliveries! Many of the Breakfast, Brunch, and Lunch recipes make great dinners, too. Review "How to Choose the Freshest Meat, Poultry, and Seafood" in Chapter 5, as well as "Safe Food Handling" in Chapter 6.

ADDITIONAL VEGETARIAN ENTRÉES IN:
BREAKFAST, BRUNCH, LUNCH
PASTA AND PASTA SAUCES
SOUP, STEW, CHILI

FISH AND SEAFOOD

Fresh seafood can be expensive depending on where you live. Look for sales and check fish for freshness. Some seafood freezes well, so buy frozen (typically more economical) when appropriate.

BAKED FISH WITH PESTO AND TOMATOES

2 to 4 servings   Easy $$ to $$$

No more excuses—dinner doesn't get much easier than this. Buy a jar of prepared pesto sauce, and you'll be able to throw this recipe together even after a tough day at work. Our recipe is based on using cod, a relatively thick cut. If your choice of fish is thinner, you might need to adjust the cooking time.

Prep Time: 10 minutes   **Cook Time:** 20 to 25 minutes
Tools: 8×8-inch baking dish, knife and cutting board, measuring cups and spoons
Special Supplies: aluminum foil

1 pound white fish fillets (e.g., cod, flounder, tilapia, snapper)
1/4 cup broth, or white wine
4 teaspoons pesto sauce

1 medium tomato, or 12 cherry tomatoes
2 tablespoons grated Parmesan cheese
Ground black pepper, to taste

Preheat oven to 375°F. Spray or rub oil into an 8×8-inch baking dish.

1. Cut fish into four pieces. Place evenly in baking dish.
2. Pour broth (or wine) over fillets.
3. Spread a teaspoon of pesto sauce over each piece of fish.
4. Chop tomato (or cut cherry tomatoes in half), then scatter on top.

TIP

If using thin fillets like flounder, you can roll up each one so they'll fit into the dish and look pretty too! To roll, place fillet on a plate or cutting board with the pointed end away from you. Spread some pesto on top of each fillet, then roll up starting at the wide end. Place in the baking dish, seam-side down. Pour broth over fish, then top each roll with a small dollop of pesto and spread to cover the top. Continue per recipe directions.

5. Sprinkle Parmesan on top and season with pepper.

6. Cover with foil and bake 10 minutes. Uncover and bake another 10 to 15 minutes, or until the fish is opaque and flakes when pierced with a fork.

VARIATION:

- Substitute 1/4 cup chopped, marinated artichoke hearts and 1 tablespoon capers for pesto. Spoon equal amounts over each piece of fish. Follow all other recipe instructions.

BAKED GINGER SALMON

1 serving   Easy $$ to $$$

"This dish was inspired by a friend whose parents are from China. They often steam a whole fish covered with sliced ginger and scallions. For a small portion, we seal a salmon fillet in foil and steam it in the oven. Of course, you can make as many as you want. It's always best to buy wild-caught, Alaskan (or Pacific) salmon if you can afford it." GREG

Prep Time: 5 minutes
Cook Time: 15 to 20 minutes
Tools: knife and cutting board, measuring spoon, rimmed baking sheet
Special Supplies: aluminum foil

1 (6-ounce) salmon fillet
Spray oil
4 thin slices peeled, fresh ginger, or pickled ginger
1 small **scallion,*** or 2 thin slices onion
1 teaspoon soy sauce
Pinch red pepper flakes

*Scallion is another name for a small green onion. The top green portion is often used as a garnish, but the entire scallion can be used. They are milder than regular onions. One small scallion should yield 1 to 2 tablespoons when the whole thing is thinly sliced.

Preheat oven to 375°F.

1. Tear off a sheet of foil, about 15 inches long. Lay on a flat surface and spray with oil.

2. Place a piece of salmon in the center, skin-side down. Spray oil to cover the top of the fillet.

3. Lay ginger slices over salmon. Cut green top of scallion into 1/2-inch-thick pieces (slice on the diagonal for a more attractive presentation). Scatter over salmon.

4. Drizzle soy sauce and sprinkle red pepper flakes on top.

5. Form a packet by bringing two parallel sides of foil together in the center. Fold over or crease edges together to seal. Repeat with the other two sides.

6. Place packets onto a rimmed baking sheet and into preheated oven. Bake 15 minutes, or until fish flakes when pierced with a fork.

7. Remove ginger and serve.

SERVING SUGGESTION:

- Add a side of BASIC BROWN RICE and GARLICKY GREEN BEANS or CHINESE CABBAGE STIR-FRY.

BAKED SHRIMP SCAMPI WITH ARTICHOKES

2 to 3 servings   Easy $$

We like to prepare our scampi in the oven, but feel free to cook everything in a skillet on the stovetop if you prefer. The addition of artichokes is a nice touch, but it's not necessary. If serving with brown rice remember to prepare it ahead of time (or use leftovers). The cost of fresh shrimp can vary, so we usually pick up a bag of frozen, peeled shrimp when it's on sale. It works well in this recipe, although fresh is always best. If using fresh shrimp ask for enough to make one pound after it's been peeled.

Prep Time: 10 minutes   **Passive Time:** 30 minutes (if thawing shrimp)
Cook Time: 15 minutes
Tools: medium bowl, 8×8-inch baking dish, knife and cutting board, measuring cups and spoons, grater

1 pound shrimp

1/2 teaspoon salt

1/8 teaspoon ground black pepper

1/8 teaspoon red pepper flakes

2 tablespoons butter

4 to 6 garlic cloves

1/2 cup marinated artichokes (optional)

1 lemon

1/2 teaspoon dried oregano leaves

2 tablespoons grated Parmesan cheese (optional)

*TIPS

- Shrimp have a "vein" down the back that might be black. **Cleaning**, or deveining, the shrimp involves removing the shell, making a small incision with a sharp knife along the vein, then pulling it out. This is an optional step. Some grocery stores will shell and clean them for you, often at no extra charge, if you order them in advance.

- If you want more intense lemon flavor, zest the lemon before juicing and add zest as well as juice.

Preheat oven to 375°F.

1. If using fresh shrimp, peel and **clean.*** If using frozen shrimp, thaw by placing in a baggie then submerging it in a bowl of warm water for 30 minutes.
2. Place shrimp in a medium bowl and season with salt, pepper, and red pepper flakes. Toss and let stand while you continue.
3. Put butter in the baking dish, then place dish in the oven to melt butter.
4. Mince garlic. When butter has melted but not yet turned brown, remove dish from oven and add garlic. Let stand while you continue.
5. Coarsely chop optional artichokes and add to baking dish, along with shrimp, juice from half the lemon, and oregano. Stir.
6. Bake in preheated oven (uncovered) 15 minutes, or until shrimp is pink and opaque. Sprinkle Parmesan on top with about 5 minutes left to cook.
7. Remove from oven. Garnish with wedges from remaining lemon half if desired.

SERVING SUGGESTION:

- Serve with pasta, rice, or a crusty bread. Add a salad or vegetable on the side, and you'll have an amazingly simple yet delicious meal!

VARIATION:

- Cook in a skillet on the stovetop.

CANCUN COD

3 servings   Easy $$

"Here's a simple way we prepared fish when the whole family rented a condo in Cancun. It's perfect for a quick weekday meal, and it doesn't require much space or equipment. We use fresh cod, which is fairly economical, but frozen cod (or any white fish) can be substituted." BOBBI

Prep Time: 2 minutes   **Cook Time:** 15 to 20 minutes
Tools: knife and cutting board, large (10-inch) skillet, measuring cups and spoons

1 small onion
1 tablespoon butter, or high-heat cooking oil
1 medium tomato (about 1 cup chopped)
1/4 teaspoon salt

1/8 teaspoon ground black pepper
1/8 teaspoon hot pepper sauce
1 pound cod, or other white fish
1 tablespoon capers (optional)

Garnish:
1/4 cup chopped cilantro
1 lemon

1. Slice onion in half then cut across to form half rounds. Melt butter in a large skillet over medium-low heat, then add onion slices. Cook and stir about 5 minutes, or until they are very soft and smell sweet.
2. While onion cooks, chop tomato. Add to onion, along with salt, pepper, and hot sauce. Cook and stir another 2 to 3 minutes.
3. Cut cod into smaller pieces for the number of servings desired (using a cutting board dedicated to raw meats/fish if possible). Place cod in the tomato mixture, spooning some over fish. Season with a little more salt and pepper, then sprinkle optional capers on top.
4. Cover and simmer on low 7 to 10 minutes, or until fish is opaque and comes apart with a fork. *Note:* If using thin fish fillets like flounder, cook 2 to 3 minutes.
5. While fish cooks, chop cilantro.
6. When done, squeeze the juice of <u>half</u> a lemon over fish. Garnish with cilantro and serve with a wedge or slice of lemon from the remaining half.

SERVING SUGGESTION:
- Serve with a simple steamed vegetable and boiled new potatoes or BAKED POTATOES.

CHILI-LIME FLOUNDER

2 to 4 servings   Easy $$ to $$$

This is a quick, but very flavorful way to cook flounder, or any white fish. We also use this recipe to make fish tacos—just add corn tortillas and your favorite coleslaw.

Prep Time: 5 minutes   **Passive Time:** 15 minutes   **Cook Time:** 4 minutes
Tools: measuring cups and spoons, large (10-inch) skillet (or grill)

Marinade:

1/2 lime, or 1-1/2 tablespoons juice
2 tablespoons high-heat cooking oil
1 teaspoon chili powder
1 teaspoon ground cumin

3/4 teaspoon salt
1/4 teaspoon ground black pepper
1/4 teaspoon red pepper flakes

Fish:

1 pound flounder fillets, or similar white fish
1 tablespoon butter

Garnish:

1/2 lime

1. Squeeze juice from half a lime into a liquid measuring cup. Add other marinade ingredients and mix well.
2. Place flounder on a plate. Pour marinade on top, spreading to coat evenly. Turn fillets over several times to coat both sides. Cover and let stand 15 minutes.
3. Heat skillet over medium heat. Add butter and swirl around skillet to melt and coat the bottom.
4. Place flounder in skillet and cook 2 minutes on each side, or until fish is opaque and comes apart with a fork.
5. Cut remaining lime half into wedges or slices, and garnish.

SERVING SUGGESTION:
- Serve with CORN ON THE COB and REBECCA'S CHUNKY GUACAMOLE.

VARIATION:
- Use a firm fish, like swordfish or halibut, and cook outdoors on the grill.

COCONUT SHRIMP STIR-FRY

4 to 6 servings   Moderate $$

This is technically not a stir-fry, since we don't use high heat. Keeping the heat lower gives you more time to chop as you go. For time savers, we use frozen, peeled shrimp and frozen sliced mushrooms. The cooking time includes cooking rice while you prepare everything else. Add red or green Thai curry paste, or sriracha hot sauce.

Prep and Cook Time: 1 hour, start to finish
Tools: colander, large (4-quart) saucepan, measuring cups and spoons, medium bowl, knife and cutting board, large (10-inch) skillet

Rice:
1 cup brown rice (dry, uncooked)
2 cups water
1/2 teaspoon salt

Shrimp:
1 pound peeled shrimp (fresh or frozen)
Salt and pepper

TIP
Letting salted shrimp rest about 15 minutes before cooking improves the texture and flavor.

*Reduce – to simmer a liquid for a period of time, allowing some of the water to evaporate. The result is a thicker and more flavorful sauce.

Vegetables:

1 large carrot

1 cup chopped broccoli (fresh or frozen)

1 cup sliced mushrooms (fresh or frozen)

1 tablespoon high-heat cooking oil (coconut oil recommended)

3 garlic cloves

1/2 tablespoon minced fresh ginger (optional)

3 to 4 cups chopped bok choy, or Napa cabbage

1 (13.5-ounce) can coconut milk

1 tablespoon Thai curry paste, or 1 teaspoon hot pepper sauce

1 tablespoon soy sauce

1 lime (or lemon)

For rice:

1. Rinse rice, then cook in water with salt. See our recipe for BASIC BROWN RICE, or prepare according to package instructions.

For shrimp:

1. If using frozen shrimp, thaw by placing in a baggie, then submerging bag in a medium bowl of warm water for 30 minutes.

2. Empty bowl and place thawed shrimp in it. Season generously with salt and pepper. Toss and set in the refrigerator if not ready to use right away.

For vegetables:

1. Slice carrot on the diagonal into 1/4-inch-thick pieces, chop broccoli, and slice or thaw mushrooms.

2. Heat oil in a large skillet over medium-low heat. Add carrot, broccoli, and mushrooms. Cook and stir while you continue.

3. Mince garlic and optional ginger, then add to skillet. Cook about 2 minutes. Add a teaspoon of water if too dry.

4. Chop bok choy (or Napa cabbage) and set aside.

5. Add shrimp to skillet and cook about 2 minutes. Stir in bok choy (in two batches if necessary). Cook another 2 minutes, or until bok choy is somewhat wilted and reduced in volume.

6. Stir in coconut milk, curry paste (or hot sauce), and soy sauce.

7. Simmer (uncovered) over medium-low or low heat for 5 minutes, or until liquid has been **reduced*** by about a quarter.

8. Remove from heat and add juice from the lime. Adjust seasonings, to taste.

9. Serve in a bowl over brown rice.

VARIATION:

- Substitute chicken for shrimp. Cut 1/2 to 1 pound of boneless, skinless chicken into bite-size pieces. Cook in oil until mostly done, then add vegetables.

FISH WITH CREAMY MUSHROOM SAUCE

2 to 4 servings   Easy $$ to $$$

"This recipe was inspired by a dish I had in France when I was an au pair (nanny). The host father was a chef, and often made something quite similar. I've simplified it and lightened up the sauce, without sacrificing flavor. I make this when turbot is available, a popular French fish with a buttery flavor. However, any white fish will do." BOBBI

Prep and Cook Time: 20 minutes, start to finish

Tools: knife and cutting board, large (10-inch) skillet, measuring cups and spoons

1 small onion

2 tablespoons butter

2 cups (1 pint) fresh mushrooms, or 1-1/2 cups frozen, sliced mushrooms

1/4 cup white wine

1 pound turbot, cod, or other white fish

Salt and pepper, to taste

1 teaspoon Dijon mustard

1/4 cup cream, or half-and-half

1. Cut peeled onion in half, top to bottom, then thinly slice to form half-rounds. Melt butter in a large skillet over medium-low heat, then add onion slices. Cook and stir 3 to 5 minutes.
2. While onion cooks, slice mushrooms (or thaw frozen mushrooms in microwave and drain). Add to onion and cook another 2 to 3 minutes.
3. Add wine and push vegetables to outer edges of the skillet. Place fish in the center and season with salt and pepper. Cover and simmer on low 3 to 5 minutes, or until fish is done and most of the liquid has cooked off.
4. Transfer fish (not vegetables) to serving plates and place in a warm oven or cover with foil. Add Dijon mustard and cream to vegetables. Cook and stir 1 to 2 minutes.
5. Pour vegetables over fish.

SERVING SUGGESTION:

*   Serve with green beans (or French haricots verts) and roasted potatoes. Garnish with parsley and a wedge of lemon if desired.

TIP

Place discarded shrimp shells in a plastic bag and take directly out to the trash. They can stink up a whole house overnight if left in the kitchen trash!

LAZY CAJUN SHRIMP
WITH RICHARD'S COCKTAIL SAUCE

2 (1/2-pound) servings   Easy $$ to $$$

"Richard (aka Dad) is half Cajun, and shrimp with cocktail sauce is his specialty. He never actually uses a recipe for the sauce, but we pinned him down on his estimates and believe we have replicated it. One pound of fresh shrimp serves two Cajuns as a main meal, but it can be stretched out to serve three light eaters or more as an appetizer. You'll have plenty of sauce, so feel free to cook 2 pounds of shrimp and invite some friends over!" BOBBI

Prep Time: 5 minutes   **Cook Time:** 3 to 5 minutes
Tools: large (4-quart) saucepan, colander, small bowl, measuring cups and spoons

1 pound fresh shrimp (in the shell)
Water (for cooking)
1 teaspoon salt

Cocktail Sauce:

1/4 cup ketchup

2 tablespoons prepared horseradish

1/2 tablespoon lemon juice

1 teaspoon Worcestershire Sauce

1/2 teaspoon hot pepper sauce (Tabasco recommended)

1/2 teaspoon salt

For shrimp:

1. Fill large saucepan about half full of water. Add salt, then bring to a boil over high heat.
2. Gently lower shrimp into the water with a large spoon.
3. Leave in water about 1 to 2 minutes, or just until they turn pink and opaque. Turn heat down if needed.
4. Immediately pour the shrimp into a colander and rinse briefly with cold water.

For sauce:

1. While waiting for water to boil, combine all cocktail sauce ingredients and stir to blend well. Adjust seasonings if desired. Refrigerate until ready to use. *Note:* Sauce can be made up to two days in advance.

SERVING SUGGESTION:

- Transfer shrimp to a large serving bowl or platter, with a small bowl of sauce and a bottle of Tabasco on the side. Provide an empty container for discarding the shells and plenty of paper towels or napkins. Peel one, dip in sauce, and pop into your mouth, like a Cajun!
- Serve with RED POTATO SALAD, MANGO COLESLAW, and/or watermelon.

MISO GLAZED COD

2 to 4 servings   Easy $$ to $$$

This is a very simple yet elegant dish. Make it for yourself, or double or triple it for a dinner party. If you don't have rice vinegar, use the lightest vinegar you have and add 1/4 teaspoon honey or 1/2 teaspoon sugar. Cod is an economical fish and works well in this recipe, but you can substitute any thick, white fish like halibut or sea bass.

Prep Time: 5 minutes   **Passive Time:** 30 minutes (optional)   **Cook Time:** 8 to 10 minutes

Tools: small bowl (or measuring cup), measuring spoons, knife and cutting board, large (10-inch) skillet

Glaze:
1 tablespoon **miso paste***
1 tablespoon rice vinegar
1 teaspoon fresh minced ginger, or ground ginger
Pinch red pepper flakes

Fish:
1 pound cod, or similar white fish
1 tablespoon butter, or coconut oil

Garnish:
Cilantro sprig
Orange slices (optional)

***Miso paste** is a fermented soy and/or barley product found in the refrigerated section of grocery stores, often by tofu. It's a good source of natural probiotics, which help gut and immune system health. Miso is salty, so you will probably not need to add salt.

1. Combine glaze ingredients in a small bowl or measuring cup and stir well.
2. Cut cod into four pieces and place on a plate. Using a pastry brush or spoon, spread the glaze evenly on both sides of fish.
3. Cover and marinate in the refrigerator up to 30 minutes, although it's not necessary.

To cook:

1. Melt butter (or oil) in a large skillet over medium-low heat, then add fish. Cook 3 minutes on first side. Gently turn over with a food turner and cook the second side about 5 to 7 minutes or until done. Lower heat if necessary to prevent burning. *Note:* This can also be cooked on a grill.
2. Garnish with a sprig of cilantro and a slice of orange if desired.

SERVING SUGGESTION:
- Serve with KALE SALAD WITH AVOCADO ORANGE DRESSING, steamed green beans, or braised bok choy. Add a side of BASIC QUINOA.

PAN-SEARED SALMON

2 servings   Easy $$ to $$$

This is our go-to way to prepare salmon indoors. However, it tends to splatter, so wear an apron or old t-shirt. If possible, buy wild Alaskan (or Pacific) salmon, not farmed Atlantic salmon. We've also listed some of our favorite spice combinations to sprinkle on the fish.

Prep Time: 2 minutes   **Cook Time:** 4 to 6 minutes   **Passive Time:** 5 minutes
Tools: large (10-inch skillet), measuring spoon, food turner

2 (5 to 6-ounce) salmon fillets
1 tablespoon high-heat cooking oil (for cooking)

Seasoning choices: (choose one)
a) salt and pepper
b) salt, pepper, dill
c) salt, Chinese 5-spice
d) salt, pepper, paprika (smoked recommended)

1. Season fillets generously with one of the above combinations, or make up your own.
2. Heat oil in large skillet over medium to medium-high heat. Use a food turner to place salmon fillets in skillet, skin-side down (if there's skin on one side). Press down lightly with the back of the food turner to flatten. **Sear*** about 2 to 3 minutes, or until skin (or flesh) has browned and will easily lift from skillet. Turn over and cook 2 to 3 minutes on the other side, or until fish is <u>almost</u> done according to your preference. (It will continue to cook as it stands.)
3. Transfer fillets to a plate and cover with foil. Let stand 5 minutes to reabsorb juices and finish cooking.

SERVING SUGGESTIONS:
- Keep it simple and serve plain, with a green salad (or cooked vegetable) and roasted new potatoes.
- Serve with RED PEPPER SAUCE on top.

*Sear – to quickly cook foods with a little oil over high heat, turning the outer layer brown. Food item is left undisturbed to sear on one side, then flipped to sear on the other side. Typically used for foods that cook quickly, or are served rare. To finish cooking throughout, lower the heat or add a liquid, depending on the food item and recipe.

POACHED SALMON

2 servings   Easy $$ to $$$

Prep Time: 2 minutes   **Cook Time:** 7 to 10 minutes
Tools: large (10-inch) skillet, measuring spoons

2 (5 to 6-ounce) salmon fillets

Water (for poaching)

1 tablespoon vinegar, or 2 tablespoons
white wine

1 teaspoon dried dill

1 teaspoon salt

1/8 teaspoon ground black pepper

4 thin slices onion (optional)

1 lemon

1. Fill a large skillet with water about 1 inch deep. Stir in vinegar (or white wine), dill, salt, and pepper. Add optional onion slices.

2. Heat on medium-high until water just begins to simmer. Turn to medium-low and place salmon gently in the water. (We use our tongs, but a large spoon or food turner also works.) Bring back to a simmer, then lower heat as needed to keep just below a simmer. Do not boil. **Poach*** about 10 minutes, or until fish flakes easily when tested with a fork in the thickest part.

3. Remove from water with a slotted spoon or food turner and set on a paper towel to absorb the excess water, if it's not too fragile. Use the food turner or paper towel to carefully transfer it to a serving plate.

4. Squeeze juice from half a lemon over the cooked salmon and serve. Garnish with wedges cut from the other half.

SERVING SUGGESTIONS:

- Keep it simple and serve with a dollop of mayonnaise or aioli and a green salad.
- Serve with RED PEPPER SAUCE on top and boiled potatoes (or pasta) and steamed or roasted asparagus on the side.

> ***Poach** – to cook submerged in a liquid that is not quite simmering. The heat is lower than that used for simmering or boiling. Usually used for fish or eggs. Vinegar improves the taste and texture of seafood.

SHRIMP À LA CRÉOLE

3 servings   Easy to Moderate $$

"This is a simpler and more healthful version of one of our Cajun family favorites. Although we usually buy fresh shrimp and let Richard (aka Dad, the Cajun) peel them, using frozen, peeled shrimp will save time and perhaps money. Creole cuisine is characterized by its reliance on tomatoes rather than peppers for red sauces. It can be a little spicy, but not super hot like Cajun food. However, we still place a bottle of Tabasco (the authentic Louisiana hot sauce) on the table for those who want more heat, like Richard, Greg, and Nick." BOBBI

Prep and Cook Time: 20 to 25 minutes, start to finish (not including rice)

Tools: medium bowl, knife and cutting board, large (10-inch) skillet, measuring cups and spoons

2 cups cooked brown rice

Shrimp:

1 pound shrimp

1/2 lemon

1/2 teaspoon salt

Pinch ground black pepper

Vegetables:

1 small onion, or large shallot

4 garlic cloves

2 tablespoons butter

3 large Roma (plum) tomatoes, or 1 (14.5-ounce) can diced tomatoes

1/2 tablespoon dried thyme leaves

1/4 teaspoon hot pepper sauce (Tabasco recommended)

1/4 cup heavy cream, or half-and-half

> **TIP**
> Always choose shrimp caught in the U.S., which has stricter controls. Many other countries raise shrimp in unhealthy environments and have limited to no controls or testing for toxins.

Garnish:

2 tablespoons chopped fresh parsley

For rice:

1. Use leftover rice and warm up right before serving, or cook now. See our recipe for BASIC BROWN RICE, or prepare according to package instructions.

For shrimp:

1. If using fresh shrimp, **peel*** and clean. If using frozen, peeled shrimp, thaw by placing in a baggie, then submerging it in a bowl of warm water for 30 minutes.

2. Place shrimp in a medium bowl, and add juice from the lemon half. Season with salt and pepper, then toss. Set aside while you follow the next steps.

*To **peel** fresh shrimp, start at the top (the thicker end where the head was cut off) and turn it over to the underneath side, where the legs are. Just "flip" the shell sections up with your thumb and keep moving down to the tail. At that point you can take the shell off. Next, squeeze the remaining shell on the tail section and pull it off (or leave it on if you like that look). This technique also works for peeling cooked shrimp in the shell.

For vegetables:

1. Chop onion, to yield no more than 1 cup. Mince garlic.
2. Melt butter in a large skillet over medium-low heat, then add onion and garlic. Cook and stir frequently 3 to 5 minutes, or until onions are soft and translucent.
3. While onion mixture cooks, chop tomatoes (should yield about 1-1/2 cups, or use canned). Add to onions, along with thyme and hot pepper sauce. Cook and stir another 3 to 5 minutes to reduce the liquids and intensify the flavor.

To assemble:

1. Add shrimp and simmer (uncovered) over low heat, stirring frequently for 3 to 5 minutes, or until shrimp is done.
2. Remove from heat and stir in cream. Add more hot sauce if desired.
3. Serve on top of rice and garnish with fresh parsley.

SERVING SUGGESTIONS:

- Skip the rice and serve over pasta, or with crusty bread to soak up the sauce.
- Add a simple green salad or vegetable like BROCCOLI WITH DIJON GARLIC DRESSING on the side.

VARIATION:

- GREEK SHRIMP – Add 2 tablespoons white wine along with tomatoes. Substitute oregano for thyme and leave out hot sauce and cream. In final minute of cooking stir in 1/2 cup feta cheese crumbles, 1/4 cup plain Greek yogurt, and 1/4 cup chopped Kalamata olives (optional).

SMOKED PAPRIKA SHRIMP KABOBS

2 to 4 servings   Easy $$

"This recipe is from my niece Elizabeth, and it's a winner in our house as well as hers. The shrimp is flavorful, attractive, easy to prepare, and versatile. Elizabeth sautés hers, but we like to place them on skewers and cook them outside or broil them in the oven. The recipe yields two large servings or four smaller ones. To serve as an appetizer, remove cooked shrimp from skewers and provide toothpicks." BOBBI

Prep Time: 10 minutes   **Passive Time:** 0 to 30 minutes   **Cook Time:** 5 minutes
Tools: medium bowl, measuring spoons, grill (or oven)
Special Supplies: skewers

1 pound fresh shrimp, with tail intact

1 lime

1/2 tablespoon smoked paprika

1/2 tablespoon high-heat cooking oil

1/2 teaspoon salt

1/4 teaspoon ground black pepper

Hot pepper sauce, to taste

1. Peel shrimp, leaving the tail intact. Place in a medium bowl.
2. Squeeze juice of lime over shrimp and stir.
3. Add remaining ingredients and toss to coat evenly.
4. Cook right away, or cover and marinate 15 minutes. (Do not leave in marinade more than 15 minutes or it will become dry and tough—acids like lime juice break down seafood over time.)
5. Thread shrimp on skewers by piercing each one through the thick end first, then through the tail end. (Each shrimp will be in the shape of a letter C.) If possible, leave a small amount of space between each shrimp.
6. Heat grill to medium, or 350°F. Cook 4 to 5 minutes, or until done. Turn over after 2 minutes.

SERVING SUGGESTION:

- Serve with CORN ON THE COB and a salad of spinach, mango slices, and red grapes with VINAIGRETTE.

VARIATIONS:

- Add cherry tomatoes, mushrooms, bell peppers, or chunks of squash and zucchini to the skewers, between each shrimp. Toss vegetables with shrimp to coat in sauce first.
- SAUTÉED – Follow directions, but heat an additional 1/2 tablespoon cooking oil in a large skillet over medium heat. Add seasoned shrimp. Cook and stir until shrimp is pink and opaque, about 3 to 5 minutes.
- BROILED – Follow directions but broil in the oven (with skewers or not) on a baking sheet placed about 6 inches below heat source. Cook 4 to 5 minutes, or until done.

SPANISH MACKEREL

2 servings   Easy $$

"During a trip to Spain, I was inspired to eat more mackerel, which is a good source of omega 3s, low in mercury, and relatively inexpensive. I put this together, using the most common ingredients we encountered in Barcelona: paprika, garlic, and olive oil. We like to line our baking sheet with parchment paper, which makes cleanup easier." BOBBI

Prep Time: 5 minutes   **Cook Time:** 10 to 15 minutes
Tools: baking sheet, knife and cutting board
Special Supplies: parchment paper

2 (5 to 6-ounce) mackerel fillets
Olive oil*
1 garlic clove

Paprika (smoked recommended)
Salt and pepper

Preheat oven to 450°F.

1. Line a baking sheet with a piece of parchment paper, then spray it with oil. Place mackerel fillets on the paper. (Alternatively, cook directly on the greased baking sheet.)
2. Drizzle olive oil over the fillets and brush or rub to evenly coat surface.
3. Mince garlic and sprinkle over mackerel.
4. Season generously with paprika, salt, and pepper.
5. Place in hot oven and cook 10 to 15 minutes, or until fish flakes when pierced with a fork.

SERVING SUGGESTIONS:

- Garnish with a lemon wedge and fresh herbs if desired.
- Serve with SPANISH RICE and a salad.
- Serve with CORN ON THE COB and green beans.

*TIP
This is not quite the same without olive oil, but because it's cooked at a high temperature we try to use refined (or virgin olive oil). The fatty acids in extra virgin olive oil can be damaged at temperatures over 375°F, but Spanish cooks will use extra virgin olive oil for just about everything, including this.

TUNA SALAD WITH APPLES

2 cups   Easy $

"This is the way my mother and her mother always made tuna salad, and it's still my favorite. We usually add a hard-boiled egg and cook up another for garnish, but you can save time and skip them if you need to. Use sweet or sour pickles, depending on your taste preference. We go fairly light on the mayonnaise, but feel free to add more if you prefer." BOBBI

Prep Time: 10 minutes   **Cook Time:** 20 minutes (optional—for eggs)
Tools: small (1-quart) saucepan (for eggs), medium bowl, knife and cutting board, measuring spoons

2 hard-boiled eggs (optional)

1 (5-ounce) can tuna (packed in water)

1 small apple

1 stalk celery

2 tablespoons finely chopped pickles, or relish

3 tablespoons mayonnaise

1 tablespoon pickle juice (optional)

Salt and pepper, to taste

Garnish: (optional)

2 tablespoons chopped pecans (raw or toasted)

1. Prepare hard-boiled eggs (see our recipe for BOILED EGGS).
2. Drain tuna and place in a medium bowl. Separate with a fork.
3. Cut apple into quarters, removing the core but not the peel. Chop two of the quarters and add to tuna. Slice the remaining quarters for garnish (or chop and add to tuna).
4. Finely chop celery (to yield about 1/4 cup) and pickles. Add to tuna, along with mayonnaise and optional pickle juice. Stir to combine well.
5. Chop one hard-boiled egg and stir into salad. Slice or quarter the other egg for garnish.
6. Season with salt and pepper, to taste.
7. Toast pecans if desired.

SERVING SUGGESTIONS:

- Place a scoop of tuna on top of salad greens. Garnish plate with a few slices of apple and egg, then sprinkle pecans on top.
- Eat in a sandwich.

VARIATIONS:

- Substitute grapes or pear for the apple.
- Add half an avocado and 1 tablespoon lemon juice instead of pickle juice. Substitute thinly sliced scallions (or chives) for pickles.
- Use Greek yogurt for all or part of the mayonnaise.

MEAT (BEEF, PORK, LAMB)

BEEF AND VEGETABLE STIR-FRY

2 to 3 servings   Easy $$

"I got this simple recipe from a Chinese friend. They use about three times more black pepper and red pepper flakes, but we've cut it down for the average American palate. I suggest you make it as written, then add more spices as desired. Stir-fry is cooked quickly, so it's best to cut all of the vegetables first, as we've instructed." GREG

Prep Time: 10 minutes   **Cook Time:** 10 to 15 minutes
Tools: knife and cutting board(s), medium bowl, measuring cups and spoons, large (10-inch) skillet

Vegetables:

1 small onion

1 large carrot

2 cups chopped broccoli (or other **dense*** vegetable)

1 cup sliced fresh or frozen mushrooms (or other **quick-cooking*** vegetable)

1 tablespoon minced garlic

Beef and spices:

1 pound beef **strips*** or cubes

2 tablespoons high-heat cooking oil

3 tablespoons soy sauce

1/3 cup water

1 teaspoon Chinese 5-spice

1/2 teaspoon ground black pepper

1/2 teaspoon red pepper flakes

---

*TIPS

- **Dense** vegetables that can be substituted for the broccoli include cauliflower, green beans, Brussels sprouts, etc., or a combination.

- **Quick-cooking** vegetables that can be substituted for the mushrooms include snow peas, bok choy, Napa cabbage, zucchini, bell peppers, spinach, etc., or a combination.

- If you can't find beef **strips**, buy a flat iron, skirt, or flank steak and cut into thin strips.

For vegetables:

1. Chop onion. Slice carrot into 1/4 to 1/2-inch-thick slices. Chop broccoli (or other dense vegetable), then combine all three in a medium bowl.
2. Slice mushrooms (or prepare other quick-cooking vegetable) and mince garlic. Set aside, but don't combine with other vegetables.

To cook:

1. On a cutting board dedicated to raw meat, cut beef into strips (if not purchased as strips or cubes).
2. Heat skillet over medium-high heat. Once hot, add oil.
3. Carefully add meat (it might splatter, so wear an apron). Cook and stir just until browned, about 3 to 5 minutes depending on the size of the pieces. Transfer to a plate and cover with foil to keep warm.
4. Add onion, carrot, and broccoli mixture to the skillet without cleaning it first (the brown bits from the beef are very flavorful). Cook and stir 1 to 2 minutes.
5. Add mushrooms and garlic, then cook and stir another minute.
6. Stir in soy sauce, water, 5-spice, black pepper, and red pepper flakes.
7. Return cooked meat to skillet.
8. Cook and stir another 2 to 3 minutes, or until vegetables are crisp-tender. Remove from heat and serve immediately.

SERVING SUGGESTION:

- Serve with BASIC BROWN RICE. In the Chinese tradition, follow meal with fresh fruit.

VARIATION:

- Substitute chicken for beef and cook thoroughly before transferring to a plate.

HAMBURGERS

4 (4-ounce) patties   Easy $$

There's nothing wrong with simply shaping some ground beef into patties and throwing them on the grill, but why not make them a little special? Try this easy way to dress up a burger and impress your friends.

Prep Time: 5 minutes   **Cook Time:** 6 minutes   **Passive Time:** 5 minutes
Tools: knife and cutting board, large bowl, measuring cups and spoons, grill (or large skillet)

Patties:

1/4 cup finely chopped onion, or
  2 tablespoons minced garlic

1 pound ground beef (80% lean
  recommended)

1 tablespoon Worcestershire sauce

1 tablespoon horseradish (optional)

1 teaspoon chili powder, or **garam masala***

1 teaspoon dried oregano leaves

1/2 teaspoon salt

1/4 teaspoon ground black pepper

> ***Garam masala** is a special Indian blend of spices, but can vary somewhat. Although it's typically made by toasting whole spices then grinding as needed, we have developed a quick version using our Finite Foodie spices. See our recipe in Miscellaneous.

Extras: (optional)

4 whole grain hamburger buns,
  or English muffins

4 slices cheese
Lettuce, tomatoes, pickles, onions, etc.

For patties:

1. Chop onion or mince garlic, then place in a large bowl.
2. Add meat and all other patty ingredients. Mix with hands (or with a large spoon), just until combined. Don't overwork the meat, or it will become tough.
3. Form into four patties. Flatten slightly, but don't pack down too hard.

To grill:

1. Make sure grill surface is clean. Spray with oil before turning on. Turn grill to high (around 400°F). If using a charcoal grill, prepare coals according to package instructions.
2. Place patties on grill, away from flame. Lower flame to medium-high and cook patties about 4 minutes. Flip over, turn heat to medium, and cook 2 minutes on the other side, or to desired doneness. To keep moisture in the meat, do not press down on the patties while they're on the grill. *Note:* The patties will continue to cook after being removed from the heat, so remove a little before they're done to your preference.
3. Top with a slice of cheese in the last minute of cooking if desired.
4. Transfer to a plate and lightly cover with foil. Let rest for 5 minutes before serving, for a juicier hamburger.
5. Toast bun if desired, then assemble. We like to add lettuce, tomatoes, pickles, etc., or serve with a salad.

VARIATION:

- To cook inside, heat large (10-inch) skillet over medium-high heat. Add patties and press down once to flatten. Do not press down again, as it will push out the juices. Lower heat to medium and cook until browned, about 3 to 4 minutes. Turn over and cook on other side 3 to 4 minutes, or until done almost to your preference. Remove patties and cover with foil to rest and reabsorb juices for 5 minutes.

JAMBALAYA

6 to 10 cups   Involved $$ to $$$

"Although we have rated this Involved, it's a simplified variation of my original Jambalaya and easy enough for anyone to complete in about an hour. Choose one or more of the proteins. I usually use all of them, like I do with my more complicated version. Now we don't have to wait for a special Mardi Gras celebration to enjoy this delicious Creole dish, and the leftovers freeze well too." BOBBI

Prep Time: 30 minutes   **Cook Time:** 30 minutes or longer
Tools: measuring cups and spoons, colander, large (4-quart) saucepan, small and medium bowls, knife and cutting board, large (10-inch) skillet

Rice:

1 cup brown rice (dry, uncooked)
1-1/2 cups chicken broth

Proteins: (Choose one* or more)

2 cups cooked, chopped chicken
1 cup cooked, chopped ham (about 8 ounces)

1/2 pound shrimp
1 (12-ounce) package precooked sausage (andouille recommended)

Vegetables:

1 small onion
1 tablespoon butter, or grease from sausage
2 stalks celery
1 red bell pepper
1 (8-ounce) can **tomato sauce***
1/4 cup broth, or water
1 tablespoon Worcestershire sauce
1 teaspoon dried thyme leaves

1 teaspoon paprika (regular, not smoked)
1/2 teaspoon salt
1/4 teaspoon ground black pepper
1/4 teaspoon ground cloves
Hot pepper sauce, to taste (Tabasco recommended)
1/4 cup chopped fresh parsley (optional)

*If you only have tomato paste, you can make your own **tomato sauce**. Use 3 parts tomato paste and 4 parts water (i.e. 3/4 cup tomato paste and 1 cup water), or simply use equal amounts. To make 1 cup tomato sauce (as the recipe states) measure a little over 1/2 cup water in a liquid measuring cup, then add enough paste to make 1 cup. Stir well.

For rice:

1. Rinse brown rice in a colander. Bring chicken broth to a boil in a large saucepan over medium-high heat. Stir in rice and bring to a boil again. Lower heat to medium-low or low, then cover and simmer 20 minutes. Remove from heat and let stand 10 minutes. Fluff with fork. (Rice should be somewhat firm, but it will absorb more moisture when everything is combined.)

For proteins:

1. While rice cooks, prepare chosen proteins:
a) **Chicken*** – If you need to cook some chicken, use a boneless, skinless chicken breast. Brown in a large skillet over medium heat, then cook on low until done. Remove from skillet and chop into bite-size pieces. Place cooked, chopped chicken in a medium bowl.
b) Shrimp – If using fresh shrimp, peel and remove tail. If using frozen peeled shrimp, thaw by placing in a baggie and then putting the baggie in a bowl of warm water for 15 to 30 minutes.
c) Ham – Chop ham into bite-size pieces. Brown in the large skillet you plan to use for the vegetables. Transfer to the bowl with chicken.
d) Sausage – Slice sausage into 1/2-inch-thick pieces. Brown in the skillet, along with the ham (if using). Transfer to the bowl with chicken, reserving about 1 tablespoon of the grease in the skillet.

2. Set aside all cooked proteins, or place in the refrigerator if not continuing right away.

---

*TIPS

- We like to chop up leftover roast **chicken** and freeze it in baggies, which can later be thawed and used in recipes like this one.

- You can choose one protein to turn this into Shrimp or Chicken Jambalaya, but you'll need to increase the amount. Chicken andouille sausage is available, if you don't want pork. Be sure to add extra hot sauce if you leave out the sausage. Add extra salt if you omit the ham.

For vegetables:

1. Chop onion. Heat grease or melt butter in the same skillet used above over medium-low heat. (No need to clean it first.) Add chopped onion and stir occasionally while you continue.

2. Chop celery and bell pepper, adding to onion as you finish each. Cook and stir another 2 to 3 minutes, or until vegetables are soft.

3. Add tomato sauce, water, Worcestershire sauce, thyme, paprika, salt, pepper, and cloves. Stir in shrimp and cook about 3 minutes, or until shrimp turns white.

4. Pour the mixture into the saucepan with rice. Add other proteins. Cover and cook over medium-low heat until moisture has been absorbed and everything is warm, 3 to 5 minutes.

5. Turn to low and keep warm on the stovetop or in the oven for an additional 30 minutes (or more if possible). This allows the flavors to meld and intensify. Taste to determine if you need hot sauce, which depends on how spicy the sausage is. If you did not use sausage, you'll definitely want extra hot sauce. *Note:* We often make this in advance and store in the refrigerator, reheating when ready to serve. It also freezes well.

6. Stir in chopped parsley right before serving.

PORK CHOPS WITH HONEY MUSTARD

2 servings   Easy $$

"Richard is a big pork fan, and this has been one of his favorite meals over the years. Our philosophy is to eat all meats rarely, but to buy the best quality you can afford when you do. Purchasing from small, local farmers is a good option. Cooking times are approximate since it depends on the thickness of the cut. Use your judgment or a meat thermometer. Try **brining*** *the meat first for a more tender and moist chop if you have the time. It will require an additional 1 to 2 hours, but is well worth it."* BOBBI

Prep Time: 5 minutes   **Passive Time:** 5 minutes   **Cook Time:** 10 minutes
Tools: measuring spoons, small bowl, grill (or oven)   **Special Supplies:** aluminum foil

2 (1-inch-thick) pork chops
Salt and pepper
1 tablespoon honey

1 teaspoon Dijon mustard
1 teaspoon rosemary leaves (fresh or dried)

Preheat grill to high, or oven to broil. If cooking in the oven, spray or rub oil onto a baking sheet.

1. Season both sides of pork chops generously with salt and pepper.

2. Mix honey, mustard, and rosemary in a small bowl. Set aside.

To cook on grill:

1. Cook chops on grill 3 to 4 minutes on one side, then turn over. Brush half of the honey-mustard sauce on the cooked side. After 3 to 4 more minutes turn over again, and brush remaining sauce on the other side. Cook 1 additional minute on the first side to brown. Check with a meat thermometer (should be 145°F), or cut through one piece and check that meat is pinkish-white and juices run clear.

To cook under broiler:

1. Place top oven rack about 6 inches from the top heating element. Preheat oven to broil.
2. Arrange chops on greased baking sheet. Brush half of the honey-mustard sauce on the top, then **broil*** 5 to 7 minutes. Turn over and brush remaining sauce on the other side. Cook another 5 to 7 minutes, or under done.

Before serving:

1. Remove from heat, cover with foil, and let rest 5 minutes before serving to reabsorb juices.

SERVING SUGGESTION

- Serve with GARLICKY GREEN BEANS and ROASTED BUTTERNUT SQUASH SLICES.

*Brine – to soak a food item in brine (a salty water solution) with the goal of tenderizing and adding flavor.

*Broil – to cook with dry, direct heat from a heating source located above the food. Place the item on a broiling pan (ideally), or on a rimmed baking sheet. The food should be about 6 inches away from heat source, depending on the food. Typically broil both sides.

VARIATIONS:

- BRINED – Dissolve 2 tablespoons salt and 1 tablespoon sugar in 2 cups water. Pour brining solution into a bowl or resealable baggie, then place chops in it. Keep in refrigerator about 1 to 2 hours. Remove from brine to prepare, but do not rinse. Do not season with salt—only pepper. Follow remaining instructions.
- PAN-SEARED – Heat oil in a skillet over medium heat. Add chops and cook per recipe.

PORK LOIN ROAST WITH MAPLE GLAZE

4 (3 to 4-slice) servings   Easy $$ to $$$

"This is one of my favorite recipes. It's simple, requires few ingredients, and doesn't mess up many dishes. Buy or mix up our GARAM MASALA spice blend, or use Chinese 5-spice instead. For a juicier and more tender roast, brine it first—it's easier than you might think, but you'll need to plan ahead. Use a skillet with an ovenproof handle to finish cooking this in the oven, or transfer it to a baking dish." GREG

Prep Time: 20 minutes   **Passive Time:** 10 minutes (or more to brine)

Cook Time: 40 to 50 minutes

Tools: liquid measuring cup and measuring spoons, large (10-inch) skillet (with ovenproof handle), tongs, knife and cutting board

Special Supplies: kitchen twine (optional), aluminum foil

TIP

To brine a 2-pound pork loin roast, mix 4 cups water, 1/4 cup salt, 2 to 4 table-spoons sugar, and 1/2 teaspoon red pepper flakes, until salt and sugar are dissolved. Place roast in a shallow dish or a large resealable plastic baggie and pour brine over it. Cover dish or seal baggie and keep in the refrigerator 2 to 6 hours. When ready to use, drain off liquid, but do not rinse. Season with pepper, but no extra salt. Follow all other instructions.

1/4 cup maple syrup

1 teaspoon garam masala, or Chinese 5-spice blend

1 (2-pound) pork loin roast

Salt and pepper

1/2 tablespoon high-heat cooking oil

Sprigs of fresh mint, cilantro, or parsley (optional)

Preheat oven to 325°F.

1. Mix syrup and garam masala (or 5-spice) in a liquid measuring cup.

2. *Optional step:* Cut 5 (15 to 18-inch) pieces of kitchen twine. Lay across a flat surface about 1 inch apart, parallel to each other. Lay the roast across the strings, and tie tightly around the pork. The first and last strings should be about 1 inch from the ends of the roast, and the others evenly spaced in between. Although optional, this step keeps the roast in a nice, cylindrical shape.

3. Season all sides with salt and pepper (use pepper and no salt if it's been brined first). Heat oil in a large skillet over medium heat. Use tongs to place pork in the skillet. Cook about 3 to 5 minutes on one side to brown, then turn with tongs and cook another 3 to 5 minutes on the other side. Use tongs to turn pork and lightly brown the other sides for a few minutes.

4. Transfer roast to a plate. Turn heat to low and pour syrup mixture into the skillet to **deglaze.*** Stir and scrape to loosen the brown bits. Remove from heat.

5. Place roast back in the skillet and turn it over several times to coat completely with the maple glaze. (If your skillet does not have an ovenproof handle, move roast and syrup to a greased 8×8-inch baking dish at this point.)

6. Place skillet (or baking dish) into preheated oven and roast 20 minutes, then turn over. Cook another 20 to 30 minutes. Check with a meat thermometer (interior should be 145°F), or cut through the middle and check that meat is pinkish-white and juices run clear.

*Deglaze – to create a sauce from the browned scraps that have accumulated in a hot skillet after sautéing, browning, or caramelizing certain foods. Add some liquid like water, wine, vinegar, or broth and loosen up any brown bits of food stuck to the pan. This incorporates the flavors into the sauce. Scrape the pan as the liquid boils, then turn heat to low.

7. Remove from oven. Turn pork to coat again with glaze, then cover lightly with foil and let rest about 10 minutes.

8. Transfer to a cutting board. Cut into 1/2-inch-thick slices. Drizzle any extra juices left in the skillet over pork to serve.

9. Garnish with a sprig of mint or other herb if desired.

SERVING SUGGESTION:
- Serve with a mixture of ROASTED VEGETABLES, like Brussels sprouts and carrots.

TEXAS-STYLE OVEN-ROASTED BRISKET

4 (3 to 4-slice) servings   Easy (but takes time) $$

"If you don't have a grill, this option is perfect. Ask the butcher for a flat cut brisket, which has less fat (better for indoor cooking). A 3-pound brisket should just fit into your 8×8-inch baking dish. Growing up in Texas, we ate our brisket cooked with a few spices and no barbecue sauce. I've updated my family recipe a bit, but the idea is the same. We brine the brisket in soy sauce, using 3 tablespoons of regular or 4 tablespoons of low-sodium soy, shōyu or tamari sauce. Next, we apply a dry rub for added flavor. Finally, we add a vinegar-based marinade to make it extra moist. Feel free to double the recipe if you have a larger baking dish, since leftovers are even more flavorful." BOBBI

Prep Time: 15 minutes   **Passive Time:** 1 hour   **Cook Time:** 3 hours
Tools: knife and cutting board(s), 8×8-inch baking dish, measuring cups and spoons, small bowl
Special Supplies: aluminum foil

3-pound brisket (flat cut with fat trimmed)
3 to 4 tablespoons soy sauce

Dry Rub:

2 teaspoons brown sugar

2 teaspoons dried oregano leaves

2 teaspoons paprika (smoked recommended)

1 teaspoon chili powder

1/2 teaspoon ground black pepper

1/2 teaspoon red pepper flakes

Marinade:

6 garlic cloves

1/4 cup vinegar

2 tablespoons water

2 tablespoons Worcestershire sauce

*TIP

The **grain** on a cut of meat refers to the direction of the bundles of muscle fibers that run parallel to each other and across a cut of meat. They are obvious in a brisket. If you cut the meat in the same direction (parallel) to the fibers, the cut will be chewy. If you cut across (perpendicular) to the fibers, you'll end up with a tender piece. This is called, cutting against the grain.

1. Trim excess fat from the brisket if needed, or ask the butcher to trim it for you. Leave a thin (about 1/4-inch-thick) layer of fat on top. *Note:* The more fat on it, the more tender the meat, but it will be greasier.

2. Place brisket in an 8×8-inch baking dish. Pour soy sauce onto both sides and spread over all surfaces. Make sure the side with a layer of fat is on top. Cover with foil and place in the refrigerator to brine at least 1 hour, or up to 12 hours. Turn over at least once.

To prepare and cook:

1. Preheat oven to 300°F.

2. Mix sugar, oregano, paprika, chili powder, pepper, and red pepper flakes in a small bowl. Rub <u>half</u> of the spice mixture onto the top of the brisket (side with the layer of fat). Turn over. Rub other half of spices onto the other side. Leave brisket with fat-side down.

3. Coarsely chop garlic. Combine with vinegar, water, and Worcestershire sauce in a liquid measuring cup. Pour over the brisket.

4. Cover tightly with foil and cook 3 hours.

5. Remove from oven and loosen foil to vent. Let stand at room temperature (loosely covered with foil) 10 to 30 minutes.

6. Transfer brisket to a cutting board, and slice into 1/4 to 1/2-inch-thick pieces, cutting against (or across) the **grain.***

7. Arrange slices on a plate and pour some of the juices from the baking dish over the brisket.

SERVING SUGGESTIONS:

- SUMMER – Serve with CORN ON THE COB, APPLE CABBAGE SLAW, and fresh watermelon.

- WINTER – Serve with ROASTED CABBAGE WEDGES, BAKED POTATOES, and carrot sticks.

TURKISH SPICED LAMB

5 cups   Moderate $$

"I was never a fan of lamb, until Greg took me to a Turkish restaurant in Dallas during his days in graduate school. I was pleasantly surprised (shocked is more like it) by how delicious the lamb dishes were! I began experimenting at home, and finally recreated those rich aromatic flavors, drawing only from our list of 20 recommended spices. I've also made this with ground beef and bison, but I have to admit, lamb is best (bison comes in second). When Greg can't find ground lamb, he buys lamb shoulder, which is often less expensive than ground, then he cuts it into chunks." BOBBI

Prep and Cook Time: 40 minutes, start to finish
Tools: large (10-inch) skillet, knife and cutting board, measuring cups and spoons

3 tablespoons **pine nuts*** (optional)
1 pound ground lamb
1 small onion
4 large garlic cloves
1 tablespoon ground cumin
1 tablespoon paprika
1 tablespoon ground coriander
1/4 cup water

1 tablespoon dried oregano leaves
3 tablespoons Worcestershire sauce
1 teaspoon salt
1/2 teaspoon ground black pepper
2 medium carrots
1 cup chopped broccoli
1 teaspoon ground cinnamon
2 tablespoons chopped parsley, or mint (optional)

1. Heat an <u>empty</u> large skillet over medium heat. Add pine nuts and stir continually until fragrant and golden, about 2 to 3 minutes. Transfer immediately to a plate or towel to cool.

2. Heat the same skillet over medium heat, then add lamb. Stir frequently to brown and break apart, about 3 to 5 minutes.

3. While meat cooks, chop onion and mince garlic.

*TIP
Pine nuts are expensive and can be skipped, but they add a lot to this dish. We recommend buying a small quantity in the bulk section if possible.

4. When lamb is done, remove from heat and **drain*** off excess fat, leaving a small amount (about 1 teaspoon).

5. Return skillet to stove over medium-low heat. Stir in onions and garlic. Add cumin, paprika, and coriander. Cook and stir 1 minute. Add water, oregano, Worcestershire sauce, salt, and pepper. Stir well then cover. Turn heat to low and simmer while you continue.

6. Thinly slice, chop, or grate carrots. Add to meat and replace lid.

7. Chop broccoli into small bite-size pieces and stir into meat mixture. Cover and simmer 5 to 7 minutes, or until most of the liquid has been absorbed and the vegetables are crisp-tender.

8. Remove from heat and stir in cinnamon. Adjust seasonings if desired. Cover and keep warm until ready to serve.

9. Chop optional parsley (or mint) and add right before serving. Garnish with toasted pine nuts.

SERVING SUGGESTION:

- Serve with couscous or BASIC MILLET.

VARIATION:

- Substitute 2 cups fresh (or 1 cup frozen) chopped greens for broccoli.

PASTA AND PASTA SAUCES

CHEESY MAC AND CHEESE

6 cups   Easy $

If you're a mac and cheese fan, you probably fall into one of two camps: creamy or cheesy. This is our cheesy version, with a surprising kick of chipotle peppers. Feel free to use hot sauce or red pepper flakes instead, or leave out the heat altogether.

Prep Time: 20 minutes   **Cook Time:** 15 minutes
Tools: large (4-quart) saucepan, measuring cups and spoons, colander, 8×8-inch baking dish, knife and cutting board, small (8-inch) skillet, grater

Pasta:
8 ounces elbow macaroni (about 2 cups)
Water (for cooking)
1 teaspoon salt

Cheesy sauce:
1 small onion, or 1 large shallot
4 garlic cloves
2 tablespoons butter
1 tablespoon flour (all-purpose white flour recommended)
2 teaspoons minced chipotle pepper in adobo

1/4 teaspoon salt
1/4 teaspoon ground black pepper
8 ounces grated Monterey Jack cheese (2 to 3 cups, lightly packed)
8 ounces grated Cheddar cheese, <u>divided</u>
Paprika

For pasta:

1. Prepare pasta according to package instructions, or fill a large saucepan about half full of water and add salt. Cover and bring to a boil over high heat. Add macaroni, stir, then lower heat to keep at a gentle boil. Cook (uncovered) 5 to 7 minutes, or until **al dente.***

> ***Al dente** – term used for cooking pasta, meaning soft on the outside but still firm (but not hard) in the center. It is the most common way to cook pasta.

2. Remove 1/2 cup cooking liquids. Drain pasta then return to saucepan. Stir in reserved cooking liquids. Cover to keep warm.

3. Preheat oven to 450°F. Rub or spray oil in an 8×8-inch baking dish.

For sauce: (can begin while pasta cooks)

1. Chop onion and mince garlic. Melt butter in small skillet over medium-low heat, then add onion and garlic. Cook and stir 2 to 3 minutes, or until soft. Stir in flour, chipotle pepper, salt, and pepper. Cook 1 more minute.

2. Grate cheeses. Set aside about half of the Cheddar for topping. Stir remaining cheese into pasta, along with onion mixture.

To assemble and bake:

1. Transfer pasta to greased baking dish.

2. Sprinkle reserved grated cheese over pasta, then dust with paprika.

3. Bake (uncovered) 15 minutes.

FENNEL AND WALNUT PASTA

6 cups   Easy $$

Serve this delicious and attractive pasta as a main dish or as a side. The delicate sauce works especially well with egg noodles or angel hair pasta.

Prep Time: 10 minutes   **Cook Time:** 15 to 20 minutes

Tools: knife and cutting board, measuring cups and spoons, large (10-inch) skillet, large (4-quart) saucepan, colander

1 small onion

2 tablespoons butter

1 bulb fennel

3/4 cup half-and-half, or cream

1 teaspoon salt

1/4 teaspoon ground black pepper

1/4 teaspoon ground nutmeg

Pasta:

8 ounces egg noodles, or similar

Water (for cooking)

1/2 tablespoon salt

1 tablespoon butter

1/4 cup chopped parsley

Garnish:

1/2 cup walnut pieces

Fennel fronds

> ***Caramelize** – to slowly cook food, usually vegetables, until the carbohydrates turn into sugars. Stir frequently to prevent burning and add a small amount of water, wine, or broth for extra moisture if necessary. Cook until vegetables are lightly browned and smell sweet. Add salt <u>after</u> they have caramelized, as it impedes the process.

1. Cut a peeled onion in half, then thinly slice across to form half circles. Melt butter in a large skillet over medium-low heat. Add onion and cook 5 minutes, stirring frequently.

2. Cut stalks off fennel and remove a few feathery fronds for garnish. Cut bulb into quarters and remove core. Thinly slice across each quarter. *Note:* Refrigerate or freeze unused fennel stalks for making soup stock at a later time.

3. Add fennel to onion and continue cooking another 5 to 10 minutes, or until very soft and slightly **caramelized.*** Lower heat if needed.

4. Add half-and-half and seasonings. Stir and continue simmering to reduce sauce and thicken.

5. While vegetables cook, prepare pasta according to package instructions, or fill a large saucepan about half full of water and add salt. Cover and bring to a boil over high heat. Add pasta and lower heat to simmer about 7 to 9 minutes, or until al dente.

6. When pasta is done, remove 1/4 cup cooking liquids and add to vegetables in cream sauce. Drain pasta and return to saucepan. Toss with butter. Cover to keep warm until sauce is ready.

To assemble and serve:

1. When sauce is thick and vegetables soft, pour into saucepan with pasta.

2. Add chopped parsley and toss.

3. Serve and garnish with walnuts and fennel fronds.

SERVING SUGGESTIONS:

- Serve with CANTALOUPE BERRY SALAD.
- Serve as a side dish to POACHED SALMON.

GARLIC-PEPPER PASTA

4 cups   Easy $

This extremely simple pasta tastes great as a side dish to just about anything. We suggest long pasta shapes like spaghetti, linguine, or fettuccini, but any type will do. Toss with a green vegetable if desired (see Variation).

Prep Time: 2 minutes   **Passive Time:** 15 minutes   **Cook Time:** 10 minutes

Tools: knife and cutting board, measuring cups and spoons, small (8-inch) skillet, large (4-quart) saucepan, colander, grater (optional)

Garlic-pepper sauce:

6 large cloves garlic

3 tablespoons olive oil (extra virgin recommended)

1/2 teaspoon red pepper flakes

Pasta:

8 ounces spaghetti, or similar

Water (for cooking)

1/2 tablespoon salt

1/2 cup grated **Parmesan cheese***

1/2 teaspoon salt

1/8 teaspoon ground black pepper

For garlic-pepper sauce:

1. Peel garlic cloves and smash, using the flat side of a knife and the heel of your hand. Heat oil in a small skillet over low heat and add garlic cloves. Cook and stir 2 to 3 minutes, or until golden and fragrant.

2. Remove from heat and stir in red pepper flakes. Set aside to cool at least 15 minutes, or up to several hours. This infuses the oil with the garlic and pepper taste. The longer it stands the more flavorful it will be.

*TIP

Avoid the finely grated, shelf-stable **Parmesan** cheeses found in canisters. Most contain added preservatives and fillers. If possible, purchase a wedge of fresh Parmesan. The flavor is far superior, and it goes a long way. Grate it as needed, using the fine to medium holes of a grater. Alternatively, look for freshly grated (or shredded) Parmesan in the cheese section of grocery stores. Romano, Asiago, or similar hard cheese is an acceptable substitute.

For pasta:

1. Prepare pasta according to package instructions, or fill a large saucepan about half full of water and add salt. Cover and bring to a boil over high heat. Add pasta and lower heat to simmer about 7 to 9 minutes, or until al dente.

2. Drain pasta then return to saucepan. Cover to keep warm.

To assemble:

1. Toss pasta with garlic-pepper sauce, Parmesan, salt, and pepper.

2. Adjust seasonings, to taste.

VARIATION:

• Add 1 to 2 cups fresh arugula or steamed green vegetables like broccoli or green beans. Add extra cheese and seasonings, to taste.

KASHA VARNISHKAS

4 to 8 servings   Easy $

Move over, mac and cheese! This classic Jewish dish is not only soul-satisfying, but can be made gluten-free with the right pasta (or by substituting cauliflower—see Variations). Buckwheat groats (aka kasha) are perfect for gluten-restrictive diets, and can be found at most grocery stores in the bulk or grain section. Be sure to use chicken broth for a more authentic taste. Simple and savory, Kasha Varnishkas is one of our favorite comfort foods, and we think it will become one of yours too.

Prep and Cook Time: 30 minutes, start to finish

Tools: measuring cups and spoons, large (4-quart) saucepan, colander, knife and cutting board, large (10-inch) skillet with lid (or foil) to cover, medium bowl

Pasta:

8 ounces bow-tie pasta, or similar size	1/2 tablespoon salt
Water (for cooking)	1 tablespoon butter

Kasha:

1 small onion	1 teaspoon salt
2 tablespoons butter	1/4 teaspoon ground black pepper
2 eggs	1/4 teaspoon ground nutmeg
1 cup buckwheat groats (kasha)	1/2 cup parsley leaves (lightly packed)
2 cups chicken broth	

For pasta:

1. Prepare pasta according to package instructions, or fill a large saucepan about half full of water and add salt. Cover and bring to a boil over high heat. Add pasta and lower heat to simmer 7 to 9 minutes, or until al dente.

2. Remove 1/2 cup cooking liquids and set aside. Drain pasta, then return to saucepan and toss with butter. Cover to keep warm.

For kasha:

1. While pasta cooks, chop onion. Melt butter in a large skillet over medium-low heat and add onion. Cook and stir 3 to 5 minutes, or until onion is soft and smells sweet.

2. Break eggs into a medium bowl and beat lightly with a whisk (or fork). Add buckwheat and stir to coat.

3. Turn heat under skillet to medium. Add kasha-egg mixture and cook, stirring frequently until the eggs are done and grains are dry and separate.

4. Stir in chicken broth, salt, pepper, and nutmeg. Cover skillet and simmer 10 to 15 minutes, or until all liquid has been absorbed.

To assemble and serve:

1. Add pasta and reserved cooking liquids to buckwheat mixture. Cook over low heat 1 to 2 minutes to heat through and absorb cooking liquids.

2. Coarsely chop parsley.

3. Remove skillet from heat and stir in parsley. Adjust seasonings, to taste.

SERVING SUGGESTIONS:

- Serve with carrot sticks and a wedge of cabbage with salt and pepper.
- Serve as a side to ROAST CHICKEN and steamed vegetables.

VARIATIONS:

- CAULIFLOWER KASHA VARNISHKAS – Omit pasta. Cut the florets off of one small head of cauliflower and slice them. After stirring broth and seasonings into kasha, add cauliflower on top. Cover and cook per recipe instructions.
- Stir in 1 to 2 cups cooked, chopped chicken at the end.
- Add 1 (15-ounce) can white beans along with broth.

MARINARA SAUCE

3 cups   Easy $

"I like to make this in the summer when I have a plethora of tomatoes in my garden, or when they're cheap at the farmers markets. We think fresh tomatoes make the best sauce, but we have substituted canned tomatoes in the winter months. When possible, I add a little red wine at the end. If the sauce is too tart (depending on the acidity of the tomatoes), 1/2 to 1 teaspoon sugar can mellow it out. However, we try to avoid added sugar unless the sauce really needs it." BOBBI

Prep Time: 10 minutes   **Cook Time:** 20 to 35 minutes

Tools: knife and cutting board, large (4-quart) saucepan, measuring cups and spoons

4 garlic cloves

2 tablespoons high-heat cooking oil

1 small onion

3 cups chopped fresh tomatoes, or 1
   (28-ounce) can crushed tomatoes

2 tablespoons tomato paste

1 bay leaf

1 teaspoon dried oregano leaves

1 teaspoon dried thyme leaves

1/2 teaspoon dried rosemary leaves

1/2 teaspoon salt

1/4 teaspoon ground black pepper

1/4 teaspoon red pepper flakes (optional)

2 tablespoons red wine (optional)

1. Slice garlic. Heat oil in a large saucepan over medium-low heat, then add garlic. Cook and stir 1 to 2 minutes, or until golden and fragrant. (Do not burn—turn heat down if needed.)

2. Remove from heat. Set aside to cool while you continue. This infuses the oil with the garlic flavor—the more time it stands the more intense it will taste.

3. Chop onion. Add to garlic, and return to medium-low heat. Cook and stir 3 to 5 minutes, until soft and translucent.

4. Chop tomatoes then add to saucepan (along with their juices), tomato paste, bay leaf, oregano, thyme, rosemary, salt, pepper, and optional red pepper flakes. Simmer on low (uncovered) 15 to 30 minutes.

5. Add wine if desired, and cook another few minutes or longer.

SERVING SUGGESTION:

- Serve over pasta or vegetable spirals. Top with freshly grated Parmesan cheese and add a green salad on the side.

VARIATION:

- TOMATO-BASIL SAUCE – Eliminate oregano, thyme, and rosemary. Add 1/4 cup chopped fresh basil.

MEAT SAUCE (TEXAS-STYLE) WITH PASTA

7 cups sauce   Easy $$

"I've been making this meat sauce since I was in high school, with very few changes over the years. It quickly became one of Richard's most asked-for meals. This is a chunky sauce, reminiscent of Texas-style chili, but with an Italian flair. It can also be made with ground bison, ground turkey, or Italian sausage. If you're trying to add extra vegetables to your diet (and stretch your meat dollars) add some mushrooms, grated carrots, broccoli, and/ or chopped greens. This makes a large amount of sauce, so you can freeze the leftovers for a quick mid-week meal." BOBBI

Prep and Cook Time: 45 to 60 minutes, start to finish
Tools: large (10-inch) skillet, knife and cutting board, measuring cups and spoons, large (4-quart) saucepan, colander, grater (optional)

1 pound ground beef

1 medium onion

4 garlic cloves

2 stalks celery (about 1 cup chopped)

1 bell pepper, or 1 (4-ounce) can mild chili peppers

1 (28-ounce) can crushed tomatoes

1/4 cup tomato paste

2 tablespoons Worcestershire sauce

2 bay leaves

1 teaspoon dried thyme leaves

1 teaspoon dried oregano leaves

1/2 teaspoon dried rosemary leaves

1/2 teaspoon salt

1/4 teaspoon ground black pepper

1/8 teaspoon hot pepper sauce

1/4 cup chopped parsley (optional)

Pasta:

8 ounces pasta (spaghetti recommended)

Water (for cooking)

1/2 tablespoon salt

Garnish:

Grated Parmesan cheese

TIP

*Reserve some of the cooking liquids from the pasta right before draining. Adding these starchy liquids to your sauce improves its ability to stick to and coat the pasta.

For sauce:

1. Place a large skillet over medium heat, then add ground beef. Stir and brown, breaking meat up into small pieces.
2. Chop onion and mince garlic.
3. Drain excess fat from the meat, but leave about 1 tablespoon in the skillet. Turn heat to medium-low, then add onion and garlic. Cook and stir as you continue.
4. Chop celery and bell pepper (or canned chili peppers), adding them to the skillet as you finish each one. Cook and stir about 5 minutes, or until vegetables are soft.
5. Add all remaining sauce ingredients. Simmer about 30 to 45 minutes (uncovered), or longer if desired.

For pasta:

1. Prepare pasta according to package instructions, or fill a large saucepan about half full of water and add salt. Cover and bring to a boil over high heat. Add pasta, and lower heat to keep at a gentle boil 7 to 9 minutes, or until al dente.
2. **Reserve*** 1/2 cup of the cooking water and add to sauce. Drain pasta in a colander.
3. Combine pasta with as much of the sauce as you want, or serve sauce over pasta. (You should have enough extra sauce for leftovers.)
4. Sprinkle Parmesan on top.

SERVING SUGGESTION:
- Serve with a mixed green salad and VINAIGRETTE.

PASTA WITH SPINACH, BEANS, AND TOMATOES

12 cups   Moderate $

"Finding a good, vegetarian pasta recipe that is satisfying can be a challenge! That's why we love this recipe. It is the perfect one-dish meal that will easily fill you up without weighing you down. When we have time, we'll chop one bunch of Swiss chard to replace the spinach, as noted in Variations." REBECCA

Prep and Cook Time: 30 minutes, start to finish

Tools: large (4-quart) saucepan, measuring cups and spoons, colander, knife and cutting board, large (10-inch) skillet, grater (optional)

Pasta:

1 (8-ounce) package spiral pasta, or penne (about 4 cups)	Water (for cooking)
	1/2 tablespoon salt

Vegetables:

5 ounces fresh baby spinach

1 small onion

4 garlic cloves

1 tablespoon high-heat cooking oil

1 (14.5-ounce) can diced tomatoes,
    or 2 medium tomatoes

1 (15-ounce) can white beans

1 teaspoon dried dill

1 teaspoon dried rosemary leaves

1 teaspoon salt

1/4 teaspoon ground black pepper

Pinch red pepper flakes

1/2 cup grated Parmesan cheese, <u>divided</u>

For pasta (and spinach):

1. Prepare pasta according to package instructions, or fill a large saucepan about half full of water and add salt. Cover and bring to a boil over high heat. Add pasta and lower heat to keep at a gentle boil about 7 to 9 minutes, or until al dente. **Add*** spinach in final 2 minutes.

*TIP
If pot is too full, **add** spinach to vegetable mixture a few minutes before combining it with the pasta.

2. When pasta is done, remove 1/2 cup of the cooking liquids and set aside for use later. Drain remaining liquids from pasta, then return to saucepan and cover to keep warm.

For vegetables:

1. While pasta cooks, chop onion. Heat oil in a large skillet over medium-low heat, then add onion. Cook and stir occasionally while you continue.

2. Slice garlic and chop tomatoes (if using fresh). Add to skillet. Cook and stir an additional 2 to 3 minutes.

3. While tomato mixture cooks, drain and rinse beans in a colander. Stir into vegetables, along with reserved cooking liquids, dill, rosemary, salt, pepper, and red pepper flakes. Cook another 2 minutes.

4. Remove from heat and combine vegetables with pasta.

5. Stir in half of the Parmesan. Garnish each serving with the remainder.

VARIATIONS:

- Substitute fresh Swiss chard for spinach. Remove large stem-ends from chard (no need to removed center stem). Slice across leaves to form 1-inch-wide strips. Cut across strips to form smaller pieces (should yield about 5 to 6 cups). Place in a colander and rinse thoroughly to remove all dirt and grit.

- Add 1 cup chopped, cooked chicken along with beans and heat through.

- Slice 2 to 4 pre-cooked sausage links and brown in oil. Remove and keep warm. Continue following recipe and add sausage with beans at end.

PESTO PASTA WITH GREEN BEANS, CHICKPEAS, AND SPINACH

9 cups   Easy $

Eat your pasta and salad together in this healthy dish that uses pesto instead of tomato sauce. Choose fresh or frozen green beans (French-cut if possible).

Prep Time: 15 minutes   **Cook Time:** 12 to 15 minutes

Tools: large (4-quart) saucepan, measuring cups and spoons, knife and cutting board (optional), colander, grater (optional)

Pasta:

8 ounces whole wheat or gluten-free pasta (penne, ziti, or similar size)

Water (for cooking)

1/2 tablespoon salt

Other ingredients:

3/4 pound green beans, or 1 (10-ounce) package frozen **French-cut*** green beans

1 (15-ounce) can chickpeas

1/2 cup pesto

2 cups fresh baby spinach

1/8 teaspoon ground black pepper

1/8 teaspoon red pepper flakes

1/2 cup grated Parmesan cheese

1. Prepare pasta according to package instructions, or fill a large saucepan about half full of water and add salt. Cover and bring to a boil over high heat. Add pasta and lower heat to keep at a gentle boil about 7 to 9 minutes, or until al dente. (Add other ingredients in final 5 minutes, as indicated below.)

2. While preparing pasta, rinse green beans then snap off the stem ends. Snap beans in half (or smaller pieces), or cut in half on the diagonal. (Alternatively, thaw frozen beans.)

3. Drain and rinse chickpeas in a colander.

4. When pasta has about 5 minutes left to cook, add green beans and chickpeas. Continue cooking until beans are crisp-tender and pasta is done.

*Use frozen **French-cut** green beans for a more attractive dish and to save time. To French-cut your own beans, cut each bean in half on the diagonal, then slice each piece down the middle lengthwise to expose the inside.

5. Remove about 1/4 cup of the cooking water and set aside. Drain pasta in a colander and return to saucepan.

6. Stir in pesto and reserved cooking water.

7. Add spinach, pepper, and red pepper flakes. Cook and stir on low until spinach has wilted. Remove from heat.

8. Stir in Parmesan, then garnish with more if desired.

SERVING SUGGESTION:
- Serve with tomato slices seasoned with salt and pepper.

POULTRY

BOURSIN-STUFFED CHICKEN

4 servings   Easy $$

"One year I hosted a foreign exchange student from Denmark. She and a friend cooked this simple dish for my family, and we couldn't believe how delicious it was! Boursin® is a whipped cream cheese with herbs and spices, but similar brands can be substituted." BOBBI

Prep Time: 5 minutes   **Cook Time:** 30 to 35 minutes
Tools: knife and cutting board, measuring spoon, 8×8-inch baking dish

2 boneless, skinless **chicken breast halves*** (about 1 pound)

4 tablespoons Boursin cheese, or similar

4 slices bacon (pork or turkey)

Preheat oven to 375 °F. Spray or rub oil into an 8×8-inch baking dish.

1. Cut chicken breasts in half. Make a slit in each piece, either on the top or on the side. Insert a tablespoon of Boursin cheese.

2. Wrap a piece of bacon around each chicken piece and place in baking dish (ends of bacon underneath).

3. Bake (uncovered) 30 minutes.

4. Set oven to broil and move dish about 6 inches under the heat source for another 5 to 7 minutes, or until cooked through. Bacon should be browned and crisp. A meat thermometer should read 165°F, or cut one piece in half to see that juices run clear.

*One chicken breast consists of two halves (the left and right). However, it is common to refer to one side (or half) as one breast. To avoid confusion, we use the terms **whole chicken breast** and **chicken breast half** to differentiate the two. When the meat is still on the bone, the chicken breast half is called a **split chicken breast**.

 *TIP
This recipe can also be made with boneless, skinless thighs. They should be laid out flat then folded over a spoonful of Boursin that has been placed in the center.

SERVING SUGGESTIONS:

- Serve with spaghetti, spaghetti squash, or zucchini spirals tossed in olive oil, salt, pepper, and fresh herbs.

- Cook 8 ounces spaghetti according to package directions. Reserve 1/4 cup cooking liquids and set aside. Drain pasta and return to saucepan. Add 1 cup cream (or half-and-half) and reserved cooking liquids. Simmer on low until cream has been mostly absorbed. Place chicken on top of pasta. Top with grated Parmesan cheese if desired.

CHICKEN FRIED BROWN RICE

6 cups Easy $

Here's a great way to use up leftover roast (or rotisserie) chicken and rice. Whip up this delicious meal in no time—it's much more healthful than most Chinese takeout, and will take less time than waiting for your delivery!

Prep Time: 5 minutes **Cook Time:** 10 to 15 minutes
Tools: measuring cups and spoons, knife and cutting board, large (10-inch) skillet

2 cups cooked brown rice	3 eggs
2 cups cooked chicken (**chopped***)	2 tablespoons soy sauce
1/2 cup frozen corn	1 to 2 tablespoons vinegar (rice wine vinegar recommended)
1/2 cup frozen peas	
1 small onion	1 teaspoon Chinese 5-spice blend
2 garlic cloves	1/8 teaspoon ground black pepper
1 tablespoon high-heat cooking oil	Hot pepper sauce (sriracha recommended)

1. Measure frozen vegetables and set aside, or thaw in microwave if desired.

2. Chop onion and mince garlic. Heat skillet over medium heat, then add oil and swirl around to coat bottom. Add onion. Cook and stir 2 to 3 minutes. Add garlic and cook 1 minute.

3. Break eggs directly into skillet and stir just until thickened, but not too dry.

4. Add all remaining ingredients and stir until heated through.

---

*TIP

We usually **chop** up leftover ROAST CHICKEN and freeze it in baggies of 2 cups each. Sometimes, we'll cook a whole chicken in our slow cooker, then debone and chop it before freezing some in baggies. If you don't have any leftovers, buy a rotisserie chicken and cut up what you need.

CHICKEN MANGO SALAD

7 to 8 cups   Involved $$

"My cousin Cindy made this for us many years ago, and we've been hooked ever since. It's Greg's favorite and one of the first recipes he asked for when he was away at college. Although it involves a number of steps, they're all easy—it just takes a little time to debone a chicken. We often do that step the day before, especially if we're cooking our own chicken instead of buying a rotisserie chicken." BOBBI

Prep Time: 1 hour, start to finish
Tools: knife and cutting board, large bowl, measuring cups and spoons

1 rotisserie **chicken*** (about 5 cups chopped)

2 cups diced **mangos*** (1 to 2 mangos)

1/2 cup chopped cilantro

1 small, fresh jalapeño pepper

2 to 3 scallions (about 1/3 cup sliced)

1 to 2 limes

1/2 cup mayonnaise

1-1/2 teaspoons ground cumin

1/2 teaspoon salt

1/4 teaspoon ground black pepper

1/4 teaspoon red pepper flakes

3/4 cup pecans (toasted recommended)

1. Remove chicken from the bone and chop into bite-size pieces. Place in a large bowl.

2. Peel and dice mango. Add to chopped chicken.

3. Coarsely chop cilantro. Slice the jalapeño pepper in half lengthwise and remove seeds and pith, then mince. Add to chicken mixture. *Note:* We usually start with half of the pepper and add more at the end if desired.

4. Thinly slice scallions (both green and white parts). Add to chicken mixture and toss.

5. Juice <u>one</u> lime directly into the mixture, then add mayonnaise, salt, pepper, and red pepper flakes. Toss to combine well. Add more mayonnaise, jalapeño, and juice of the other lime if desired. Adjust other seasonings, to taste.

6. Toast pecans if desired. Chop and sprinkle on top, or stir into salad.

> ***How to Peel then Chop a Mango** – Keep in mind that the mango seed is thin and flat and runs down the center from top to bottom and edge to edge of the wider part. It will take a little practice to know where the seed is. If you want to peel the mango before chopping (works best on firm mangos), slice a thin layer off the bottom. Remove peeling with a paring knife or vegetable peeler, then place the flat bottom on a cutting board. Holding the mango upright, slice down with a knife close to the center, but just far enough off-center to miss the thin, flat seed. Next, slice down the other side. Trim off any of the fruit left on the seed. Slice or dice flesh as needed. To chop a mango before peeling, see technique on p. 182.

TIP

If cooking your own **chicken**, do so the day before or give yourself plenty of time earlier that day to not only prepare it, but to let it cool before deboning. You can roast, simmer in water, or cook the chicken in a slow cooker.

SERVING SUGGESTIONS:

- Place a mound of greens in the center of a plate. Top with the salad. Sprinkle pecans on top and surround with pita bread, pita chips, or toasted pita triangles. (To make the pita triangles, cut pita into wedges, opening each wedge up and toasting lightly in oven or toaster oven.)
- Serve inside a pita (as a sandwich), with arugula or sprouts and sliced avocado.

VARIATIONS:

- CHICKEN PEACH SALAD: Substitute diced peaches for diced mango, parsley for cilantro, and lemons for limes. Substitute almonds for pecans.
- CHICKEN GRAPE SALAD: Substitute halved grapes (green, red, or combo) for mango, mint for cilantro, and walnuts for pecans.

CHINESE 5-SPICE CHICKEN

4 servings   Easy $$

One of Greg's favorite spices, Chinese 5-spice is the perfect addition to this quick and easy dish. Adding a little rice wine vinegar brightens the dish, or use any light vinegar (or lemon juice) with a pinch of sugar. Frozen green beans are convenient and work very well in this dish if you don't have fresh.

Prep and Cook Time: 30 minutes, start to finish

Tools: knife and cutting board(s), measuring cups and spoons, large (10-inch) skillet with lid (or foil) to cover

1 small onion

1 tablespoon high-heat cooking oil

2 carrots

4 garlic cloves

1-1/2 pounds boneless skinless chicken thighs, or breasts

2 tablespoons soy sauce

1/2 tablespoon Chinese 5-spice blend

1/2 tablespoon vinegar (rice wine vinegar recommended)

1/8 teaspoon ground black pepper

1/8 teaspoon red pepper flakes

1 cup green beans (fresh or frozen)

1. Chop onion. Heat oil in a large skillet over medium-low heat, then add onion. Cook and stir occasionally while you continue.

2. Slice carrots on the diagonal into 1/4-inch-thick pieces and mince garlic, adding to the skillet as you finish each one. Turn heat to low and stir occasionally while you continue.

3. Snap green beans in half (if using fresh). Set aside.

4. Cut chicken into large bite-size pieces, using a **cutting board*** dedicated to raw meats if possible. Push onions and carrots to the outer edges of the skillet. Place chicken pieces in the center. Sprinkle soy sauce, 5-spice, vinegar, pepper, and red pepper flakes over chicken and stir gently, keeping vegetables on the outer edges as much as possible. Cover and simmer about 5 minutes.

5. Stir in green beans. Cover and simmer on low another 5 minutes, or until beans are crisp-tender and chicken is done.

> ***TIP**
> If you only have one **cutting board**, identify one side for cutting raw meats and the other side for vegetables. When doing so, always chop vegetables first, then meat. Clean thoroughly with soap and water and rinse or spray with a bleach solution. Better yet, buy two cutting boards.

SERVING SUGGESTION:
- Serve over BASIC BROWN RICE, other grain, or rice noodles.

GREEN CHILI CHICKEN ENCHILADAS

12 enchiladas   Involved $$

We love chicken enchiladas, so we prepare a dozen at a time by making two layers in our 8×8-inch baking dish. However, you can use a larger dish and make one layer, or cut the recipe in half if you prefer. Be sure to use firm corn tortillas so they'll keep their shape. If the tortillas are too soft they'll break apart, in which case you can simply call it Chicken Enchilada Casserole! We use leftover chicken, but you can quickly cook boneless chicken pieces (grill, boil, or pan-sear), or pick up a rotisserie chicken and debone it. Buy pre-grated cheese to save time.

Prep Time: 30 minutes   **Cook Time:** 40 minutes   **Passive Time:** 15 minutes
Tools: 8×8-inch baking dish, measuring cups and spoons, large bowl, knife and cutting board, grater
Special Supplies: aluminum foil

1 cup frozen chopped kale, or spinach

1 avocado

1/2 cup cilantro leaves, lightly packed

8 ounces grated Monterey Jack cheese (about 3 cups), <u>divided in half</u>

1/2 cup Greek yogurt

1 teaspoon ground cumin

2 cups cooked chicken (chopped)

12 (6-inch) corn tortillas, or 1 (8-ounce) package

2 (8-ounce) pouches green enchilada sauce, or 1 (14 to 16-ounce) can

Preheat oven to 375°F. Spray or rub oil into an 8×8-inch baking dish.

1. Place frozen kale in a large, microwave-safe bowl and thaw in the microwave for 1 minute on high. Chop avocado and cilantro, then add to kale.

2. Grate cheese. Add <u>half</u> to vegetable mixture and reserve other half for topping.

3. Stir in yogurt and cumin.

4. Chop cooked chicken and add to mixture.

5. Scoop about 1/3 cup of filling onto 6 tortillas, rolling up and placing them in the baking dish in one layer, side by side. Pour one pouch (or a little less than half of a can), over the first layer. Sprinkle half of the remaining cheese over them.

6. Repeat with remaining tortillas, laying them in the same direction on top of the first layer. (You might need to cut one in half to squeeze it in.) Pour remaining sauce evenly over enchiladas and sprinkle remaining cheese on top. Cover with foil, making sure it doesn't touch the cheese, and bake 25 minutes.

7. Remove foil and bake another 15 minutes, or until golden brown and bubbling.

8. Let stand at least 15 minutes before serving. Garnish with extra cilantro if desired.

SERVING SUGGESTION:

- Keep the sides simple and colorful. Serve with carrot sticks and/or fresh fruit.

VARIATIONS:

- BLACK BEAN ENCHILADAS – Substitute 1 (15-ounce) can black beans (rinsed and drained) for the chicken.

MOROCCAN CHICKEN KABOBS

4 kabobs   Easy $$

"This is one of my favorite dishes to make for company because it's so simple to put together and tastes amazing (just double or triple it to fit the crowd). We've cooked the kabobs in the oven and on the grill, with equally good results." BOBBI

Prep Time: 30 minutes   **Cook Time:** 20 to 25 minutes

Tools: knife and cutting board(s), measuring cups and spoons, large bowl, baking sheet

Special Supplies: skewers

Chicken:

3 garlic cloves

1/2 cup parsley leaves (lightly packed)

1 tablespoon ground cumin

1 tablespoon paprika (smoked recommended)

1 teaspoon salt

1/8 teaspoon ground black pepper

1 pound boneless, skinless chicken thighs, or breasts

Naan, pita bread, or cooked grain

Garnish:

1/2 cup chopped tomatoes

1/2 cup plain Greek yogurt, or aioli

For chicken:

1. Finely chop garlic and parsley then place in a large bowl.

2. Add cumin, paprika, salt, and black pepper. Stir.

3. Cut each chicken thigh into two or three pieces, using a cutting board dedicated to raw meats if possible. Add to the herb mixture and toss to coat well.

4. Cover bowl and store in refrigerator 15 to 30 minutes.

5. Preheat oven (or grill) to 400°F. Spray or rub oil on a baking sheet if cooking in the oven.

6. Thread chicken pieces onto a skewer. Cook in preheated oven (or on the grill) 10 minutes on each side.

To assemble:

1. Heat naan (or pita) in a toaster oven, oven or microwave. (Alternatively, heat up some cooked rice or other grain.)

2. Chop tomatoes.

3. **Remove*** meat from one kabob and place in the center of a piece of naan (or pita), or on a bed of rice. Add a spoonful of yogurt (or aioli) and chopped tomatoes.

SERVING SUGGESTIONS:

- Serve with CUCUMBER RAITA and roasted or steamed vegetables.

- Serve with a green salad and fresh fruit.

*TIP

To easily **remove** meat (and/or vegetables) from a kabob, hold the skewer by one end with the point-side down. Take a fork and push everything down and off.

PORTUGUESE CHICKEN

2 (2-piece) servings   Easy $$

"When Rebecca and Greg were in elementary school, a Portuguese friend showed me how to make this, and it instantly became a family favorite. Not long afterward, we went to Portugal and found this dish on almost every menu. It's considered peasant food, but we think it's fit for a king! You can make it with chicken wings, legs, or a combination of cuts. We updated our recipe to fit into an 8×8-inch baking dish, but if you have a larger dish make the recipe with a whole, cut-up chicken, doubling the other ingredients." BOBBI

Prep Time: 10 to 15 minutes   **Cook Time:** 55 to 60 minutes

Tools: knife and cutting board, large bowl, measuring cups and spoons, 8×8-inch baking dish

Special Supplies: aluminum foil

1 small onion

8 garlic cloves

1 large russet potato (about 2-1/2 cups cubed, or 3/4 pound*)

1/2 cup coarsely chopped cilantro

3 tablespoons vinegar, or white wine

1 tablespoon high-heat cooking oil

2 teaspoons dried oregano leaves

1 teaspoon salt

1/4 teaspoon ground black pepper

4 thighs (bone-in, with skin), or 1-3/4 pounds chicken pieces

Paprika

*TIP
When shopping for potatoes, use scales found in the produce section to weigh them. When possible, add a food scale to your kitchen equipment. You'll be surprised how much you use it!

Preheat oven to 400°F.

1. Cut peeled onion in half, then cut each half into four pieces. Place in a large bowl.

2. Slice garlic and add to onion.

3. Scrub potatoes, but don't peel. Cut into 1-inch cubes and place in bowl.

4. Chop cilantro and add.

5. Drizzle vinegar (or wine) and oil over vegetables. Add oregano, salt, and pepper. Stir to coat well.

6. If needed, cut large chicken pieces so everything is about the same size (i.e., separate thighs and drumsticks, and cut split breasts in half crosswise). Add chicken to vegetables and stir again. Transfer to the baking dish. Arrange chicken pieces skin-side up, on top of the vegetables.

> ***Baste** – to apply moisture to a food (usually meat) as it cooks in an oven. Use a baster or spoon to take some of the juices in the bottom of the dish and pour over the meat occasionally.

7. Sprinkle paprika and more salt generously over chicken. *Note:* You can refrigerate now, until ready to cook.
8. Cover dish with foil. Cook in preheated oven 30 minutes. Remove foil. Use a spoon (or baster) to **baste*** the chicken. Cook (uncovered) an additional 25 to 30 minutes, or until browned on top and chicken is done. A meat thermometer should read 165°F, or cut into the thickest piece to see that the juices run clear (not pink).

SERVING SUGGESTION:
• Serve with steamed broccoli and carrots, or a mixed salad.

ROAST CHICKEN

4 to 8 servings   Easy $$

We roast a chicken at least two times a month. If you do it properly, you don't need much more than salt and pepper, although a few simple ingredients can jazz it up (see Variations). We recommend spending a little extra to buy organic, local, or hormone and antibiotic-free chicken (at least).

Prep Time: 5 minutes   **Passive Time:** 5 to 10 minutes   **Cook Time:** 60 to 75 minutes
Tools: 8×8-inch baking dish
Special Supplies: kitchen twine (optional), aluminum foil

1 chicken
Salt (kosher salt recommended)
Ground black pepper

Place oven rack in the middle of the oven, or slightly below. Preheat to 450°F.

1. Place chicken in an 8×8-inch baking dish. **Truss*** the chicken if desired.
2. Generously sprinkle salt and pepper over the chicken.
3. Roast in oven (uncovered) 30 minutes.
4. Turn heat down to 350°F and cook another 30 to 45 minutes. Use a meat thermometer (should read 165°F) to determine if it's done, or cut into meaty part of thigh to see that the juices run clear (not pink).

5. Sprinkle more pepper on the chicken in the last few minutes of cooking if desired, since high heat causes pepper to lose some of its flavor.

6. Cover lightly with a tent of foil and let stand 5 to 10 minutes before cutting, for juicier chicken.

VARIATIONS:

- LEMON-PEPPER ROAST CHICKEN – Follow basic instructions, but after placing in the baking dish (and before trussing), squeeze juice of 1 lemon all over the chicken, then place spent lemon halves inside the cavity. Cut 1 small onion into quarters. Place in cavity with lemon halves. Truss and season with salt and lots of pepper.

- ROAST CHICKEN WITH GARLIC AND ROSEMARY – Loosen skin by working fingers under it and along the breasts, being careful not to tear the skin. Insert garlic cloves and rosemary sprigs (or other fresh herbs) under the skin, placing one sprig at the base of each leg and on each breast. Follow all other instructions.

- LAVENDER LEMON ROAST CHICKEN – Place sprigs of fresh lavender under the skin. Squeeze juice of 1 lemon over chicken then place spent halves and more lavender in the cavity. Follow all other instructions.

*Truss – to tie poultry legs (half-truss) and wings (full-truss) together for a better presentation. A half-truss is usually sufficient. To **half-truss** a chicken, cut a 12-inch piece of kitchen twine. Wrap the center of it around the tail of the chicken and tie. Cross the drumsticks and bring one end of the twine up and wrap around the point where the legs cross. Then bring the other end of the twine up and wrap around the opposite side of the legs in the other direction. Bring both ends to top and tie in a knot. This holds the chicken together, but increases the necessary cooking time by 5 to 10 minutes depending on the size of the chicken.

TIP
There's no need to rinse a chicken and contaminate your nice, clean sink. If needed, pat dry with paper towels to remove juices. Observe safe food handling tips found in Chapter 6.

SALSA CHICKEN WITH SPINACH

2 to 4 servings   Easy $$

We love recipes that only use one pan—it makes cleanup so easy! This dish can be as spicy as you want, based on your choice of salsa or by adding hot sauce. If using fresh or homemade SALSA *drain excess juices (there's no need to drain jarred salsas, which are usually cooked and thicker). We recommend serving this over rice or other grain, to soak up the flavorful juices.*

Prep Time: 10 minutes   **Passive Time:** 5 to 10 minutes   **Cook Time:** 45 to 50 minutes
Tools: 8×8-inch baking dish, 2-cup glass measuring cup, measuring spoons, grater
Special Supplies: aluminum foil

5 ounces fresh baby spinach

4 bone-in chicken thighs, or 2 large chicken breast halves

1-1/2 cups frozen corn

1 teaspoon ground cumin

1 teaspoon chili powder

3/4 cup salsa

3 tablespoons sour cream, or Greek yogurt

Hot pepper sauce, to taste

4 ounces grated Monterey Jack cheese (about 1-1/2 cups)

Preheat oven to 400°F. Spray or rub oil into an 8×8-inch baking dish.

1. Spread spinach evenly in baking dish and press down. *Note:* The spinach will fill the dish almost to the top, but it will shrink substantially when cooked.

2. Remove skin from chicken if desired. Place chicken on top of spinach.

3. Measure corn in a 2-cup glass measuring cup. Thaw in microwave about 1 minute on high. Stir in cumin and chili powder, then scatter corn over chicken.

4. Drain off excess liquid from the salsa if needed. Measure in the same glass measuring cup, then stir in sour cream. Add hot sauce if desired. Spread evenly over the corn and pat down.

5. Grate cheese and sprinkle on top. Cover loosely with foil, making sure it doesn't touch the cheese.

6. Bake 30 minutes, then remove foil. Bake (uncovered) another 15 to 20 minutes, or until chicken is done. Cut into the thickest part of the meat to see that the juices run clear, or check with a meat thermometer (should be 165°). Cover loosely with foil and let stand 5 to 10 minutes to reabsorb juices.

SERVING SUGGESTION:

- Serve over BASIC BROWN RICE (or other grain), with black beans and AVOCADO MANGO SALAD.

SHEET PAN CHICKEN WITH FENNEL AND SWEET POTATOES

4 to 6 servings   Easy $$

We love this sweet and spicy meal-in-one that is cooked in a rimmed baking sheet (aka sheet pan). You can line the pan with parchment paper for easier cleanup, but the vegetables will not brown and crisp up as well. You'll be amazed at both the flavor and simplicity of this recipe.

Prep Time: 15 minutes   **Passive Time:** 5 to 10 minutes   **Cook Time:** 40 minutes
Tools: measuring spoons, small and large bowls, knife and cutting board, baking sheet
Special Supplies: aluminum foil

Spice mix:

1 tablespoon **garam masala***

1/2 tablespoon brown sugar

2 teaspoons salt

1 teaspoon ground black pepper

1 teaspoon red pepper flakes

Vegetables:

1 pound sweet potatoes (about 4 cups cubed, or 2 medium-size)

2 small or medium fennel bulbs

1 small onion

8 prunes

1/2 tablespoon high-heat cooking oil

*TIP
Garam masala spice mixes are available at most grocery stores, or make your own with our Finite Foodie spices. See our recipe for GARAM MASALA in Miscellaneous Recipes.

Chicken:

3 pounds chicken pieces (bone-in and skin)

Position oven rack in the middle of the oven. Preheat to 425°F.

1. Mix spices in a small bowl.

2. Peel sweet potatoes. Cut in half lengthwise, then slice into 1/2-inch-thick half-rounds. Place in a large bowl.

3. Remove top stalks of fennel and cut bulbs in quarters from top to bottom. Remove core, then slice across in half to make smaller pieces. Cut onion into chunks. Add both to potatoes, along with the prunes.

4. Drizzle oil over vegetables and toss. Sprinkle 1-1/2 tablespoons of the spice mixture over them and toss again. Spread the vegetables evenly in an ungreased, rimmed baking sheet.

5. Place chicken in bowl used for vegetables. (There's no need to clean the bowl first.) Add remaining spice mixture and toss well to coat all sides. Place chicken on top of the vegetables, skin-side up.

6. **Roast*** (uncovered) in preheated oven 40 minutes. Meat should read 165°F on a meat thermometer and the juices should run clear when meat is cut.

7. Remove from oven and cover loosely with foil. Let rest 5 to 10 minutes.

SMOKED PAPRIKA CHICKEN

5 (2-piece) servings   Easy $$

"This is my go-to chicken recipe for cookouts because it's full of flavor, yet very simple to make (and our Variations are just as easy). Although you can use regular or Hungarian paprika, smoked paprika has the best flavor. We usually prepare a whole chicken, but sometimes purchase specific pieces based on everyone's preferences. To use for salads, cook 2 pounds of boneless, skinless thighs or breasts." BOBBI

Prep Time: 10 minutes   **Passive Time:** 30 to 60 minutes   **Cook Time:** 20 minutes
Tools: large bowl, measuring cups and spoons, knife and cutting board, **grill***
Special Supplies: aluminum foil

1 whole chicken, cut into **10 pieces***

Marinade:

1/4 cup lime juice

2 tablespoons Worcestershire sauce

1 tablespoon smoked paprika

1/2 tablespoon salt

1 teaspoon dried thyme leaves

1/2 teaspoon red pepper flakes

1/4 teaspoon ground black pepper

1/4 teaspoon hot pepper sauce (optional)

1/4 cup high-heat cooking oil

1. Combine all marinade ingredients, <u>except oil</u>, in a large bowl.

2. Slowly beat in the oil with a whisk (or fork) to emulsify.

3. If desired, reserve 1 tablespoon of marinade and set aside to brush onto chicken after it's been grilled.

4. Place chicken pieces in the large bowl of marinade, turning to coat all sides. Cover and refrigerate at least 30 minutes but no more than 60 minutes, turning once halfway through. *Note:* The amount of time in the marinade matters. It needs enough time to absorb the flavors, but not so much that it breaks down the meat, making it mushy.

5. Heat grill on high. (Gas grills can vary, so adjust for your grill.) Turn one burner off and the other to medium. Remove chicken from marinade and shake off excess. Discard remaining marinade.

6. Place meat on the side of the grill with no burner, skin-side down. If your grill only has one burner, turn to medium or medium low. Watch carefully, so it doesn't flame up and burn.

7. Cook 10 minutes on each side (a little less for boneless cuts).

8. *Optional step:* Flip over one more time and place on hottest side of grill for 30 to 60 seconds to get the crisscross marks.

9. Chicken is done when meat thermometer reads 165°F, or cut through the thickest piece to see if the juices run clear. (The amount of time depends on the size of the chicken piece, whether you're using bone-in or boneless chicken, and the temperature of the grill.)

10. Transfer chicken to a plate and cover loosely with a tent of aluminum foil. Let rest 5 minutes. *Note:* This step is important! While resting, the juices are reabsorbed, resulting in juicier meat.

11. If you reserved some of the unused marinade, brush it over chicken pieces before serving. Garnish with sprigs of fresh thyme, or sprinkle some dried thyme on top.

SERVING SUGGESTION:

- Serve with steamed vegetables and RED POTATO SALAD or CHIPOTLE SWEET POTATO SALAD.

VARIATIONS:

- ASIAN MARINATED – For marinade use 1 tablespoon minced garlic, 1/4 cup lemon juice (1 to 2 lemons), 3 tablespoons soy sauce, 2 teaspoons ground ginger, 1/2 tablespoon honey, 1/4 teaspoon red pepper flakes, and 3 tablespoons high-heat cooking oil. Follow all other directions, and garnish with cilantro. Serve with MANGO COLESLAW.

- MEDITERRANEAN MARINATED – For marinade use 3 tablespoons lemon juice, 2 teaspoons Dijon mustard, 1 tablespoon minced garlic, 2 tablespoons dried or fresh oregano leaves, 1/2 tablespoon salt, 1 teaspoon paprika (regular), 1/4 teaspoon ground black pepper, 1/8 teaspoon red pepper flakes, and 3 tablespoons high-heat cooking oil. Follow all other directions, and garnish with flat (Italian) parsley. Serve with APPLE CARROT SALAD.

- KABOBS – Use 2 pounds boneless, skinless thighs or breasts and cut into smaller pieces. Thread onto skewers and cook about 10 minutes each side—on the grill, or in the oven. Add vegetable chunks to skewers if desired.

- TO COOK INSIDE, preheat oven to 400°F. Remove chicken from marinade and place on a greased baking sheet. Cook 25 to 35 minutes, or until done, turning once halfway through. Internal temperature should read 165°F on a meat thermometer, or cut through the thickest piece and see if the juices run clear. Follow all other instructions.

SOUP, STEW, CHILI

BEEF STEW WITH FENNEL AND SWEET POTATOES

4 to 6 servings   Moderate $$

We don't eat beef often, but when we do, we try to buy local grass-fed beef, which is more expensive than conventional. However, stew meat is typically more economical than other cuts, making it a good option for tight budgets. Beef stew can be simmered for as little as an hour, but the longer it cooks, the more tender and flavorful it will be.

Prep Time: 15 minutes   **Cook Time:** 1 to 3 hours
Tools: measuring cups and spoons, large (4-quart) saucepan, knife and cutting board
Special Supplies: paper bag or plastic baggie

Beef:

1 pound beef stew meat

2 tablespoons flour

1 teaspoon salt

1/4 teaspoon ground black pepper

1 tablespoon high-heat cooking oil

Vegetables:

1 medium onion

1 medium fennel bulb

3 to 4 cups beef broth

1/4 cup red wine, or 1 tablespoon vinegar

2 tablespoons Worcestershire sauce

1 bay leaf

1 teaspoon dried rosemary leaves

1 teaspoon ground coriander

1 medium sweet potato (about 1/2 pound), or 2 large carrots

1 cup chopped broccoli

For beef:

1. Check beef to make sure the pieces are no larger than 1-inch cubes. Cut into uniform pieces if needed.

2. Place flour, salt, and pepper in a paper bag or plastic baggie. Shake to mix, then add beef and shake again to **dust*** all sides.

*Dust – to coat food in a very light layer of flour, cornmeal, tapioca starch, etc. Examples: Used to coat fish, chicken, beef, and vegetables in some recipes. Also, to sprinkle the top of an item with a powdery substance for a nice finish. Examples: Paprika, nutmeg, and powdered sugar.

3. Heat oil over medium to medium-high heat in a large saucepan, then add beef. **Brown*** on all sides, stirring occasionally. This should take about 5 minutes.

4. In the meantime, coarsely chop onion. Turn heat down to medium-low, then add onion, stirring frequently.

5. While onion is cooking, cut the tops off the fennel bulb. Slice bulb in quarters from top to bottom and cut out the core. Thinly slice across each quarter, then add to saucepan. Cook and stir 1 to 2 minutes.

6. Add 3 cups broth, red wine (or vinegar), Worcestershire sauce, bay leaf, rosemary, and coriander. Bring to a gentle boil, then lower heat and simmer (uncovered) while you continue.

> ***Brown** – to cook foods over (or under) high heat quickly, turning the outer layer brown. Also used for cooking ground meat until it is brown throughout.

> ***TIP**
> Cooking stew **uncovered** reduces the liquid and intensifies the flavor. Add up to 1 additional cup broth if needed.

7. Peel sweet potato and cut into 1-inch cubes (or cut carrots into 1/2-inch-thick slices). Add to stew.

8. Continue simmering (**uncovered***) at least 1 hour, or up to 3 hours, stirring occasionally. Add another cup of broth if desired.

9. Chop and stir in broccoli during the last 15 to 30 minutes.

VARIATION:

- CLASSIC BEEF STEW – Substitute white potatoes for sweet potatoes, and omit fennel. Use 2 cups frozen pea and carrot mixture instead of broccoli.

CHINESE 5-SPICE CHICKEN SOUP

10 cups   Moderate $$

We make this soup grain-free, then serve it over brown rice or rice noodles. The soup freezes well, making it another one of Greg's favorites. It's quite simple to put together, but does require a fair amount of chopping.

Prep and Cook Time: 45 minutes, start to finish

Tools: knife and cutting board(s), large (4-quart) saucepan, measuring cups and spoons, colander

1 small onion

1 tablespoon high-heat cooking oil

2 medium carrots

2 cups crimini mushrooms (1 pint),
    or 1-1/2 cups frozen

4 garlic cloves

1 tablespoon minced fresh ginger (optional)

1 (32-ounce) box or can chicken broth
    (4 cups)

1 cup water

1 medium bok choy or 3 baby bok choy

1 pound boneless, skinless chicken (dark or
    white meat)

1 to 2 tablespoons soy sauce, to taste

1/2 tablespoon **Chinese 5-Spice blend***

1/4 teaspoon red pepper flakes

2 tablespoons rice wine vinegar (optional)

1. Chop onion. Heat oil in a large sauce-pan over medium-low heat, then add onion. Cook and stir occasionally while you continue.

2. Cut carrots on the diagonal into 1/4-inch-thick slices, and add to onion.

3. Slice mushrooms and stir in.

4. Mince garlic and optional ginger. Add to vegetables. Cook and stir 2 to 3 minutes, or until vegetables are soft. Add a little water if too dry.

*TIP
Chinese 5-spice blends can vary, so we suggest starting with a small amount and adding more at the end after tasting.

5. Add broth and water. Raise heat to bring to a boil, then lower again to keep at a simmer (uncovered) while you continue, or at least 15 minutes.

6. Slice bok choy into 1-inch-wide strips, then cut across to form bite-size pieces. Place in a colander and rinse thoroughly to remove dirt and grit. Set aside to drain.

7. Cut chicken into 1/2-inch-wide strips, using a cutting board dedicated to raw meats if possible. Add chicken pieces, soy sauce, **5-spice*** and red pepper flakes to saucepan. Adjust heat to keep at a gentle simmer about 5 minutes.

7. Add bok choy and simmer another 3 to 5 minutes.

8. Stir in optional vinegar. Adjust seasonings, to taste.

SERVING SUGGESTION:

- Serve as-is, or over your favorite grain or rice noodles.

VARIATION:

- Substitute 2 to 3 cups leftover Thanksgiving turkey for chicken, and add along with bok choy.

CHIPOTLE BLACK BEAN SOUP

10 cups   Easy $

"Chipotles in adobo pack an extra punch and a smoky flavor. Use a small amount if you're unfamiliar with them. My husband usually puts a whole chipotle on top of his soup, but he's crazy when it comes to spice! I would recommend 1/2 tablespoon for mild, 1 tablespoon for medium, and 1-1/2 to 2 tablespoons for spicy. This is one of our favorite soups and most frequent meals. It's not only tasty, but inexpensive as well. We have a large soup pot, so we usually double the recipe and freeze part of it in small batches." REBECCA

Prep Time: 15 minutes   **Cook Time:** 30 minutes, or longer

Tools: colander, knife and cutting board, large (4-quart) saucepan, measuring cups and spoons, blender (optional)

2 (15-ounce) cans black beans

1 (15-ounce) can **refried black beans***

1 small onion

1 tablespoon high-heat cooking oil

2 garlic cloves

1 large carrot

1 teaspoon ground cumin

3 cups broth, or water

1 (14.5-ounce) can diced tomatoes

1/2 tablespoon minced **chipotle pepper in adobo***

1 teaspoon salt

1/8 teaspoon ground black pepper

1. Drain and rinse whole beans in a colander.

2. Chop onion. Heat oil in a large saucepan over medium to medium-low heat, then add onion. Cook and stir frequently while you continue.

3. Slice (or chop) carrot and mince garlic. Add both to saucepan and continue cooking 2 to 3 minutes.

4. Add cumin and stir continually about 1 minute to release flavors.

5. Add broth, tomatoes, whole beans, and refried beans. Bring to a gentle boil, then lower heat to keep at a simmer.

---

*What are chipotle peppers? And what is adobo?

- A **chipotle** (sometimes spelled chilpotle) is a smoke-dried jalapeño pepper, usually made from red jalapeños. It is quite spicy! These peppers are easy to find in the Mexican food section of the grocery store—dried, or stored in adobo sauce in a small can or jar.

- **Adobo** is Spanish for marinade or sauce, so it's actually redundant to say adobo sauce. Adobo is usually made with vinegar and paprika (to give it the red coloring), along with other seasonings for flavor.

*TIP
Refried beans give this soup a creamy texture. Refried pinto beans can be substituted if you have difficulty finding refried black beans. You can also make the soup using all whole beans (3 cans total), mashing some of the beans with a spoon, or blending some or all of the soup.

6. In the meantime, finely mince chipotle pepper and add to soup, along with salt and pepper. Simmer (uncovered) at least 30 minutes, or until ready to serve.
7. Adjust seasonings, to taste.

SERVING SUGGESTIONS:
- Serve with a dollop of CILANTRO-LIME SOUR CREAM, plain sour cream, or yogurt. Garnish with cilantro sprigs. *Note:* Dairy helps neutralize the heat, so add more if the soup is too spicy for you.
- Substitute grated Monterey Jack cheese for sour cream/yogurt toppings.
- Sprinkle crushed tortilla chips and/or avocado slices on each serving.

CURRIED CHICKEN SOUP

10 cups   Easy to Moderate $$

This relatively simple chicken soup is moderately spicy—perfect for cold winter days. Use frozen chopped cauliflower to save time.

Prep and Cook Time: 40 minutes, start to finish
Tools: knife and cutting board(s), large (4-quart) saucepan

1 medium onion
2 tablespoons high-heat cooking oil
3 large garlic cloves
2 medium carrots
4 cups chopped cauliflower florets (fresh or frozen)
1 tablespoon curry powder
1 teaspoon ground cumin

1 pound boneless, skinless chicken (dark or white meat)
4 to 5 cups broth, or water
1/4 cup tomato paste
1 teaspoon dried thyme leaves
1 teaspoon salt
1/8 teaspoon ground black pepper
1/8 teaspoon red pepper flakes

1. Chop onion. Heat oil in a large saucepan over medium-low heat, then add onion. Cook and stir 3 to 5 minutes.

2. While onion cooks, mince garlic and slice carrots on the diagonal into 1/2-inch-thick pieces. Add to onions, stirring occasionally.

3. If using fresh cauliflower, cut florets off and coarsely chop. Add cauliflower to vegetables.

4. Stir in curry powder and cumin.

4. Cut chicken into bite-size pieces, using a cutting board dedicated to raw meat if possible. Add to vegetable mixture. Turn heat up to medium or medium-high. Cook and stir 3 to 5 minutes, or until chicken starts to turn white.

5. Add 4 cups broth (or water), tomato paste, thyme, salt, pepper, and red pepper flakes. Stir well.

6. Bring to a simmer, then turn heat to low or medium-low to keep at a simmer (uncovered) at least 20 minutes, or longer. Add up to 1 additional cup broth if desired. *Note:* Don't allow to boil, as that will make the chicken tough.

7. Adjust seasonings, to taste.

SERVING SUGGESTION:
- Serve with pita bread on the side, or over couscous or your favorite grain.

VARIATIONS:
- Substitute 1 cup cubed, peeled sweet potatoes for the carrots.
- Substitute chopped broccoli for cauliflower.

GINGERY TURKEY MEATBALL SOUP WITH BOK CHOY AND SOBA NOODLES

11 to 12 meatballs   Moderate $$

Our ginger meatballs were inspired by a Bon Appétit recipe, which we simplified substantially. You can cook them ahead of time and freeze for use later on if desired. We add quick-cooking soba noodles to make this a filling meal-in-a-bowl.

Prep and Cook Time: 1 hour, start to finish

Tools: large bowl, knife and cutting board, measuring cups and spoons, large (10-inch) skillet, colander, large (4-quart) saucepan

Meatballs:

1 pound ground turkey or chicken
   (dark or white meat)

4 garlic cloves

1 tablespoon minced fresh ginger

1/4 cup chopped cilantro (lightly packed)

2 scallions

1-1/2 tablespoons soy sauce

1/4 teaspoon hot pepper sauce (sriracha
   recommended)

1/2 cup bread crumbs (optional)

Oil (for cooking)

2 cups chicken broth, or vegetable broth

Vegetables:

1 large bok choy, or 3 baby bok choy

2 cups fresh mushrooms, or 1 cup frozen

Hot pepper sauce, to taste

Noodles:

Soba* noodles

Water (for cooking)

*TIP

Soba noodles are a Japanese noodle made with buckwheat (soba). Some brands add wheat flour, but we prefer 100% buckwheat noodles. They are brown in color and look something like spaghetti, but usually thinner. Fresh soba is also available. The time to cook varies depending on the thickness of the noodle, so follow package instructions.

For meatballs:

1. Place ground turkey in a large bowl.
2. Mince garlic and ginger, chop cilantro, and thinly slice scallions (using both the green and white parts). Add to turkey, along with soy sauce and hot sauce, then stir well to combine. (The mixture will be very wet.)
3. Add bread crumbs if desired. Form into 1- to 2-inch diameter balls.
4. Heat oil in a large skillet over medium heat and add meatballs. Cook until browned, 3 to 5 minutes on two sides.
5. Leave meatballs in skillet and add broth. Lower heat to medium-low, then cover and **simmer*** 10 minutes.

For vegetables:

1. Slice mushrooms, or use frozen. Add to meatballs.
2. Chop bok choy into 1-inch pieces, discarding the bottom few inches. Rinse in a colander to remove dirt. Add to skillet and simmer another 5 minutes, or until bok choy has wilted but is still bright green. Meatballs should be cooked through by this time.
3. Adjust seasonings, to taste.

*Simmer – to cook over medium to low heat with some liquid. There will be small bubbles, but it will not quite come to a boil.

For noodles:

1. When dish has about 10 minutes left, fill a large saucepan about half full of water and bring to a boil. Rinse desired amount of soba noodles, then add to boiling water and cook per package instructions, until **molto al dente.***

2. Drain in a colander then place some in a soup bowl. Spoon broth, vegetables, and meatballs on top and serve.

VARIATIONS:

- Substitute parsley, basil, or mint for cilantro.
- Add 1 cup snow (or sugar snap) peas.
- Serve over rice noodles or brown rice instead of soba.

> ***Molto al dente** – term used primarily for cooking pasta. The pasta will be pliable but still somewhat firm all the way to the center. Used for pasta that will be cooked further, like the noodles in this soup or in baked dishes like ziti and lasagna.

LEMONY CHICKEN RICE SOUP WITH CAPERS

10 to 11 cups   Easy $$

Use up leftover chicken and frozen vegetables for a quick and easy soup. Although we call for kale in this recipe, you can use whatever vegetable you have in the refrigerator or freezer. We make this tangy and nutritious soup anytime someone has a cold or just needs some TLC.

Prep Time: 15 minutes   **Cook Time:** 45 minutes

Tools: knife and cutting board, large (4-quart) saucepan, measuring cups and spoons, colander

1 onion

1 tablespoon high-heat cooking oil

2 medium carrots

4 garlic cloves

1/2 cup brown rice (dry, uncooked)

7 cups chicken broth

3 cups finely chopped fresh kale, or 1-1/2 cups frozen

2 cups cooked chicken (chopped)

1/4 cup capers

1 teaspoon dried thyme leaves

1 teaspoon salt

1/2 teaspoon dried rosemary leaves

1/4 teaspoon ground black pepper

1/8 teaspoon red pepper flakes

1 lemon

1. Chop onion. Heat oil in a large saucepan over medium-low or low heat. Add onion. Cook and stir occasionally while you continue chopping.

2. Cut carrots on the diagonal into 1/4-inch-thick slices, and chop the garlic. Add to onion and stir.

3. Rinse and drain rice in a colander. Add to vegetables, along with broth. Bring to a boil over high heat, then turn to low. Cover and simmer 15 minutes.

TIP

Whenever you've made a dish that is too salty, add lemon juice to counteract it. If a dish has too much lemon, stir in a pinch of baking soda to neutralize it. This recipe should be nicely balanced, but just in case, you now know how to adjust it.

4. In the meantime, chop fresh kale or any other vegetable of your choice (like broccoli, cauliflower, cabbage or other leafy greens), or simply use frozen.

5. Add vegetables and all remaining ingredients, except lemon. Bring to a gentle boil again over medium-high heat, then turn to low and simmer (uncovered) another 30 minutes, or until rice is soft.

6. Remove from heat. Add juice from lemon. Adjust seasonings, to taste.

VARIATION:

• Reduce broth to 6 cups. Add 1 (15-ounce) can diced tomatoes (or 1-1/2 cups fresh, with juices), along with kale.

LENTIL SOUP

11 cups   Easy $

*"This is a tasty vegetarian version of lentil soup, and it's been one of our family favorites since Rebecca and Greg were toddlers. Slicing the carrots is easier, but we like to grate ours—you choose. We sometimes add peanut butter for a rich **umami*** taste without pork. If you happen to be a bacon or ham lover, see our Variations. The flavor intensifies over time, so this is a great make-ahead soup that also freezes well."* BOBBI

Prep Time: 15 minutes   **Cook Time:** 60 to 90 minutes

Tools: knife and cutting board, large (4-quart) saucepan, measuring cups and spoons, colander

1 large onion

2 tablespoons butter, or high-heat cooking oil

4 garlic cloves

3 to 4 stalks celery

2 medium carrots

1-1/2 cups brown lentils

7 cups no or low-sodium broth (vegetable, chicken, or beef)

2 bay leaves

1 tablespoon paprika (smoked recommended)

1 teaspoon dried thyme leaves

1 teaspoon dried oregano leaves

1/4 teaspoon red pepper flakes

1/8 teaspoon ground black pepper

1-1/2 teaspoons salt

2 tablespoons peanut butter (optional)

1. Chop onion. Heat butter (or oil) in a large saucepan over medium-low heat, then add onion. Cook and stir while you continue.

> ***Umami** is called the fifth taste, after sweet, sour, bitter, and salty. It is best described as meaty and savory.

2. Mince garlic, chop celery (about 2 cups), and slice (or grate) carrots (about 2 cups), adding each to the onion as you finish. Cook and stir another 2 to 3 minutes, or until softened.

3. Sort lentils: Measure, then spread onto a plate or cutting board. Discard any pieces of pebbles, grains, or discolored lentils. Rinse lentils in a colander, to remove sand or grit, then stir into vegetables.

4. Add all remaining ingredients, <u>except</u> salt.

5. Raise heat to medium to bring to a boil. Stir and turn heat to low or medium-low to keep at a simmer (uncovered) until lentils are very tender, 30 to 60 minutes. Once the lentils are tender, add salt and extra broth if desired. Cover and simmer another 30 minutes, or longer for more intense flavor.

6. Discard bay leaves. Stir in peanut butter and adjust seasonings, to taste.

7. Soup can be served as-is, or blended to desired consistency with an immersion stick blender or regular **blender.***

SERVING SUGGESTION:

- All you need is a simple green salad and some crusty bread!

VARIATIONS:

- WITH BACON – Cook 4 to 8 pieces of bacon in the saucepan before you begin. When crisp but not burned, remove bacon and place on a paper towel to drain. Reserve about 2 tablespoons bacon fat and use in place of butter (or oil). Follow the recipe, but eliminate peanut butter. To serve, crumble a piece of bacon on top of each serving.

- WITH HAM – Add about 1/2 cup chopped ham, along with the garlic and other vegetables. Follow the recipe, but eliminate peanut butter and do not blend.

*TIP

To purée hot soups in a **blender**, cool slightly first. Pour a small batch into the blender container. Remove the center section of the lid. Place lid on the container firmly, then cover with a towel folded over 3 or 4 times. Hold the towel firmly in place with one hand, then turn blender on low. Heat expands the air in the blender container, which can push the lid off—along with the contents!

MOROCCAN RED LENTIL SOUP

7 to 8 cups   Easy $

This soup is even better when simmered longer or served the next day. It also freezes well. When reheated, we recommend adding additional ground cinnamon, to taste, since the flavor tends to dissipate over time.

Prep and Cook Time: 1 hour, start to finish

Tools: knife and cutting board, large (4-quart) saucepan, measuring cups and spoons, colander

1 medium onion

1 tablespoon high-heat cooking oil

3 stalks celery

1 red bell pepper (optional)

3 garlic cloves

2 teaspoons ground cumin

1 teaspoon ground ginger

1 teaspoon paprika

1/2 teaspoon ground black pepper

4 to 5 cups water, or unsalted broth

1 cup red lentils (dried, uncooked)

1 (15-ounce) can chickpeas

1 (15-ounce) can tomato sauce

2 tablespoons **tomato paste*** (optional)

1 teaspoon salt

1/2 teaspoon ground cinnamon

1/4 cup chopped parsley, or cilantro

1/2 lemon, or 1-1/2 tablespoons lemon juice

Hot pepper sauce, to taste (optional)

1. **Chop*** onion. Heat oil in a large saucepan over medium-low heat, then add onion. Cook and stir while you continue.

2. Chop celery, optional red pepper, and garlic. Add to onion. Cook and stir an additional 2 to 3 minutes.

3. Stir in cumin, ginger, paprika, and pepper. Cook 1 minute.

4. Add 4 cups water (or broth) and turn heat up to medium-high.

5. Sort lentils: Measure, then spread onto a plate or cutting board. Discard any pieces of pebbles, grains, or discolored lentils. Rinse lentils in a colander, to remove sand or grit, then add to saucepan.

*How to Slice or Chop Onions – Cut off stem end to create a flat surface. Place on a cutting board and slice in half. Remove papery peeling (and the next layer if tough or slippery). Place cut-side down on the cutting board and slice off root end. Hold onion half with thumb on one side and fingers on the other, with your palm arched up over the onion. Bring the knife under the palm of that hand and start carefully slicing as you hold it together. To chop, rotate and do the same thing in the other direction.

6. Bring to a gentle boil, then turn heat down to keep at a simmer (uncovered) about 15 minutes, or until lentils are soft.

7. Drain and rinse chickpeas. Add to soup along with tomato sauce and salt. Add up to 1 additional cup of water (or broth) if desired. Cook an additional 30 minutes. *Note:* Can serve right away or cook longer, which intensifies flavor.

8. Chop parsley (or cilantro). Remove soup from heat and stir in parsley, cinnamon, and lemon juice. Add hot sauce if desired.

*TIP

Tomato paste is a great flavor-enhancer that adds a little sweetness and color to this soup. We keep a tube of tomato paste in the refrigerator for recipes like this one, but the soup will be fine without tomato paste if you don't have any.

SERVING SUGGESTIONS:

- Garnish with additional parsley (or cilantro) and a dollop of Greek yogurt if desired. Serve with crackers or toast, and fruit or green salad.

- Serve with CUCUMBER RAITA and pita bread.

POTATO SALMON CHOWDER

8 cups   Easy $$

We usually use 2% milk to make a light broth, unlike many thick chowders. It's still flavorful, and it's chock-full of omega 3-rich red salmon. Canned salmon is relatively economical and provides additional calcium as well. Since most of the nutrition in a potato is found in and right under the skin, we like potatoes that don't need to be peeled. That makes this soup quicker and easier to make as well. If you prefer a richer chowder, use whole milk or substitute cream for part of the milk.

Prep and Cook Time: 30 minutes or longer, start to finish

Tools: knife and cutting board, large (4-quart) saucepan, measuring cups and spoons

1 medium onion

1 tablespoon butter, or high-heat cooking oil

2 stalks celery

2 to 3 garlic cloves

2 large Yukon Gold potatoes (about 1 pound)

1 cup frozen peas

1 cup broth (vegetable or chicken)

2 cups milk, or unsweetened non-dairy milk

1 tablespoon dried or fresh dill

1/2 tablespoon capers (optional)

1/2 teaspoon salt

1/4 teaspoon ground black pepper

1 (15-ounce) can wild-caught, Alaskan red salmon (not drained)

1. Chop onion. Melt butter in a large saucepan over medium-low heat, then add onion. Cook and stir while you continue.

2. Chop celery and mince garlic, adding to saucepan as you finish each one. Cook and stir while you continue.

3. Cut the potatoes into quarters, then cut across to form 1/4-inch-thick slices. Add to other vegetables, along with all remaining ingredients except salmon.

4. Heat on medium or medium-high just until it starts to bubble. <u>Watch carefully so it doesn't boil over.</u> Immediately lower heat to keep at a simmer (uncovered) about 10 to 15 minutes, or until potatoes are soft.

5. *Optional step:* If you want to thicken the chowder, take out about half of the potatoes once they're soft and mash them in a bowl with a fork or potato masher. Stir back into chowder.

6. Place salmon and the juices in a small bowl and break apart with a fork. Add to soup and heat through. Do not boil, but keep on low until ready to serve. Adjust seasonings, to taste.

SERVING SUGGESTION:
- Serve with a green salad and NANA'S THIN CORNBREAD.

VARIATIONS:
- POTATO CHOWDER – Omit salmon altogether. Another option is to divide the soup in half right before adding the fish, use a smaller can of salmon and add to one half. That way, you can serve both options if desired.
- Use a frozen pea and carrot mixture instead of just peas.

SPLIT PEA SOUP

10 cups   Easy $

"Rebecca and Greg's first babysitter usually made this soup when she took care of them. (This is probably how they learned to love green food.) She finally shared her recipe with me, so we could enjoy it once the kids no longer needed a sitter." BOBBI

Prep Time: 15 minutes   **Cook Time:** 1 to 2 hours
Tools: knife and cutting board, large (4-quart) saucepan, grater (optional), colander, measuring cups and spoons

1 medium onion

1 tablespoon high-heat cooking oil

3 stalks celery

3 medium carrots

4 garlic cloves

2 cups split peas

7 cups water, or low sodium broth

1 teaspoon dried thyme, or rosemary

1/4 teaspoon ground black pepper

Pinch red pepper flakes

2 bay leaves

1 teaspoon salt

4 slices ham (optional)

1. Chop onion. Heat oil in a large saucepan over medium-low heat, then add onion. Cook and stir occasionally while you continue.

2. Chop celery and grate (or slice) carrots to yield about 2 cups of each, adding to the saucepan as you finish each one.

3. Mince garlic and add to vegetables. Cook and stir another 1 to 2 minutes.

4. Sort split peas: Measure and spread onto a plate or cutting board. Discard any pieces of pebbles, grains, or discolored peas. Rinse in a colander to remove sand or grit.

5. Stir in water (or broth), thyme, black pepper, red pepper flakes, and bay leaves. Do NOT add salt or ham yet. Turn heat up and bring to a boil, then immediately lower to keep at a simmer (uncovered) 1 to 2 hours. Add up to 1 additional cup of liquid and/or cover, as needed. Once peas are soft, add salt.

6. When soup is done, remove pan from heat and discard bay leaves.

7. If not **blending*** soup, chop ham and add to soup now. Cook another 3 to 5 minutes. If planning to **purée,*** do not add ham yet. Use an immersion stick blender, or purée (all or some) of the soup in a regular blender, then add ham.

SERVING SUGGESTIONS:

- Serve with crusty bread, cornbread, or crackers. Add a mixed salad if desired.
- Omit ham and cook bacon separately. Crumble on top of each serving. (This way, you can please the vegetarians and meat eaters alike.)

*What's the difference between blend and purée?

- **Blend** – to combine two or more ingredients until well mixed. The term is also used for mixing ingredients in a blender.
- **Purée** – French term used for a cooked food that has been blended or pushed through a sieve until smooth. Can also be used as a verb.

SUPER BOWL CHILI

9 cups   Moderate $$

"Over the years, this has become our main Super Bowl meal. Hide vegetables in it to fool even the pickiest eaters, and let family or guests serve themselves when they're ready. Double the recipe and freeze in smaller containers for a quick mid-week meal." BOBBI

Prep Time: 15 minutes   **Cook Time:** 1 hour, or longer

Tools: large (4-quart) saucepan, knife and cutting board, grater (optional), measuring cups and spoons, colander

1 pound ground turkey, beef, bison, or a combination

1 large onion

4 large garlic cloves

3 stalks celery

2 medium carrots

1 (28-ounce) can diced tomatoes, or 4 cups fresh, chopped

2 (15-ounce) cans red beans, or kidney beans

1 cup frozen chopped spinach (optional)

1/4 cup tomato paste

2 tablespoons brown sugar

1 tablespoon chili powder

1 tablespoon ground cumin

1 tablespoon vinegar

1 teaspoon minced chipotle pepper in adobo (optional)

1-1/2 teaspoons dried thyme leaves

1 teaspoon salt

1 teaspoon paprika (smoked recommended)

1/2 teaspoon ground allspice

1/4 teaspoon ground black pepper

1/8 teaspoon ground cloves

1. Heat a large saucepan over medium heat and add meat. Cook and stir, breaking up clumps until browned. *Note:* If using ground turkey, you might need to add a little oil.

2. Chop onion and mince garlic. Add to meat, then turn heat down to medium-low. Cook and stir occasionally while you continue.

3. Chop celery (about 1-1/2 cups) and slice, dice, or grate carrots (about 2 cups), adding to saucepan and stirring after each one.

4. Stir in tomatoes. Drain and rinse beans in a colander, then add to the mixture, along with all remaining ingredients.

5. Simmer (covered, but with lid ajar) on low at least 1 hour. Adjust seasonings, to taste.

TIP

For a party, transfer chili to a slow cooker (if you have one) to keep warm.

SERVING SUGGESTIONS:

- Serve with NANA'S THIN CORNBREAD and a mixed salad or crudité platter.
- Serve a scoop of chili on top of a baked potato.

VARIATION:

- CAULIFLOWER VEGETARIAN CHILI – Cook onion in 1 tablespoon oil. Substitute 1 (16-ounce) bag frozen, chopped cauliflower (or 5 cups fresh) for the meat. Add cauliflower to chili along with tomatoes.

TUSCAN KALE AND WHITE BEAN SOUP

10 cups   Moderate $

"My husband likes to shop with a list. I like to be spontaneous. One day we found beautiful, crisp Tuscan* kale at the farmers market, and even though it wasn't on our list, I had to have it! We brought it home and came up with this recipe, which is now a regular in our dinner repertoire. This soup can be ready to eat in less than an hour, but it's even better if simmered longer. It also freezes well—always a plus in my book!" REBECCA

Prep and Cook Time: 45 to 60 minutes, start to finish
Tools: colander, knife and cutting board, large (4-quart) saucepan, measuring cups and spoons

2 (15-ounce) cans white beans (cannellini, Great Northern, navy)

1 medium onion

1 tablespoon high-heat cooking oil

1 large carrot

6 large garlic cloves

4 cups low-sodium broth (vegetable or chicken)

2 tablespoons tomato paste

1 teaspoon dried rosemary leaves

1 teaspoon dried thyme leaves

1 teaspoon salt

1/4 teaspoon ground black pepper

1/4 teaspoon red pepper flakes

2 bay leaves

1 bunch fresh Tuscan kale, or 2 cups frozen chopped kale

1 (14.5-ounce) can diced tomatoes, or 2 cups fresh, chopped

1/4 cup grated Parmesan cheese

1 lemon (optional)

Garnish:
Grated Parmesan cheese

*TIP
Tuscan kale is also called lacinato or dinosaur kale. If it's not available in your grocery store, regular (curly) kale will also work.

1. Drain and rinse beans in a colander.

2. Chop onion. Heat oil over medium-low heat in a large saucepan, then add onion. Cook and stir while you continue.

3. Slice carrot on a diagonal into 1/4-inch-thick pieces, then add to saucepan. Cook and stir another 2 to 3 minutes.

4. Mince garlic. Stir into vegetables and cook another minute.

5. Add broth, tomato paste, rosemary, thyme, salt, pepper, red pepper flakes, and bay leaves. Bring to a gentle boil, then reduce heat to keep at a simmer (uncovered) about 5 minutes.

6. Add beans and cook another 5 minutes.

7. While soup simmers, remove kale leaves from the center stem. Chop into small pieces to yield 4 to 6 cups (lightly packed). Place in a colander and rinse well. *Note:* If using frozen kale, thaw in the microwave now.

8. Use the back of a spoon (or a food masher) to mash some of the beans for a thicker broth. Add kale. Cover and simmer 15 minutes.

9. Add tomatoes and simmer (uncovered) at least another 15 to 30 minutes, or longer if desired.

10. Remove from heat and take out bay leaves. Stir in Parmesan and juice from half the lemon. Add more lemon juice and adjust seasonings, to taste.

11. Sprinkle additional Parmesan on top of each individual serving.

VARIATIONS:

- FRENCH COUNTRY SOUP – Use 6 cups broth and 2 large carrots. Eliminate diced tomatoes.

- WITH SAUSAGE – Slice and brown precooked Italian (or similar) sausage in the large saucepan before you begin. Transfer sausage to a plate and cover to keep warm. Use the drippings to cook onion, adding more oil if needed. Continue with recipe, adding sausage in the last 15 minutes.

VEGETARIAN MAINS

CABBAGE AND POTATOES

8 cups   Involved $

This dish is found in many cultures with slight variations. It's called Colcannon in Ireland and Rumbledethumps in Scotland. Bubble and Squeak is a British variation that includes sausage. Another reason we love this recipe—it's easy to make ahead of time and reheat when ready to serve.

Prep Time: 45 minutes   **Passive Time:** 10 minutes   **Cook Time:** 20 minutes
Tools: knife and cutting board, large (4-quart) saucepan, measuring cups and spoons, colander, large (10-inch) skillet, grater, food masher, 8×8-inch baking dish

Potatoes:

2 pounds potatoes (5 to 6 tennis ball-size)

Water (for cooking)

1 teaspoon salt

2 tablespoons butter

1/2 cup Greek yogurt

1/2 cup milk, or reserved cooking liquids

TIP
If you have leftover mashed potatoes (from Thanksgiving), use 3 to 4 cups in this dish.

Cabbage:

1 small onion

1 tablespoon butter

5 cups chopped green cabbage

1/2 teaspoon salt

1/2 teaspoon ground black pepper

1/4 teaspoon hot pepper sauce (optional)

4 ounces grated cheddar cheese (about 1-1/2 cups, lightly packed), <u>divided in half</u>

Garnish: (optional)

1/4 cup parsley leaves

For potatoes:

1. Scrub potatoes, removing dark spots, sprouts, and any areas that are green under the skin. Peel russet potatoes, but not thin-skinned potatoes like red or Yukon Gold. Cut into 1- to 2-inch chunks.

2. Place potatoes in a large saucepan and **cover with water*** (about 6 cups). Add salt. Cover pan and bring to a boil over medium-high heat. Watch carefully so it doesn't boil over. Immediately reduce heat to medium-low and simmer (uncovered) until

potatoes are just becoming soft, about 5 to 7 minutes. *Note:* While potatoes cook, skip down and begin to prepare cabbage.

3. When potatoes are done, remove 1/2 cup cooking liquids (if using), then drain in a colander. Return potatoes to the pan. Immediately add 2 tablespoons butter to melt.

4. Add yogurt and milk (or reserved cooking liquids). Mash with a food masher (or kitchen spoon) to desired consistency. (Alternatively, beat with a mixer if you want a very smooth texture, but don't overdo it or they will become gummy.) Cover to keep warm.

For cabbage:

1. While potatoes are cooking, chop onion. Melt butter in a large skillet over medium-low heat, then add onion. Cook and stir while you continue.

2. Cut cabbage into 1/4-inch-thick slices, then coarsely chop. Add cabbage, salt, pepper, and hot sauce to skillet. Cook and stir until tender, about 5 to 7 minutes.

To assemble and bake:

1. Preheat oven to 450°F (unless you plan to cook it later). Spray or rub oil into baking dish.

2. Stir cabbage mixture into mashed potatoes.

3. Grate cheese. Add half to the potato-cabbage mixture, then pour into baking dish. Smooth off the top and sprinkle remaining cheese evenly over it. *Note:* At this point, you can bake it, or cover and refrigerate up to one day ahead.

4. Bake (uncovered) until top is brown and bubbling, about 20 minutes. *Note:* If you made this ahead and refrigerated it, cook at 375°F for 40 to 45 minutes, to heat through thoroughly.

5. Let stand about 10 minutes before serving. Sprinkle chopped parsley on top if desired.

SERVING SUGGESTIONS:

- Serve with carrot sticks.
- This can be a vegetarian meal, or a side dish for ham, PORK CHOPS WITH HONEY MUSTARD, LEMON PEPPER ROAST CHICKEN, or corned beef (on St. Patrick's Day).

*Cover with water – to add enough water to a pan so the food item is completely immersed. Used to boil vegetables and to soak and cook dried beans.

CURRIED LENTILS

4 cups   Easy $

All of the ingredients are cooked together in the same pan, making cleanup easy! Cooking with broth adds more flavor, but be sure to choose low or no sodium, as salt can prevent the lentils from softening. To further simplify, use a frozen pea and carrot mixture (see Variations).

Prep Time: 10 minutes   **Cook Time:** 30 minutes
Tools: measuring cups and spoons, colander, knife and cutting board, large (10-inch) skillet with lid (or foil) to cover, grater (optional)

2/3 cup brown lentils (dried, uncooked)

1/2 onion

2 tablespoons butter, or high-heat cooking oil

1 large carrot

1/2 tablespoon curry powder

1/2 teaspoon chili powder

1-1/2 cups water, or no/low sodium broth

1 cup frozen peas

1/2 tablespoon vinegar

1 teaspoon salt

1/8 teaspoon ground black pepper

Hot pepper sauce, to taste

1. Chop onion. Melt butter in a large skillet over medium-low heat, then add onion. Cook and stir frequently while you continue.

2. Grate or chop carrot. Add to skillet, along with curry and chili powder. Cook and stir another 2 to 3 minutes.

3. Sort lentils: Measure, then spread onto a plate or cutting board. Discard any pieces of pebbles, grains, or discolored lentils. Rinse lentils in a colander, to remove sand or grit, then add to skillet, along with water (or broth). Raise heat just until it begins to bubble. Cover, then simmer on low 20 minutes, or until lentils are soft.

4. Add all remaining ingredients, then continue cooking (uncovered) 5 to 10 minutes, or until most of the water has been absorbed.

SERVING SUGGESTIONS:

- Serve with naan, BASIC BROWN RICE, or in a BAKED POTATO (sweet or white). Add a green salad.

VARIATIONS:

- Substitute 1 (15-ounce) can lentils (rinsed) for dried lentils and water. Cook onions and carrots 5 minutes, then add lentils, peas, vinegar, spices, and 2 tablespoons water. Cook another 5 to 10 minutes.

- Substitute 1 cup chopped broccoli (fresh or frozen) for peas.

- Omit fresh carrot and add 2 cups frozen carrot and pea mixture in place of 1 cup peas.

LENTIL RICE CASSEROLE

6 cups   Easy $

"This was a stand-by for us when Rebecca and Greg were young, and it's still part of our core group of go-to recipes. Although it takes 2 hours to cook, you don't have to watch it. You can get some work done or run on errands, then pull out a warm dinner when you get home! If you don't have broth, make this with water, but add extra salt and seasonings at the end." BOBBI

Prep Time: 10 to 15 minutes   **Passive Time:** 5 minutes   **Cook Time:** 2 hours
Tools: 8×8-inch baking dish, measuring cups and spoons, colander, knife and cutting board, grater
Special Supplies: aluminum foil

1 cup brown lentils (dried, uncooked)
1/2 cup brown rice (dried, uncooked)
1/4 cup minced onion
4 garlic cloves
1/2 teaspoon dried oregano leaves
1/2 teaspoon dried thyme leaves

1/2 teaspoon hot pepper sauce (optional)
1/4 teaspoon ground black pepper
3-1/2 cups low-sodium broth, or water
1/2 teaspoon salt
4 ounces grated cheese (about 1-1/2 cups), divided in half

Garnish: (optional)
2 tablespoons chopped parsley

Preheat oven to 325°F. Spray or rub oil into an 8×8-inch baking dish.

1. Sort lentils: Measure, then spread onto a plate or cutting board. Discard any pieces of pebbles, grains, or discolored lentils. Rinse lentils in a colander to remove sand or grit, then transfer to baking dish.
2. Rinse brown rice in the colander, then add to lentils.
3. Mince onion and garlic. Add to lentil mixture along with oregano, thyme, hot sauce, and pepper. Add broth (or water) and stir gently.
4. Cover with foil and bake 1 hour and 45 minutes.
5. Grate cheese. Remove casserole from oven and add salt. Fluff and stir with a fork.
6. Fold in half of the cheese. Sprinkle remainder on top. Return lentils to oven (uncovered) and cook an additional 15 minutes.
7. Garnish with chopped parsley if desired.

SERVING SUGGESTION:
- Serve with a simple green salad or one of our slaw recipes.

MIXED VEGETABLES AND RICE

2 servings   Easy $

"One year I escaped my busy life in New York City, and took a job at a small inn in Pennsylvania that had a vegetarian restaurant. When I wasn't cleaning rooms, I was waitressing or working in the kitchen. This was one of their most popular dishes, and it was probably the first time I considered eating vegetables and rice as a meal. It's not only easy and tasty, but is a great way to use up an overabundance of vegetables in your refrigerator." BOBBI

Prep Time: 10 minutes   **Cook Time:** 10 minutes (or more for cooking rice)

Tools: knife and cutting board, measuring cups and spoons, large (10-inch) skillet with lid (or foil) to cover

2 cups **cooked brown rice***

Vegetables:

1 small onion

1 tablespoon high-heat cooking oil

1 large carrot

2 garlic cloves

1 tablespoon water

2 cups dense vegetables (broccoli, cauliflower, green beans, Brussels sprouts, cabbage, kale)

1 cup quick-cooking vegetables (bok choy, spinach, Swiss chard, snow peas, mushrooms, bell peppers)

1/2 tablespoon soy sauce (optional)

Toppings: (choose one)

1/2 cup grated cheese

1 recipe PEANUT/CASHEW SAUCE

---

*TIPS

- Cook BASIC BROWN RICE and freeze in containers of about 2 cups, so you'll always have some rice that can be thawed in the microwave and used in recipes like this one.

- **Adding a little water** (or broth) when cooking vegetables cools down the temperature and keeps the oil from becoming damaged by high heat. It also cuts down on calories, but don't leave oil out altogether—it's important to use some oil for proper absorption of the fat-soluble nutrients found in vegetables. Use this trick in any recipe that starts with **sautéing*** onions, garlic, etc.

For rice:

1. Heat up **leftover rice*** or make some in advance.

For vegetables:

1. Cut peeled onion in half, then slice across each to form half rounds. Heat oil in a large skillet over medium to medium-low heat, then add onion. Cook and stir while you slice the carrots and mince the garlic, adding each to the skillet as you finish.

2. Cook another 1 to 2 minutes. Add **water.*** Turn heat to low, then cover and steam while you continue.

3. Cut 2 cups of dense vegetables. Stir into onion mixture and cover again. Add a little more water if needed.

4. Chop quick-cooking vegetables and stir into other vegetables. Cover and cook another 2 to 3 minutes, or until vegetables are crisp-tender.

5. Season with soy sauce, to taste. (Omit soy sauce if topping with PEANUT/CASHEW SAUCE.)

To assemble and serve:

1. Serve vegetables over brown rice.

2. Sprinkle cheese on top, or drizzle PEANUT/CASHEW SAUCE over it.

> ***Sauté** – French word meaning "to jump." Used for cooking food quickly in a skillet or pan with a small amount of oil, over medium to high heat (unless the recipe calls for sautéing over a lower heat and for a longer period of time). Theoretically, the food should be kept moving (or jumping) by stirring or flipping continually. However, some chefs prefer to stir occasionally so the food browns. The phrase "cook and stir" is often used as a substitute for this term.

POLENTA VEGETABLE BAKE

4 servings   Easy $

"This is one of our favorite vegetarian meals. It's a filling dish that you can easily assemble ahead of time, then bake in the oven when you're ready. Don't want to use your oven? Check out the Stovetop Variation." REBECCA

Prep Time: 20 minutes   **Passive Time:** 10 minutes   **Cook Time:** 30 minutes

Tools: 8×8-inch baking dish, colander, knife and cutting board, large bowl, measuring cups and spoons

1 (15-ounce) can cannellini beans

1 (16-ounce) roll prepared polenta

5 ounces fresh arugula, or baby spinach (4 to 6 cups)

1 small onion

1/4 cup pesto

1 (14.5-ounce) can diced tomatoes, or 2 cups **fresh*** chopped

1 teaspoon dried thyme leaves

1/2 teaspoon dried rosemary leaves

1/3 cup crumbled goat cheese, or feta cheese

1/4 cup grated Parmesan cheese

*TIP

If using **fresh tomatoes**, cut each one in half, then squeeze over the sink to remove some of the juices, pulp and seeds, before chopping. (The final dish will have too much liquid in it if you skip this step.)

Preheat oven to 400°F. Spray or rub oil into an 8×8-inch baking dish.

1. Drain and rinse beans in a colander.
2. Cut polenta into 1/2-inch-thick slices. Make a layer with them in the bottom of the baking dish.
3. Sprinkle all of the arugula (or spinach) on top of polenta slices. Press down gently.
4. Chop onion and place in a large bowl. Drain excess juices from tomatoes then add to onion, along with beans, pesto, thyme, and rosemary. Mix well.
5. Spread bean mixture over arugula (or spinach), patting down to fit.
6. Top with goat cheese (or feta) and Parmesan.
7. Bake (uncovered) 30 minutes. Remove from oven and let stand 10 minutes before serving.

VARIATION:

- STOVETOP VERSION – Heat 1 tablespoon oil in a large skillet over medium-high heat. Cook polenta slices on each side about 3 minutes, or until browned. Transfer to a plate and cover with foil to keep warm. Use skillet to cook onions, tomatoes, and herbs for 3 to 5 minutes. Stir in beans, arugula, and pesto, then heat through. Remove from stovetop and stir in goat cheese. To serve place a few polenta slices on a plate, then top with a scoop of the vegetable mixture. Garnish with grated Parmesan.

QUESADILLAS WITH ARUGULA

6 quesadillas   Easy $

These vegetarian and gluten-free (provided you use corn tortillas) quesadillas are very easy to put together! We buy a bag of grated Mexican-blend cheeses for convenience and great flavor. Also see our ROASTED VEGETABLE AND BEAN QUESADILLAS under Variation." REBECCA

Prep and Cook Time: 20 minutes, start to finish

Tools: grater (optional), measuring cups, large (10-inch) skillet, baking sheet (optional)

2 cups grated cheese (Mexican blend recommended), <u>divided</u>

12 (6-inch) corn tortillas

Ground cumin

Chili powder

Hot pepper sauce

3 cups fresh arugula, or baby spinach (lightly packed)

Spray oil (for cooking)

Preheat oven to lowest setting.

1. Grate 2 cups cheese (if needed). Set aside 1/2 cup for garnish.

2. Lay 6 tortillas onto a flat surface. Place about 1/8 cup (2 tablespoons) grated cheese on each one, then sprinkle ground cumin and chili powder on top.

3. Mound up about 1/2 cup arugula in the center (it will wilt down substantially). Sprinkle another 1/8 cup cheese over arugula, and add a few dashes hot sauce.

4. Place another tortilla on top and lightly press down.

5. Spray skillet with oil, and heat on medium to medium-low.

6. Place a quesadilla in hot skillet and cover with a lid if possible. (This will help melt the cheese more quickly.) When the bottom tortilla is beginning to turn brown and the cheese has melted somewhat, flip quesadilla over and brown the other side. Once cheese has fully melted, remove from heat. Transfer to a baking sheet and sprinkle some of the reserved cheese on top. Keep warm in the oven until ready to serve.

7. Repeat for all quesadillas.

SERVING SUGGESTIONS:

- Serve whole or cut into quarters. Add CANTALOUPE BERRY SALAD, or your favorite fruit.

*Julienne – to cut food into small thin strips, usually around 1/4 to 1/8-inch thick by 1-1/2 to 2 inches long. Examples: Often used for vegetables and some herbs, but also for making strips of grilled meats.

- ROASTED VEGETABLE AND BEAN QUESADILLAS – Slice 1 onion, and cut 1 bell pepper into **julienne*** strips. Toss with some olive oil, ground cumin, salt, and pepper to taste, then roast 10 to 20 minutes in oven preheated to 425°F. Stir and flip at least once (see ROASTED VEGETABLES for more details). Heat 1 (15-ounce) can refried beans in a small saucepan, slice 1 avocado, and grate 2 cups cheese. Top each tortilla with a spoonful or two of refried beans, a few pieces of roasted vegetables, cheese, avocado, and another tortilla. Follow recipe instructions for cooking.

QUICK TAMALE CASSEROLE

4 to 6 servings   Easy $

"Nick and I try to make most things from scratch, but sometimes that just doesn't happen. Since we love Mexican food, this is one of our favorite meals to prepare when we don't have much time. Polenta rolls are mostly shelf-stable and located in the pasta section of the grocery store, or sometimes in the refrigerated produce section." REBECCA

Prep Time: 10 minutes   **Passive Time:** 5 to 10 minutes   **Cook Time:** 30 minutes
Tools: 8×8-inch baking dish, knife and cutting board, grater, measuring cups
Special Supplies: aluminum foil

1 (16-ounce) roll prepared polenta
1 (15-ounce) can **vegetarian chili***
1 cup salsa
1 cup lightly crushed tortilla chips
4 ounces grated Monterey Jack cheese
    (about 1-1/2 cups) divided

*TIP
Use an all-natural **vegetarian chili** with wholesome ingredients you can pronounce.

Garnish: (optional)
1 small jalapeño pepper

Preheat oven to 350°F. Spray or rub oil into an 8×8-inch baking dish.

1. Slice polenta roll into 1/2-inch-thick pieces and layer on bottom of baking dish, overlapping or breaking slices to make them fit.
2. Pour vegetarian chili evenly over polenta slices.
3. Grate cheese and sprinkle 1 cup over chili.
4. Pour salsa over the cheese, spreading out evenly.
5. Sprinkle crushed tortilla chips on top, then cover with remaining cheese.
6. Slice optional jalapeño pepper. Remove seeds for less heat. Sprinkle slices on top.
7. Cover with foil and bake in oven 15 minutes. Uncover and bake an additional 15 minutes. Cool about 5 to 10 minutes before serving.

- Serve with a salad of greens, avocados, and tomatoes.

VARIATIONS:

- QUICK TAMALE CASSEROLE CON CARNE – Substitute 2 cups leftover SUPER BOWL CHILI, or your favorite chili con carne, for the vegetarian chili.
- Substitute 1 can ranch-style (ranchero) beans for chili.
- Substitute 2 cups prepared polenta for the roll, and spread on bottom of baking dish. Polenta mixes can be found in grocery stores and some ethnic markets.

SWEET POTATO AND KALE CASSEROLE

4 to 8 servings   Involved $

This is an updated variation of Irish colcannon, made with sweet potatoes instead of white, and kale instead of cabbage. We serve this for Thanksgiving in place of the traditional yams with marshmallows on top. It's much more healthful, and tastes great!

Prep Time: 30 minutes   **Passive Time:** 10 minutes   **Cook Time:** 20 minutes
Tools: knife and cutting board, large (4-quart) saucepan, measuring cups and spoons, colander, large (10-inch) skillet, grater, food masher, 8×8-inch baking dish

Potatoes:

2 pounds sweet potatoes (about 2 large)

Water (for cooking)

1 teaspoon salt

2 tablespoons butter

1/2 cup reserved cooking liquids

1/2 cup plain yogurt, sour cream, half-and-half, or milk

2 teaspoons ground ginger

1/2 teaspoon salt

1/4 teaspoon ground black pepper

1/4 teaspoon hot pepper sauce (**sriracha*** recommended)

> ***Sriracha** is an Asian hot sauce that is slightly sweet and not as intense as Tabasco.

Kale:

1 small onion

1 tablespoon high-heat cooking oil, or butter

1/2 tablespoon minced fresh ginger (optional)

1-1/2 cups frozen chopped kale, or 1 (5-ounce) package baby kale

1/2 teaspoon salt

1/4 teaspoon red pepper flakes

Garnish:

4 ounces sharp cheddar cheese (about 1-1/2 cups grated), <u>divided in half</u>

For potatoes:

1. Wash and peel sweet potatoes. Cut into 1- or 2-inch chunks to yield about 7 cups. Place in a large saucepan and cover with water (about 6 cups). Add salt. Cover pan and bring to a boil over medium-high heat. (Watch carefully so it doesn't boil over.) Immediately reduce heat to medium-low and simmer (uncovered) just until soft, about 5 to 10 minutes.

2. When potatoes are done, remove 1/2 cup of the cooking liquids and set aside. Drain potatoes in a colander, then return to the saucepan. Immediately add 2 tablespoons of butter to melt.

3. Add yogurt, reserved cooking liquids, ground ginger, salt, pepper, and hot sauce. Mash with a food masher (or fork) to desired consistency. (Alternatively, beat with a hand-held immersion blender or an electric mixer for a smoother consistency.) Cover to keep warm until ready to use.

For kale:

1. While potatoes are cooking, chop onion. Heat oil (or butter) in a large skillet over medium-low heat, then add onion. Cook and stir while you **peel*** and mince optional ginger. Stir in ginger and turn heat to low. Cook 2 to 3 minutes.

2. Add kale, salt, and red pepper flakes. Cook, stirring occasionally, until vegetables are soft and moisture has evaporated.

To assemble and bake:

1. Preheat oven to 450°F. Spray or rub oil into 8×8-inch baking dash.

2. Stir kale mixture into mashed sweet potatoes.

3. Grate cheese. Stir in about half. Pour mixture into the baking dish and smooth off the top. Sprinkle remaining cheese evenly on top. *Note:* At this point, you can bake it, or cover and refrigerate up to one day ahead.

4. Bake (uncovered) until top is brown and bubbling, about 20 minutes. *Note:* If you assembled this earlier and refrigerated it, cook at 375°F for 40 to 45 minutes, to heat through.

5. Let stand about 10 minutes before serving.

*How to Peel Ginger – Peeling ginger without much waste can be challenging. The trick is to ditch the knife and use a small spoon instead. Turn the spoon upside down and scrape off the peeling with the tip edge. You can easily get into all the little nooks and crannies.

- This can be a vegetarian meal as-is, but also makes a nice side dish for PORK LOIN ROAST WITH MAPLE GLAZE, ROAST CHICKEN, or Thanksgiving turkey.

VARIATION:

- To substitute canned sweet potatoes for fresh, melt butter and add 2 (15-ounce) cans purée. Omit cooking liquids and use Greek yogurt or sour cream—not milk or half-and-half.

SWEET POTATO BLACK-EYED PEA BURGERS

8 burgers, or 16 sliders   Involved $

"When you're craving a good burger but don't want beef, this is an incredibly delicious swap-in. Using canned sweet potato purée and canned black-eyed peas saves a lot of time, and although involved, it's still manageable. We add cornmeal to bind the ingredients, but avoid corn flour (too fine) and coarse ground (not fine enough). Medium grind is just right! These burgers are packed with fiber, vitamins A and B, and plant protein too. Yum!" REBECCA

Prep Time: 20 minutes   **Passive Time:** 30 minutes   **Cook Time:** 6 to 8 minutes per batch
Tools: knife and cutting board, measuring cups and spoons, large (4-quart) saucepan, small bowl, large (10-inch) skillet

Burgers (patties):

1/4 cup finely chopped onion

1/4 cup finely chopped red bell pepper

1 tablespoon high-heat cooking oil

1 to 2 garlic cloves

1-1/2 teaspoons ground cumin

1 teaspoon chili powder

1 teaspoon paprika (smoked recommended)

1-1/2 teaspoons salt

1 teaspoon dried oregano leaves

1/4 teaspoon ground black pepper

1/4 teaspoon red pepper flakes

1 cup canned **sweet potato purée***

1 (15-ounce) can black-eyed peas

1 egg

3/4 cup cornmeal (medium grind)

1 tablespoon Worcestershire sauce

2 to 3 dashes hot pepper sauce (optional)

Oil (for cooking)

Optional fixings:

Whole grain buns, English muffins, or tortillas

Avocado slices

Lettuce, red onion slices, tomatoes, and/or sprouts

Mayonnaise, or TAHINI LEMON DRESSING

1. Chop onion and bell pepper. Heat oil in a large saucepan over medium-low heat, then add vegetables. Cook and stir 2 to 3 minutes, while you continue.

2. Mince garlic and add to onion mixture, along with cumin, chili powder, and paprika. Cook and stir 1 minute, then remove from heat.

3. Stir in salt, oregano, black pepper, and red pepper flakes.

4. Add sweet potato purée. Drain excess juice (if there is any) from black-eyed peas, but do not rinse. Add to sweet potato mixture and mash some of the peas with a fork (or spoon) as you stir.

5. In a small bowl, lightly beat egg with a whisk (or fork). Add to sweet potato mixture, along with cornmeal, Worcestershire sauce, and hot sauce.

6. Refrigerate mixture at least 30 minutes to give the cornmeal time to soak up some of the moisture and thicken.

7. Form patties using about 1/3 cup of the mixture for each.

8. Heat some oil in a large skillet over medium heat. Cook 3 to 4 patties at a time for 3 to 4 minutes on each side, or until browned and cooked through. Add more oil as needed to cook all patties.

SERVING SUGGESTION:

- Serve on a bun, English muffin, or in a tortilla. Top with avocado slices and any other optional toppings you like. Garnish with a dollop of mayonnaise or TAHINI LEMON DRESSING.
- Serve on a bed of greens and any toppings you like.

VARIATIONS:

- Form into smaller patties to make about 16 sliders, and serve on slider buns.
- Substitute lentils for the black-eyed peas.
- Substitute 1/2 cup finely chopped mushrooms, or 1/4 cup corn for bell pepper.
- Add 1 to 2 teaspoons minced chipotle peppers in adobo sauce instead of red pepper flakes and hot sauce.

---

*TIP

To make your own **sweet potato purée**, bake a medium sweet potato until very soft, then scoop out the inside and mash with a food masher (or fork). (Alternatively, peel the sweet potato, cut in chunks and boil in water until soft. Drain and mash.) Canned purée tends to have more liquid in it than a homemade, so decrease the amount of cornmeal to 1/2 cup if making your own purée.

TEX-MEX VEGETABLE CASSEROLE

4 to 6 servings   Moderate $

"This is another one of our favorite gluten-free, vegetarian meals. Make it and freeze to have on one of those days when you don't want to cook. You can increase the spiciness several ways (but don't do all of them!): use spicy refried beans, spicy enchilada sauce, pepper jack cheese, or increase the chipotle peppers and hot sauce. We like to bring this to potlucks, or to a friend who needs a comforting but healthful dinner. In the latter case, make our mild version and bring a bottle of hot sauce as a gift." REBECCA

Prep Time: 20 minutes   **Passive Time:** 15 minutes   **Cook Time:** 30 minutes
Tools: 8×8-inch baking dish, knife and cutting board, measuring cups and spoons, large (10-inch) skillet, grater

8 (6-inch diameter) corn tortillas

1 cup red enchilada sauce, divided in half

1 small onion

1 tablespoon high-heat cooking oil

1 (14.5-ounce) can diced tomatoes, or 1-1/2 cups fresh

1 cup frozen chopped greens

1 (6-inch-long) zucchini (about 2 cups chopped)

1/2 tablespoon minced chipotle pepper in adobo sauce

1 (15-ounce) can plain refried beans (black or pinto)

2 cups grated cheese (Monterey Jack or Mexican blend), divided in half

Garnish: (optional)
Sour cream
Avocado slices

Preheat oven to 375°F. Spray or rub oil into an 8×8-inch baking dish.

1. Tear 5 tortillas into small (about 1-inch) pieces and scatter on the bottom of baking dish. Pour half of the enchilada sauce over tortillas.

2. Chop onion. Heat oil in a large skillet over medium-low heat, then add onion. Cook and stir 2 to 3 minutes.

3. Add tomatoes and greens. Cook 3 to 5 minutes.

4. Chop zucchini by cutting it lengthwise into quarters to form four long spears. Slice each spear into 1/2-inch-thick pieces. Add to skillet.

5. Mince chipotle peppers and stir into vegetable mixture. Cook another few minutes, or until most of the liquid has evaporated.

6. Remove skillet from heat and stir in refried beans.

7. Grate cheese, then add half to vegetable mixture. Pour on top of tortillas in baking dish.

8. Tear 3 tortillas into small pieces and sprinkle on top.

9. Pour remaining enchilada sauce over the tortillas and press down lightly with the back of a spoon, so all of the tortillas are covered in sauce. Top with remaining cheese.

10. Bake 30 minutes (uncovered) or until brown and bubbling on top.

11. Let rest at least 15 minutes before serving. If desired, garnish with sour cream and/or avocado slices.

VEGETABLE FRIED RICE

6 cups   Easy $

This is a great option for cleaning out leftover rice and veggies from the refrigerator. We've specified some of our favorite vegetables to use, but feel free to choose whatever you have on hand.

Prep and Cook Time: 15 to 20 minutes, start to finish
Tools: measuring cups and spoons, knife and cutting board, large (10-inch) skillet

2 cups cooked brown rice
1/2 small onion
2 tablespoons high-heat cooking oil
1 cup chopped cabbage, or other greens
1 cup chopped broccoli, or cauliflower
1/2 cup frozen corn
1/2 cup frozen peas
1 tablespoon water

3 eggs
2 tablespoons soy sauce
1 tablespoon vinegar (rice wine vinegar recommended)
1 teaspoon Chinese 5-spice blend
1/8 teaspoon ground black pepper
Hot pepper sauce (sriracha recommended)

1. Use leftover brown rice, or prepare some now (see our recipe for BASIC BROWN RICE). Remember, brown rice takes about 50 minutes to prepare.

2. Chop onion. Heat oil in a large skillet over medium-low heat, then add onion. Cook and stir 2 to 3 minutes.

3. While onion cooks, chop cabbage and broccoli. Add to skillet, along with corn, peas, and water. Cook and stir another 3 to 5 minutes, or until vegetables are crisp-tender and all of the liquid has cooked off.

4. Turn heat to medium. Break eggs directly into skillet. Cook and stir 1 to 2 minutes, or until eggs are cooked.

5. Add rice and heat through, stirring frequently.

6. Season with soy sauce, vinegar, 5-spice, pepper, and hot sauce, to taste.

VEGGIE TACOSTADAS

9 tacostadas   Moderate $

Is it a taco or tostada? A tostada is made on a flat, crispy corn tortilla topped with refried beans, lettuce, tomatoes and cheese. However, we made this version on a soft corn tortilla, and added asparagus along with the other vegetables. We fold it in half and eat it like a soft taco, which is why we call it a tacostada. The recipe is rated Moderate due to the number of the steps, but there's nothing difficult about it.

Prep and Cook Time: 30 minutes, start to finish

Tools: knife and cutting board, large saucepan with steamer insert, small (1-quart) saucepan, measuring cups and spoons, medium bowl, grater, microwave

1 bunch asparagus

1 (15-ounce) can refried beans

1 cup chopped lettuce (lightly packed)

1 cup chopped tomatoes

1/4 cup cilantro leaves (lightly packed)

2 scallions

1 tablespoon olive oil (extra virgin recommended)

1 lime

Salt and pepper, to taste

1 cup grated Monterey Jack cheese

1 avocado

9 corn tortillas

Hot pepper sauce, to taste

Greek yogurt, or sour cream (optional)

1. Cut off the tough, bottom part of the asparagus stems, leaving the top 6 inches or so. Add about 1/2 inch of water to a large saucepan, then place a steamer insert (or colander) into it. Lay asparagus in the steamer insert then cover pan and bring water to a boil. Turn to low and steam 1 to 2 minutes, or until crisp-tender. Remove from heat and rinse with cold water.

2. While asparagus is cooking, heat refried beans in a small saucepan over low heat, stirring frequently until warm. Add a little water if too dry. Remove from heat and cover with lid.

3. Chop lettuce, tomatoes, and cilantro, and place in a medium bowl. Thinly slice scallions (both green and white parts) and add to bowl.

4. Drizzle olive oil and juice from half the lime over salad mixture. Season with salt and pepper, to taste, then toss.

5. Grate cheese, slice avocado, and cut remaining lime half into wedges for garnish.

To assemble:

1. Warm up tortillas by stacking them, then wrapping in a damp kitchen (or paper) towel. **Microwave*** for 10 to 15 seconds. Turn over and heat another 10 seconds, or until hot.

2. Place 2 to 3 warm tortillas on a dinner plate. Spread 3 to 4 tablespoons refried beans evenly over each tortilla. Sprinkle some grated cheese on top, then add a little salad mixture. Lay 2 to 3 asparagus spears over the salad and top with 2 slices avocado. Repeat with all tortillas, using up all of the ingredients. (You might have more asparagus than you need. If so, it's great on a salad the next day.)

3. Serve with a wedge of lime. Add a few dashes of hot sauce and a spoonful of yogurt (or sour cream) if desired. Fold in half and eat like a soft taco.

 *TIP
If you don't have a **microwave**, heat some oil in a large skillet over medium heat and cook each tortilla about 15 seconds on each side. Transfer to a plate and cover with foil to keep warm.

ZUCCHINI PANCAKES

8 to 10 (3-inch) pancakes   Involved $

"When a friend returned from a trip to Greece, she raved about zucchini pancakes that were served at tapas bars. At her encouragement, I've created a similar treat, which can be served as a vegetarian meal, side dish, or appetizer. These pretty pancakes can be cooked ahead of time, and warmed up in the oven at 350°F when ready to serve." BOBBI

Prep Time: 10 minutes   **Passive Time:** 30 minutes   **Cook Time:** 5 to 10 minutes per batch

Tools: grater, measuring cups and spoons, three bowls (small, medium, and large), colander, knife and cutting board, large (10-inch) skillet

Zucchini:
2 (6-inch-long) zucchinis (about 3 to 4 cups grated)
1 teaspoon salt

Batter:
1/3 cup **flour***
1 teaspoon dried dill
1/2 teaspoon dried oregano leaves
1/2 teaspoon baking powder
1/8 teaspoon red pepper flakes

2 tablespoons minced shallot, or onion
1 tablespoon chopped fresh mint (optional)
1 egg
1/4 cup plain Greek yogurt
Spray oil, or butter (for cooking)

Garnish: (optional)
Greek yogurt (plain)
Mint, dill, or oregano sprigs

For zucchini:

1. Grate zucchini and place in a medium bowl. Add salt and stir. Let stand while you continue, at least 30 minutes. This will draw out excess moisture.

2. After 30 minutes, pour zucchini into a colander and press down to squeeze out as much liquid as possible.

For batter:

1. While zucchini stands, combine flour, dill, oregano, baking powder, and red pepper flakes in a small bowl, and stir.

2. Finely chop shallot (or onion) and optional fresh mint. Set aside.

3. Lightly beat egg with a whisk (or fork) in a large bowl. Stir in yogurt until smooth. Add shallots and fresh herbs.

4. Stir in flour mixture.

To assemble and cook:

1. Fold zucchini into the batter. Let rest 2 to 3 minutes before cooking.

2. Place skillet over medium heat. When hot, spray with oil (or add about 1 teaspoon butter) to coat cooking surface. Drop batter onto skillet to form 3-inch-diameter rounds. *Note:* Make 2-inch pancakes to serve as appetizers.

3. Cook 3 to 5 minutes, or until nicely browned and beginning to firm up. Flip over and cook another 3 to 5 minutes on the other side. Repeat with remaining batter.

4. Transfer pancakes to a cooling rack or plate to cool slightly and firm up.

5. Garnish with a dollop of yogurt and herbs if desired.

SERVING SUGGESTION:

- Serve with CARROT APPLE SALAD, carrot sticks, or cantaloupe, for a more colorful meal.

VARIATIONS:

- Add 1/4 cup feta cheese crumbles to batter, and sprinkle more on top instead of yogurt.
- Remove seeds and excess juice from a plum tomato and chop. Stir into batter. Garnish with more chopped tomato.

---

 *TIP

White, whole wheat, or a combination of the two **flours** will work just fine. If substituting gluten-free flour, add an extra 1 to 2 tablespoons to hold together better, if needed.

SIDES

Side dishes are just as important as the entrée, so we've provided an assortment of recipes ranging from very easy to somewhat involved. When the main course is simple, try out a more complicated side dish, and vice versa. Think about the whole menu, the time required for everything, and the number and types of pans needed. Also make sure the flavors of your side dishes complement rather than compete with the main dish.

GRAINS AND LEGUMES

TIPS (Applies to all grains)

- Choose the right size and weight of pan. Water is absorbed more evenly and quickly if a grain is cooked in a wide-based pan, as opposed to a small, deep one. When lightweight cookware is used, water evaporates too quickly, and the grain often burns on the bottom. If possible, use a heavy saucepan, or lower the temperature.

- Electric heating elements can vary from one stove to the next, and this can affect the cooking time. If you have a gas stovetop, the water takes longer to boil than on an electric stove; however, the heat can be adjusted better.

The How and Why of Soaking Grains – Some people soak grains before cooking to improve the digestibility. Place grain in a glass (not plastic) bowl and add water. Use 1 part rice and three to four parts water (e.g., for 1 cup of grain, add 3 to 4 cups water). If desired, add 1/2 tablespoon lemon juice or apple cider vinegar per 1 cup of grain, to further break down the phytic acid and increase the absorption of nutrients. Cover and let stand overnight, or about 8 hours. Rinse, then cook according to basic instructions, cutting the cooking time in half.

BASIC BROWN RICE

3 to 4 cups   Easy $

This is our preferred way to cook rice, unless the package specifies something else. We like clear saucepan lids, which make it easy to check on the rice without uncovering.

Prep Time: 2 minutes   **Passive Time:** 10 minutes   **Cook Time:** 40 minutes
Tools: measuring cups and spoons, colander, large (4-quart) saucepan

1 cup brown rice (dry, uncooked)
2 cups water, or broth
1/4 teaspoon salt (eliminate if using salted broth)

TIP

We recommend using brown rice because of the higher levels of fiber and nutrients than white rice. Be mindful that it takes longer to cook brown rice than white rice. There are many types of brown rice from which to choose: long grain, short grain, basmati, and Texmati®. Our recipe for BASIC BROWN RICE should work for most varieties, or simply follow package directions. Long grain is typically the least expensive, but choose whichever you prefer. Buy it in the bulk section to save money.

1. Rinse brown rice in a colander to remove residue of toxins (like arsenic) found naturally in rice. Set colander in the sink to drain while you continue.

2. Use a large or wide saucepan, so the rice will have plenty of room to cook evenly. If possible, choose a heavy saucepan to prevent burning. Add water (for firmer rice, cut the liquid down by 2 tablespoons; for creamier, add 2 tablespoons) and salt, then bring to a full boil over high heat. Add rice and stir.

3. Bring water to a boil again, then turn heat to low. Cover and simmer 40 minutes. *Note:* Set the timer and resist the urge to lift the lid, but stay close by. Turn heat down if it starts to boil over.

4. Remove from heat and keep covered. Let stand 10 minutes.

5. Remove lid and fluff with a fork.

BASIC MILLET

3 to 4 cups   Easy $

Millet is an inexpensive, gluten-free grain that was actually a staple in China before rice came on the scene. In some countries, cracked millet is the grain used for couscous. It cooks quickly and provides similar nutritional benefits as other grains. Millet is particularly high in manganese and provides over one quarter of the recommended daily allowance of magnesium. Millet tastes even better when toasted before cooking.

Prep Time: 2 minutes   **Passive Time:** 10 minutes   **Cook Time:** 15 minutes
Tools: measuring cups and spoons, colander, large (4-quart) saucepan

1 cup millet (dry, uncooked)
2 cups water, or broth
1/4 teaspoon salt (eliminate if using salted broth)

The How and Why of Toasting Grains – Toasting gives grain a richer, nuttier flavor. Heat a skillet over medium heat. Add grain, stirring frequently. It will start popping and begin to smell fragrant and golden brown (about 3 to 5 minutes if dry, longer if wet from rinsing). Do not let it burn! Remove from heat and pour into a glass bowl to cool, or immediately pour into a large saucepan of boiling water. This technique works best with quinoa, millet, and buckwheat groats.

1. Rinse millet if desired.
2. Use a large or wide saucepan, so the millet will have plenty of room to cook more evenly. If possible, choose a heavy saucepan, to prevent burning. Add water and salt, then bring to a full boil. Add millet and stir.
3. Bring water to a boil again, then turn heat to low. Cover and simmer 15 minutes. (Set the timer and resist the urge to lift the lid. Turn heat down if it starts to boil over.)
4. Remove from heat and keep covered. Let stand 10 minutes.
5. Remove lid and fluff with fork.

VARIATION:

- CREAMY HOT BREAKFAST MILLET – Use 3 cups water and stir frequently as it simmers. Increase the cooking time by 5 minutes if needed. Can also serve like grits, as a side dish.

BASIC QUINOA

3 to 4 cups   Easy $$

Quinoa (keen-wah) is called the "Gold of the Incas" or "Mother Grain" even though it's not technically a grain. It's actually a seed from a plant in the same family as spinach and Swiss chard. Quinoa is more expensive than most other grains, but it's a source of high-quality protein, providing three amino acids that are typically limited in most other grains: lysine, methionine and cysteine. The seeds are coated with saponins, which have a bitter flavor if not washed off. Be sure to rinse quinoa in a fine-mesh colander for a few minutes before cooking unless it's marked "prewashed," or if the package instructions do not indicate the need to wash.

Prep Time: 2 minutes   **Passive Time:** 10 minutes   **Cook Time:** 15 minutes
Tools: measuring cups and spoons, colander, large (4-quart) saucepan

1 cup quinoa (dry, uncooked)

1-1/2 cups water, or broth

1/4 teaspoon salt (eliminate if using salted broth)

1. **Rinse*** quinoa in a colander to remove the natural saponins that give it a bitter taste. (Some quinoa is already rinsed, which should be indicated on the package.) If desired, toast quinoa first.

> ***TIP**
> If you don't have a colander with small enough holes to contain quinoa, place in a bowl of water and swish around to **rinse**. Line your colander or a large bowl with a thin dish towel (or several layers of paper towels) before pouring the quinoa into it to drain.

2. Use a large or wide saucepan, so the quinoa will have plenty of room to cook evenly. If possible, choose a heavy saucepan, to prevent burning. Add water and salt, then bring to a full boil over high heat. Add quinoa and stir.

3. Bring water to a boil again, then turn heat to low. Cover and simmer 15 minutes. (Set the timer and resist the urge to lift the lid.) Turn heat down if it starts to boil over.

4. Remove from heat and keep covered. Let stand 10 minutes.

5. Remove lid and fluff with fork.

LEMON PARSLEY QUINOA

3 cups   Easy $

Lemon, parsley, and black pepper are a winning combination, but only use parsley leaves, as the stems have an unpleasant flavor.

Prep Time: 5 minutes   **Cook Time:** 15 minutes   **Passive Time:** 10 minutes

Tools: measuring cups and spoons, colander, grater, large (4-quart) saucepan, knife and cutting board

1 cup quinoa (dry, uncooked)

1 lemon, or 2 tablespoons lemon juice

1-1/2 cups water

1/2 teaspoon salt

1/2 cup chopped parsley

2 tablespoons butter

1/4 teaspoon ground black pepper

1. Rinse quinoa if not prewashed.

2. If using a fresh lemon, grate off the yellow part of peel (zest) with the small or medium holes of grater and set aside for later. Juice the lemon to yield 2 tablespoons.

3. Place water, lemon juice, and salt into a large saucepan and bring to a boil over high heat. Add quinoa and stir.

4. Bring water to a boil again, then turn heat to low. Cover and simmer 15 minutes. Turn heat down if it starts to boil over.

5. Chop parsley while quinoa cooks.

6. Remove quinoa from heat and keep covered. Let stand 10 minutes, then fluff with a fork.

7. Place butter in pan and cover again until melted. Add parsley, lemon zest, and pepper, then toss gently with a fork. Adjust seasonings to taste.

SERVING SUGGESTION:

• Serve with LEMON-PEPPER ROAST CHICKEN, PAN-SEARED SALMON, or SPANISH MACKEREL.

VARIATION:

• Substitute lime juice for the lemon juice, cilantro for the parsley, and/or brown rice for the quinoa (cooking rice in 1-3/4 cup water for 40 minutes).

LIMA BEANS AND KALE

2-1/2 cups   Easy $

Lima beans and/or butter beans are popular in the south, especially in the summer when they're in season. (There's a big debate about whether lima and butter beans are the same thing or not, but for our purposes, they're interchangeable.) Our recipe calls for frozen lima beans, which are easy to find at the grocery store year-round. However, we recommend substituting fresh butter beans if you have access to them.

Prep Time: 5 minutes   **Cook Time:** 30 minutes
Tools: measuring cups and spoons, small (1-quart) saucepan

2 garlic cloves	1/2 cup water
1 tablespoon butter	1/2 teaspoon dried rosemary leaves
2 cups frozen lima beans	1/2 teaspoon salt
1 cup frozen chopped kale	Pinch ground black pepper

1. Mince garlic. Melt butter in saucepan over medium-low heat, then add garlic. Cook and stir 1 minute.

2. Add all remaining ingredients. Turn heat up to bring to a gentle boil, then lower to simmer (uncovered) 30 minutes or longer. Add more water if needed.

SERVING SUGGESTIONS:

• Serve as a side dish to meats, or with brown rice for a vegetarian meal.

• Cook 2 strips of bacon and crumble on top.

MILLET WITH BROCCOLI

4 cups   Moderate $

Millet is an economical, gluten-free grain that we feel is underused. It can be toasted first to bring out the nutty millet flavor, although that step is not necessary. This recipe makes a hearty side dish, which can also be served as a vegetarian main meal.

Prep Time: 10 minutes   **Passive Time:** 10 minutes   **Cook Time:** 20 minutes
Tools: large (10-inch) skillet with lid (or foil) to cover, small bowl, measuring cups and spoons, knife and cutting board

1/2 cup millet (dry, uncooked)	1 cup + 2 tablespoons broth, or water
1/2 onion	2 cups chopped broccoli
1 tablespoon high-heat cooking oil	1 tablespoon lemon juice
1 red bell pepper	1/4 teaspoon salt
2 garlic cloves	1/8 teaspoon ground black pepper
1/4 teaspoon ground cumin	1/4 cup grated Parmesan cheese
1/4 teaspoon red pepper flakes	

1. *Optional step:* Heat large skillet over medium-high heat, then add millet. Stir continually until fragrant and golden brown, about 3 to 5 minutes. The tiny seeds will begin to make popping noises. Transfer to a small bowl or plate to cool.

2. Chop onion. Heat oil in the same large skillet over low heat, then add onion. Cook and stir while you continue.

3. Slice off the top and bottom of the bell pepper and save for another use. Cut the remaining pepper (sides) into straight julienne strips, 1/4-inch thick by about 1-1/2 inches long. Combine with onion.

4. Mince garlic, then add to skillet along with cumin and red pepper flakes. Cook and stir a few minutes.

5. Add broth and millet, then turn heat to medium-high. Once it begins to boil, turn to low. Cover and cook 15 minutes. Remove from heat and let stand 10 minutes.

6. While millet cooks, chop broccoli into bite-size pieces and place in a 2-cup glass measuring cup (or small, microwave-safe bowl). Cover with a plate or plastic wrap. *Note:* Cut a few slits in plastic wrap to allow steam to escape. Microwave on high 1 minute, or until crisp-tender. (Alternatively, steam broccoli in a saucepan on the stovetop.)

7. Stir broccoli into cooked millet mixture, along with lemon juice, salt, and pepper. Add Parmesan, or serve on the side for everyone to garnish as desired.

SERVING SUGGESTIONS:

- Serve as a side dish to MEDITERRANEAN MARINATED CHICKEN, PORK LOIN ROAST, or CHILI-LIME FLOUNDER.

- Serve as a vegetarian meal. Add extra cheese or beans if desired.

SIMPLE LENTILS

3 cups   Easy $

When you go to the store to find lentils, you might see black, brown, green, white, red, and yellow lentils. This can be very confusing, but we recommend brown lentils for everyday purposes. They're the most common and least expensive. Cook a batch, or even double this recipe and freeze some in packages of about 1-1/2 to 2 cups each as a substitute for a 15-ounce can. Lentils are quick and easy to prepare, unlike some of the larger beans. They'll keep in the refrigerator up to 5 days, or frozen for 6 months. (Most recipes will indicate red, yellow, or specialty lentils if required. When not specified, use brown or green lentils.)

Prep Time: 5 minutes **Cook time:** 20 to 30 minutes
Tools: measuring cups and spoons, colander, large (4-quart) saucepan

1 cup brown lentils (dry, uncooked)
2-1/2 cups water

1 teaspoon high-heat cooking oil (optional)
1 bay leaf (optional)

1. Sort and clean lentils: Measure, then spread onto a plate or cutting board. Discard any pieces of pebbles, grains, or discolored lentils. Rinse in a colander to remove sand or grit.
2. Place in a saucepan, then add water, oil (to prevent foaming), and bay leaf (for flavor).
3. Bring to a boil over medium-high heat.
4. Immediately turn heat to medium-low or low. Cover, but keep the lid slightly ajar so it won't boil over. Simmer 20 minutes for slightly firm lentils, or 30 minutes for softer lentils. Drain off excess water.
5. These can be used in any recipe calling for canned lentils, or season as desired with herbs, salt, or butter.

TIP
Never add salt to the water when cooking lentils (or any bean for that matter), as the salt prevents the lentils from softening. Season with salt AFTER the beans have become soft.

SPANISH RICE

2 cups   Easy $

"One day I was making SPANISH MACKEREL, and I decided to add the same spices to some leftover rice. It was an instant hit, and is now one of our favorite ways to dress up plain brown rice." BOBBI

Prep and Cook Time: 10 minutes, start to finish

Tools: knife and cutting board, small (8-inch) skillet, measuring cups and spoons

1 garlic clove

1/2 tablespoon extra virgin olive oil

1/4 teaspoon paprika (smoked recommended)

1 plum tomato

Salt, to taste

1-1/2 cups cooked brown rice

1. Mince garlic.
2. Heat oil in a small skillet over low heat, then add smoked paprika and garlic, stirring frequently.
3. Chop tomato and add to skillet, along with salt. Cook and stir 1 to 2 minutes.
4. Add cooked rice and stir until warmed through.

SERVING SUGGESTION:

- Serve as a side to SPANISH MACKEREL, or any grilled fish or chicken.

TEXAS-STYLE PINTO BEANS

3 to 4 cups   Easy $

"For those days when you need to make something last-minute, try spicing up some canned pinto beans to serve as a side to leftover meat, or with rice or cornbread (see Variations) for a complete vegetarian meal. This was inspired by my Nana's pinto beans that she cooks all day. She uses dried beans, which are more economical and definitely worth the wait, but not always feasible for us. If you're interested in learning how to cook dried beans, see our website for details." REBECCA

Prep Time: 5 minutes   **Cook Time:** 20 minutes

Tools: colander, knife and cutting board, large (4-quart) saucepan, measuring cups and spoons

2 (15-ounce) cans pinto beans

1/2 small onion

1/2 tablespoon high-heat cooking oil

1/2 cup water, or broth

1/2 tablespoon chili powder

1/2 tablespoon ground cumin

1/2 teaspoon salt

1/8 teaspoon ground black pepper

1 small jalapeño, or minced chipotle pepper in adobo, to taste (optional)

1. Drain and **rinse*** pinto beans in a colander.
2. Chop onion. Heat oil in a large saucepan over medium-low heat, then add onion. Cook and stir 2 to 3 minutes, or until soft.
3. Add beans, water (or broth), chili powder, cumin, salt, and black pepper. Add the whole (uncut) jalapeño to flavor the beans without adding too much heat. If you want spicy beans, slice the jalapeño in half lengthwise, remove seeds and pith, then mince. (Alternatively, use minced chipotle peppers in adobo, to taste.)
4. Bring to a gentle boil over medium-high heat, then turn to low and simmer (uncovered) about 15 minutes, adding more water if needed.

SERVING SUGGESTIONS:

- Serve as a side dish to TEXAS-STYLE OVEN-ROASTED BRISKET.
- Serve with NANA'S THIN CORNBREAD or BASIC BROWN RICE for a complete vegetarian meal.

VARIATION:

- CUBAN BLACK BEANS – Substitute black beans for pinto beans. Add 2 minced garlic cloves and cook with onion. Use 1 teaspoon ground cumin and add 1/8 teaspoon red pepper flakes. Omit chili powder and jalapeño pepper. Add juice of 1 lime to beans right before serving. Otherwise, follow directions for pinto beans. Serve with rice and hot sauce on the side.

*TIP

We usually **rinse** canned beans to remove the thick juices that can contain hard-to-digest compounds. Do not drain if you prefer to keep the juices, but reduce the water by half.

SALADS

HOW TO BUILD A SALAD

10 cups base salad   Easy $ to $$

"I eat a huge mixed salad almost every day for lunch, with all sorts of goodies thrown in. That's a lot of salad, so I've learned how to make the process easier. It's important to know which ingredients can be prepared ahead of time and which ones to add right before serving. When you choose salad greens, mix varieties for more interest. We like to combine light and dark greens, as well as mild and spicy ones. You can purchase prewashed salad greens, but keep in mind that they tend to go bad more quickly and lose some of their flavor and freshness. Use this 'recipe' as a guide, then come up with your own combinations." BOBBI

Prep Time: varies

Tools: knife and cutting board, salad spinner (optional), grater (optional), large airtight bowl with lid

Base salad:

6 cups salad greens

1 cup sliced cabbage (red or green)

2 stalks celery

1 large carrot

4 to 6 radishes, and/or other root vegetables

Optional items to add later if desired:

Fruit and Vegetables

Avocado

Bell peppers

Broccoli or cauliflower

Cherry tomatoes

Citrus segments

Cucumbers

Fruit (e.g., berries, apples, pear, mango, papaya)

Herbs

Leftover cooked vegetables

Marinated artichoke hearts

Microgreens or sprouts

Olives

Raisins, cranberries, or other dried fruits

Sugar snap peas

Zucchini or yellow squash

Proteins

Cheese

Fish, poultry, bacon, or other meats

Hard-boiled eggs

Nuts and seeds

Miscellaneous

Rice, quinoa, or pasta

For base salad:

1. Choose your salad greens and rinse if needed. After rinsing, spin in a salad spinner, and/or pat dry before continuing. Leaving water on the greens will cause them to go bad more quickly and will prevent the dressing from coating well.

2. Place a paper towel in the bottom of a large bowl. (We use a large Tupperware container with a lid.) You will remove this towel later, but for now, it will soak up excess moisture that falls to the bottom. Place the greens in the bowl, on top of the paper towel.

3. Chop cabbage and celery. Sprinkle on top of the greens.

4. Grate or slice carrot and radishes (or other root vegetables like turnips, beets, jicama, or kohlrabi). Beets tend to stain anything they touch, so we prefer to use golden beets or keep them separate to add right before serving.

5. Grab the corner of the paper towel that's lining the bowl and pull it out. Using a salad set or a large spoon and fork, toss the salad until well mixed.

6. Place a clean paper towel gently over the salad and seal with an airtight lid or plastic wrap. Store in the refrigerator.

For extras:

1. Some of the add-ins can be prepared ahead of time and stored in airtight containers. These don't keep as long as the base salad ingredients, so they are best stored separately.

To assemble and serve:

1. When ready to eat, place the desired amount of base salad in a serving bowl. Top with desired add-ins.

2. Dress the salad with oil, vinegar, salt, and pepper, or your favorite salad dressing. See our recipes for VINAIGRETTE, TAHINI LEMON DRESSING, or AVOCADO ORANGE DRESSING.

APPLE, CABBAGE, AND FENNEL SLAW

4-1/2 to 5 cups   Easy $

"When my cousin Cindy lived in Nevada, she had a neighbor who would drop off bags and bags of apples from their orchard. Luckily, she's a big fan of apples, but she still had to find new ways to use them. This slaw was inspired by one of her creations. It's refreshing and attractive, plus it's easy to clean up afterward! The salad tastes even better the next day, so it's a great make-ahead dish for the holidays. And, you can easily double the recipe for a larger crowd." BOBBI

Prep Time: 15 minutes   **Passive Time:** 1 hour, or longer (recommended)
Tools: measuring cups and spoons, large bowl, knife and cutting board

Dressing:

2 tablespoons mayonnaise, or plain Greek yogurt

1 tablespoon lemon juice

1 teaspoon honey, or 2 teaspoons **sugar***

1/2 teaspoon dried dill, or 1-1/2 teaspoons fresh

1/8 teaspoon salt

1/8 teaspoon ground black pepper

> ***TIP**
> Honey is twice as sweet as sugar, so use twice as much **sugar** as honey, or to taste. Our slaw is just barely sweet, but mainly from the apples.

Vegetables:

2 cups chopped green cabbage

1 cup chopped fennel

1 Honeycrisp apple, or similar

1 to 2 scallions

Garnish: (optional)

Fresh dill sprigs

1. Combine dressing ingredients in a large bowl and stir.
2. Thinly slice cabbage, then cut across to chop. Measure 2 cups and add to the bowl with dressing.
3. Cut stalks off fennel. Cut bulb into quarters and remove core. Thinly slice across 2 quarters to yield about 1 cup. *Note:* Use remaining fennel bulb in a green salad, soup, or sautéed vegetables. Save stalks for making vegetable broth.
4. Cut apple into quarters, removing the core but not the peeling. Cut each quarter in half lengthwise to form 8 slices. Cut across each slice to form 1/8-inch-thick pieces. Add to cabbage.
5. Thinly slice 1 to 2 scallions (both white and green parts) to yield about 1/4 cup. Add to salad and toss.
6. Cover and chill at least 1 hour, for best flavor. Keeps well up to 3 days. Garnish with fresh dill springs or fennel fronds if desired.

SERVING SUGGESTIONS:

- Serve with CLASSIC HAMBURGERS, SWEET POTATO BLACK-EYED PEA BURGERS, or SMOKED PAPRIKA CHICKEN.

VARIATIONS:

- Use all cabbage or all fennel instead of a mixture if desired.

ASPARAGUS AND PEA SALAD

4 cups   Easy $$

"This salad was inspired by a dish I had at a charming little restaurant in the Santa Ynez Mountains of California after Rebecca's wedding. The sight of it (and the taste) always brings back memories of those mountains, wine tastings, and fun times at our daughter's wedding celebration!" BOBBI

Prep Time: 10 minutes   **Passive Time:** 2 minutes   **Cook Time:** 2 minutes

Tools: knife and cutting board, measuring cups and spoons, large microwave-safe bowl, grater (optional), small bowl (or liquid measuring cup)

Vegetables:

2 cups asparagus pieces (8 to 10 spears)

2 cups sugar snap peas, or snow peas

1 cup English peas (frozen)

1/2 tablespoon water

Dressing:

1 lemon, or 2 tablespoons juice

1/2 teaspoon honey

1/2 teaspoon dried dill, or 1 teaspoon fresh

1/8 teaspoon salt

1/8 teaspoon ground black pepper

1 tablespoon oil (extra virgin olive oil recommended)

1/2 tablespoon chopped fresh mint (optional)

Garnish:

1/2 cup ricotta cheese

Fresh dill, or mint

Honey

> ***Crisp-tender** – term used to specify the point at which vegetables should be cooked in some recipes. The vegetable is tender enough to be pierced by a fork, but it is still firm and somewhat crisp. The food item should still be a bright color.

For vegetables:

1. Remove and discard the tough, bottom portion of 8 to 10 asparagus stalks, reserving the top 6 inches or so. Cut each spear on the diagonal, into 1-inch-long pieces, to yield about 2 cups. Place in a large microwave-safe bowl.

2. Snap off the stems of the sugar snap peas (or snow peas) and remove the string that runs from end to end. Add to asparagus, along with English peas.

3. Add water, then cover with a plate, or plastic wrap that has been pierced with a knife a few times to allow steam to escape. Microwave on high for one minute. Shake the bowl to mix up the vegetables, then microwave on high another minute. Vegetables should be bright green and **crisp-tender.*** Uncover and let stand while preparing dressing.

For dressing:

1. Use the small holes of a grater to zest the lemon peel. Set aside. (Alternatively, skip this step if using bottled lemon juice.)
2. Juice the lemon and use 2 tablespoons.
3. Place all dressing ingredients except oil and lemon zest into a small bowl (or liquid measuring cup). Mix with a whisk (or fork). Slowly add oil, beating until emulsified.

To assemble and serve:

1. Drain excess water from vegetables.
2. Add lemon zest and dressing. Toss to coat well. If desired, add chopped fresh mint.
3. Serve warm, room temperature, or chilled. Place about 1 cup of vegetables on a plate then top with 2 tablespoons ricotta cheese. Garnish with fresh dill (or mint).
4. Drizzle a little honey over the ricotta.

SERVING SUGGESTION:

- Serve with salmon and roasted baby new potatoes.

VARIATION:

- Add julienne strips of 1 red bell pepper, or 1 cup cherry tomatoes cut in half, for color.

AVOCADO MANGO SALAD

2 cups   Easy $$

We love mangos and avocados, so why not combine the two? This recipe is best when the fruit (and yes, avocado is actually a fruit) is ripe but still a little firm. It will be as flavorful as your ingredients, and is best when these items are in season. We eat it as a salad or salsa.

Prep Time: 10 to 15 minutes
Tools: grater (optional), measuring spoons, large bowl, knife and cutting board

Dressing:

1 large lime, or 3 tablespoons lime juice
1 teaspoon honey, or other sweetener
1 teaspoon Dijon mustard
1/4 teaspoon salt
1/8 teaspoon red pepper flakes
1 tablespoon oil (extra virgin olive oil recommended)

Salad:

1 large avocado
1 large mango
1 tablespoon finely chopped shallot, or red onion
2 tablespoons chopped fresh basil, or mint

For dressing:

1. Use the small holes of a grater to zest the lime peel. Set aside. Juice the lime. (Alternatively, use 3 tablespoons bottled lime juice.)

2. Place all dressing ingredients except oil and lime zest into a large bowl and mix. Slowly add oil, beating with a whisk (or fork), until emulsified. Stir in lime zest.

For salad:

1. Cut avocado and **mango*** into chunks. Place in the bowl with dressing.

2. Finely chop shallot (or red onion) and basil (or mint). Add to fruit and toss.

> ***How to Chop Mangos Without Peeling Them First** – Slice a thin layer off the bottom of a mango, so it can stand upright. Holding the unpeeled mango upright, slice down with a knife close to the center, but just far enough off-center to miss the thin, flat seed. Repeat on other side. Hold one of the pieces in the palm of your hand, flesh-side up. With a knife, slice through the soft flesh, not piercing the outer peel, then slice across in the other direction. Scoop out the flesh with a spoon. Trim off the other sides of the mango, slice off the skin and cut into cubes. To peel, then chop mangos, see technique on p. 118.

SERVING SUGGESTIONS:

- Serve plain, or on a bed of greens.
- Serve with grilled salmon, shrimp, or chicken.

VARIATION:

- AVOCADO MANGO SALSA – Cut mango and avocado into small dices. Serve with tortilla chips or as a topping for grilled fish or chicken.

CANTALOUPE BERRY SALAD

8 cups   Easy $$

This is one of the prettiest and easiest salads you can make. It's especially delicious (and less expensive) during the summer when these fruits are in season. Serve it with breakfast, lunch, or dinner as a side dish or dessert.

Prep Time: 10 minutes
Tools: colander, knife and cutting board, large bowl, measuring cup

1 cantaloupe

1 cup blueberries

1 cup strawberries, or raspberries

1/2 lemon (optional)

Honey (optional)

1. Rinse berries in a colander and leave in the sink to drain.
2. Rinse cantaloupe, then cut in half and scoop out seeds with a spoon. Cut each half into wedges, then slice off the rind. Cut each wedge into 1- or 2-inch pieces and place in large bowl.
3. Remove leaves from strawberries and cut in half or in quarters, depending on the size. Add berries to cantaloupe.
4. Squeeze juice of half a lemon over fruit if desired. Add a little honey if the fruit is too tart. Toss gently to combine.

VARIATION:

- Pour some port or sweet sherry over the salad and serve for dessert.

CARROT APPLE SALAD

4 cups   Moderate $

"This is a light and refreshing carrot salad that is not too sweet. I have to admit, I typically use my Salad Shooter (an electric grater/slicer), but grating the carrots by hand only takes a few more minutes. (Watch your knuckles!) We recommend sweet, but somewhat tart apples like Honeycrisp, Pink Lady, or Fuji. See our Variations too." BOBBI

Prep Time: 15 to 20 minutes

Tools: knife and cutting board, grater, measuring cups and spoons, large bowl

3 large carrots (about 3 cups grated)

1 large apple

1/4 cup cilantro leaves, or parsley (lightly packed)

2 tablespoons orange juice

1 tablespoon oil (extra virgin olive oil recommended)

Juice of 1/2 lime, or lemon

Pinch salt

Pinch Chinese 5-spice (optional)

Garnish: (optional)

2 tablespoons sunflower seeds

1. Trim ends off carrots, then grate to yield about 3 cups. Place in a large bowl.
2. Peel apple if desired. Cut out the core. Cut into 8 wedges top to bottom. Cut across each wedge to form thin slices. Add to carrots.
3. Coarsely chop cilantro (or parsley) leaves. Add to carrots, along with orange juice, oil, lime (or lemon) juice, salt, and optional 5-spice. Toss to combine.
4. Garnish with sunflower seeds if desired.

VARIATIONS:

- Add segments of 1 orange (with or **without membrane***).
- Add a can of mandarin oranges packed in their own juice. Omit orange juice.
- Add 1/4 cup raisins (or currants).
- Substitute caraway or fennel seeds for Chinese 5-spice.
- Substitute sliced almonds for sunflower seeds.

---

*TIP

How to Remove the Membrane from Orange (or Grapefruit) Segments –
Some recipes call for segments without the membrane attached. Place the fruit
on its side and cut a slice off the top and bottom, down to the flesh. Place on
one of the flat ends and follow the curve of the fruit as you cut the peeling off
down to the flesh. Hold the peeled fruit in your hand and over a bowl to catch
the juice. Slice along the inside edge of each dividing membrane, to release and
remove the segments. Once they have all been removed, squeeze juice from the
remaining membranes into another container if desired (to save or drink).

CHIPOTLE SWEET POTATO SALAD

5 to 7 cups   Moderate $

*"I came up with this recipe as a way to use some leftover chipotles, but the spices in your
Finite Foodie pantry will also work (see Variations). Roasting potatoes brings out the sweetness, although we've had good results using boiled potatoes as well. Keep in mind that roasting reduces the volume, so you'll end up with about 5 cups (compared to 7 cups using boiled
potatoes)."* BOBBI

Prep Time: 20 minutes   **Passive Time:** 30 minutes, or longer
Cook Time: 30 to 40 minutes
Tools: knife and cutting board, measuring cups and spoons, baking sheet, large bowl

Potatoes:

2 pounds sweet potatoes (about 7 cups
    cubed)
1 tablespoon high-heat cooking oil

1 teaspoon smoked paprika
1/2 teaspoon salt
1/4 teaspoon ground black pepper

Dressing:

1/2 cup mayonnaise

1 tablespoon vinegar (apple cider vinegar recommended)

1/2 tablespoon Worcestershire sauce

2 teaspoons minced chipotle peppers in adobo

1/2 teaspoon salt

Vegetables:

2 large stalks celery

1/2 cup chopped radishes

1/2 cup cilantro leaves, or parsley (lightly packed)

1/2 cup thinly sliced scallions, or shallots

Preheat oven to 400°F. Spray or rub oil onto a baking sheet.

TIPS

- The heat intensity of peppers increases in a recipe the longer it stands, so start with less and add more right before serving if needed.

- After opening a can of chipotle peppers in adobo, freeze remaining peppers in snack-size resealable baggies (one or two peppers per bag). Label with the name and date.

For potatoes:

1. Peel and cut potatoes into 1-inch chunks. Place in a large bowl with oil, smoked paprika, salt and pepper. Toss to coat well. Spread potato chunks evenly on baking sheet, making sure they're all in one layer.

2. Roast in preheated oven 30 to 40 minutes, stirring after 15 minutes. Potatoes should be cooked through, but still firm and nicely browned. Remove from oven, stir again and set aside. (They will continue cooking for a few minutes as they cool.)

For dressing:

1. Combine all dressing ingredients in a <u>large</u> bowl and stir well.

For vegetables:

1. Chop celery, radishes, and cilantro, placing in the large bowl as you finish each one.

2. Thinly slice scallions (both green and white parts). Add to bowl and toss.

3. Add cooled roasted potatoes and toss again until well mixed.

4. Chill at least 30 minutes. (Flavor improves if chilled overnight.) Will keep up to 3 days.

VARIATIONS:

- Substitute 1/2 tablespoon chili powder, 1 teaspoon smoked paprika, 1 teaspoon ground cumin, and 1/2 teaspoon hot pepper sauce for chipotle peppers in adobo.

- Boil sweet potatoes instead of roasting. Add the seasonings used on roasted potatoes to the dressing.

- Substitute sliced and chopped kohlrabi or jicama for radishes.

KALE SALAD WITH AVOCADO ORANGE DRESSING

9 cups   Moderate $$

Use mandarin oranges packed in their own juices if possible. This salad keeps up to 3 days without wilting or turning brown, so it's a good make-ahead dish when you know you'll be busy on the day of a meal. The dressing makes about 1-1/2 cups, and it's delicious on many other salad combinations as well.

Prep Time: 10 minutes

Tools: grater (optional), measuring cups and spoons, blender, knife and cutting board, colander (or salad spinner), large bowl

Dressing:

Zest from 1 orange (optional)

1/2 cup orange juice

1 large avocado (very soft)

1 large lemon (or lime)

2 tablespoons oil (extra virgin olive oil recommended)

1/2 tablespoon honey, or 1 tablespoon sugar

1/2 teaspoon salt

Pinch ground black pepper

4 dashes hot pepper sauce

4 large leaves fresh basil, or mint (optional)

Salad:

1 bunch curly kale, or 8 cups **chopped*** (lightly packed)

1 (8 to 11-ounce) can mandarin oranges

2 tablespoons thinly sliced shallot

1/2 cup chopped pecans (raw or toasted)

For dressing:

1. If using a fresh orange, grate the zest with the medium to fine holes on a grater. Cut the orange in half and juice, using a hand juicer or simply squeezing by **hand.*** Pour 1/2 cup juice into blender.

2. Juice lemon (or lime) and scoop out the flesh of the avocado, then add to blender, along with all remaining ingredients. Blend until smooth.

3. Adjust seasonings, to taste.

---

*How to Chop Kale (or Collards) – We like to chop kale first, then rinse. Hold a leaf by the stem, vertically. Take a sharp knife and run it along one side of the stem, then the other, removing the leafy parts. Discard the stems. Cut leaves in 1/4 to 1/2-inch-wide strips, then slice across into smaller pieces as desired. This should yield about 8 cups, lightly packed. (The stems of Swiss chard and spinach are not as tough and can be cooked, removing only the wide bottom portion that is not attached to the leaves.)

For salad:

1. Cut kale leaves off the stems, then cut into bite-size pieces to yield about 8 cups (lightly packed). Rinse in a colander (or the insert of a salad spinner), then pat (or spin) dry. Place in a large bowl.
2. Combine about half the dressing and kale; toss to coat well.
3. Drain mandarin oranges and add to salad, gently tossing again. Add more dressing if desired, or serve extra on the side.
4. Coarsely chop pecans and sprinkle on top before serving.

> ***How to Juice Lemons and Limes by Hand** – Hold one half of a lemon in your hand. Squeeze it into the other hand, which is cupped with fingers slightly apart. The juice will run through your fingers, while you catch the seeds. To get a little more out of the lemon, poke the inside with a fork and twist first, then squeeze.

VARIATIONS:

- Use walnuts, cashews or pistachios instead of pecans.
- Substitute 1/4 cup dried cranberries for mandarin oranges and add 1/2 cup goat or feta cheese crumbles. Otherwise, follow recipe, using whichever nut you want.

LENTIL SALAD

5 cups   Easy $

Lentils are an inexpensive source of fiber, protein, and iron (among other nutrients), which is why they're Rebecca's favorite legume. Use canned lentils to save time, or cook some in advance (see SIMPLE LENTILS). This salad is best if made the day before, or at least 30 minutes ahead of time. Let it marinate while you prepare other things.

Prep Time: 15 minutes   **Passive Time:** 30 minutes, or longer
Tools: measuring cups and spoons, large bowl, colander, knife and cutting board

Dressing:

2-1/2 tablespoons vinegar (balsamic or red wine vinegar recommended)
1 teaspoon oregano leaves (dried or fresh)
1/2 teaspoon salt

1/4 teaspoon ground black pepper
3 dashes hot pepper sauce
1-1/2 tablespoons oil (extra virgin olive oil recommended)

Salad:

1 (15-ounce) can lentils (about 2 cups)
1 small red bell pepper
1 stalk celery
1 cup chopped parsley

1 garlic clove
3/4 cup crumbled feta cheese
1 tablespoon capers (optional)

For dressing:

1. Combine all dressing ingredients, except oil, in a large bowl. Slowly add oil, constantly beating with a whisk (or fork) until thoroughly blended. Adjust seasonings, to taste.

For salad:

1. Drain and rinse lentils in a colander.
2. Chop bell pepper and celery (about 3/4 cup each), then place in the large bowl with dressing.
3. Coarsely chop parsley and mince garlic, adding them to the bowl as you finish each.
4. Stir in lentils, feta cheese, and capers.
5. Cover bowl and place in refrigerator to marinate at least 30 minutes before serving.

SERVING SUGGESTIONS:

- Serve on a bed of arugula or other greens, with crusty bread. Add a cup of soup if desired.
- Serve as a side dish to MEDITERRANEAN MARINATED CHICKEN, PAN-SEARED SALMON, or other simple protein.

VARIATIONS:

- Add a few tablespoons finely chopped red onion or scallion.
- Substitute chopped tomatoes or halved cherry tomatoes for bell pepper.
- Add black olives and/or chopped artichoke hearts.
- Add 2 tablespoons fresh basil, and substitute cubes of mozzarella for feta.

MANGO COLESLAW

7 cups   Easy to Moderate $

This takes no time at all if you're using a coleslaw mix, although we usually chop our own (see Tip). To save even more time, make the dressing with precut frozen mango chunks that have been thawed. However, fresh mango tastes better as long as the mango is ripe and sweet. Like most slaws, the flavor improves over time. Make up to 24 hours in advance.

Prep Time: 10 to 15 minutes   **Passive Time:** 30 minutes, or longer
Tools: knife and cutting board, blender, measuring cups and spoons, large bowl

Dressing: (Yields about 2 cups)

1 large, ripe mango	1 tablespoon honey
1/4 cup lime juice (1 or 2 limes)	1/2 tablespoon ground cumin
2 tablespoons oil (extra virgin olive oil recommended)	3/4 teaspoon salt
	1/4 teaspoon red pepper flakes

Slaw:

7 cups packaged coleslaw **mix*** (16 ounces)

1/4 cup thinly sliced scallions (green and white parts)

1/3 cup chopped fresh cilantro, or parsley

For dressing:

1. Peel and cut mango, discarding seed. Place in blender container.

2. Zest one lime if desired, then juice lime(s) to yield 1/4 cup. Add juice and optional zest to blender, along with remaining dressing ingredients. Blend until smooth.

For slaw:

1. Place coleslaw mix in a large bowl (or make your own **mix***).

2. Cut scallions into thin slices, using both green and white parts. Chop cilantro. Add both to the bowl.

3. Pour about 3/4 of the dressing over slaw and toss to coat well.

4. Let stand at room temperature 30 minutes, or keep in refrigerator up to 24 hours before serving.

5. Drizzle remaining dressing over the slaw, or serve on the side.

*TIP

To make your own coleslaw **mix**, thinly slice red and/or green cabbage (6 cups) and grate a carrot to yield 1 cup.

SERVING SUGGESTION:

- Serve with SMOKED PAPRIKA SHRIMP KABOBS or TEXAS-STYLE OVEN-BAKED BRISKET.

VARIATION:

- Substitute curry powder for the cumin and use lemon juice instead of lime.

RED POTATO SALAD

5 cups   Moderate $

"This potato salad reminds us of summer holidays spent in Virginia at Grandma's house, enjoying cookouts in the backyard. We like to prepare it a day in advance to save time, but also because it tastes better the next day." REBECCA

Prep Time: 15 minutes   **Cook Time:** 20 minutes

Tools: small (1-quart) saucepan (for egg), large (4-quart) saucepan, colander, knife and cutting board, measuring cups and spoons, small bowl

1 hard-boiled egg

2 pounds small red potatoes (about 10, 2-inch-diameter)

Water (for cooking)

1 tablespoon **vinegar***

2 teaspoons salt

2 stalks celery

1/4 cup chopped pickles

1/4 cup thinly sliced scallions

1/4 cup chopped parsley (optional)

> ***TIP**
> **Vinegar** in the cooking water keeps the potatoes firm, even if you overcook them.

Dressing:

1/3 cup mayonnaise

1 tablespoon mustard

1 tablespoon pickle juice, lemon juice, or vinegar

1/2 teaspoon salt

1/4 teaspoon ground black pepper

1/4 teaspoon hot pepper sauce

1. Prepare a hard-boiled egg per our recipe for BOILED EGGS.

For potatoes:

1. While egg cooks, scrub potatoes, removing dark spots, sprouts, and any areas that are green under the skin. Do not peel. Place in a large saucepan and cover potatoes with water (5 to 6 cups). Add vinegar and salt.

2. Bring to a boil over high heat. Turn down to medium-low and simmer (uncovered) about 15 minutes, or until a fork can just begin to pierce through the potatoes. They should still be firm but not crisp.

3. Remove from heat and immediately rinse in a colander with cold water for 30 seconds. Set aside to cool.

For vegetables:

1. Finely chop celery and pickles, then place in the large saucepan that was used for potatoes (no need to wash first). Thinly slice scallions to yield about 1/4 cup, using both white and green parts. Chop optional parsley. Combine with other vegetables.

2. When the potatoes have cooled enough to handle, cut into 1-inch chunks and chop egg. Add to vegetables.

For dressing:

1. Mix dressing ingredients in a small bowl. Pour over the potato mixture and toss to coat well. Serve right away, or refrigerate until ready to eat.

VEGETABLES

ARMENIAN-STYLE CAULIFLOWER

5 cups   Easy $

Cauliflower can be boring, but not when tossed in this spicy tomato-tinged sauce! If you prepare this dish ahead of time and plan to reheat it before serving, cook cauliflower only 2 minutes.

Prep and Cook Time: 15 minutes, start to finish

Tools: knife and cutting board, colander, large bowl, large (10-inch) skillet, measuring spoons

1 head cauliflower

1 small onion

4 large garlic cloves

2 tablespoons butter

3 tablespoons water, or broth

3 tablespoons tomato paste

1 teaspoon dried thyme leaves

1/2 teaspoon ground coriander

1/4 teaspoon ground allspice

1/4 teaspoon salt

1/8 teaspoon ground black pepper

1/8 teaspoon red pepper flakes

*Italian vs. Curly Parsley – Both types are readily available in grocery stores, and are easy to grow. Italian is also known as flat-leaf parsley, and has more flavor than curly parsley, which is typically associated with garnish (but either works). Cilantro is often substituted for parsley, but the flavor is quite different, and some people don't care for the taste.

Garnish:

2 tablespoons chopped **Italian parsley,*** or cilantro

1 lemon (optional)

1. Remove outer leaves, stalk, and core from cauliflower. Divide into large florets. Rinse in a colander then pat dry with a paper towel. Slice each floret into 1/4-inch-thick slices. Place in a large bowl.

2. Chop onion. Melt butter over medium-low heat in a large skillet, then add onion. Cook and stir 2 to 3 minutes, or until onion is soft.

3. Mince garlic. Add to onion, along with cauliflower, water (or broth), tomato paste, thyme, coriander, allspice, salt, pepper, and red pepper flakes. Stir well, then turn heat to low. Cover and cook until cauliflower is crisp-tender, about 3 to 5 minutes.

4. Chop parsley. Right before serving, add parsley and toss. Squeeze juice from <u>half</u> a lemon over the cauliflower. Garnish with extra parsley and wedges from the remaining lemon if desired.

SERVING SUGGESTION:

- Serve with ROAST CHICKEN or PAN-SEARED SALMON and a green salad.

ASPARAGUS WITH EGGS MIMOSA

4 servings   Easy $

This recipe can easily be doubled to serve at a dinner party. Although simple, it makes an elegant side dish. We often serve this for Easter dinner and Mother's Day brunch, since asparagus is in season during the spring and summer. Serve it warm, room temperature, or chilled.

Prep Time: 15 minutes   **Cook Time:** 5 minutes
Tools: small (1-quart) saucepan (for egg), knife and cutting board, measuring cups and spoons, small bowl, steamer insert (or colander) with large (4-quart) saucepan

1 hard-boiled egg
1 bunch asparagus (about 1 pound)

Vinaigrette:

1 tablespoon vinegar (sherry vinegar recommended)

1 tablespoon minced shallot

1/2 teaspoon dried rosemary leaves, or fresh (chopped)

1/2 teaspoon Dijon mustard

Salt and pepper, to taste

2 to 3 tablespoons oil (extra-virgin olive oil recommended)

Garnish:

Sprigs fresh rosemary (optional)

1. Cook hard-boiled egg up to 2 days in advance. See our recipe for BOILED EGGS.

For asparagus:

1. Remove and discard the tough, bottom portion of asparagus stalks, reserving the top 6 inches or so.
2. Place a steamer insert (or colander) in saucepan with about 1/2 inch of water in it. Add trimmed asparagus, cover with lid, and bring water to a boil over medium-high heat. Once water starts to boil, turn to low and steam until crisp-tender, about 2 to 3 minutes. Remove from heat and rinse briefly with cold water. Place spears on several layers of paper towels (or a clean dish towel) to dry.

For vinaigrette:

1. While cooking egg or asparagus combine vinegar, minced shallot, and rosemary in a small bowl. If there's time, let it stand 5 to 10 minutes to develop flavors.

2. Stir in mustard and a pinch or two of salt and pepper.

3. Drizzle oil slowly into the mixture while beating with whisk (or fork). Alternatively, add 1 tablespoon at a time and whisk well after each addition. This will help emulsify the dressing so it becomes thick and creamy.

4. Adjust seasonings if desired.

TIP
Vinaigrette can be made in advance and refrigerated. Let stand at room temperature 15 to 30 minutes, then whisk again before using. Most extra virgin olive oils will thicken or solidify when chilled.

To assemble:

1. Transfer asparagus to a platter and spoon vinaigrette over the asparagus spears (or toss asparagus in half of the dressing first, then spoon the remainder on top).

2. Finely chop hard-boiled egg and sprinkle over asparagus. Garnish with a sprig of fresh rosemary if desired.

VARIATIONS:

- ROASTED – Toss trimmed asparagus in 1/2 tablespoon high-heat cooking oil and season with salt and pepper. Roast at 425°F for 10 minutes, turning over after 5 minutes. Serve with dressing and eggs per recipe.

- NO VINAIGRETTE – Toss steamed asparagus in a little butter, salt, and pepper. Squeeze some lemon juice over it instead of using vinaigrette. Serve plain, or with eggs.

- Top dish with toasted bread crumbs.

BAKED POTATOES

Easy $

"Cook potatoes (white or sweet) in the oven, crockpot, or microwave. I like to use my crock-pot, so I can come home after work to the great aroma of slow-baked potatoes. Mom prefers baking them in the oven for a crispy skin, which is her favorite part. Jab the potatoes with a fork to prevent them from bursting (and relieve stress or anger at the same time). Serve with a choice of toppings and have a potato party!" REBECCA

Prep Time: 2 minutes   **Cook Time:** varies
Tools: oven, crockpot, or microwave
Special Supplies: foil (optional)

Large russet potatoes, or sweet potatoes

Oil (optional)

Salt and pepper (optional)

1. Scrub potatoes and remove any sprouts, bad spots, or green areas (which contain toxins). Pat dry.
2. Pierce potatoes with a fork about 4 or 5 times, all the way around. It is CRITICAL that you pierce the potato—otherwise it could explode . . . literally!
3. Optional step that adds a nice, tasty finish—rub outside of potato with oil, then sprinkle with salt and pepper.

For oven-baked:

1. Preheat oven to 425°F.
2. Wrap potatoes in foil if you want a soft peeling, but leave unwrapped if you want it crispy. Place directly on the rack of a preheated oven. *Note:* If not wrapped in foil, place a baking sheet on the rack below to catch any drips, *especially* when baking sweet potatoes.
3. Bake 45 minutes, then check by piercing with a fork. Cook longer if not yet tender. The timing depends on the size and type of potato (sweet potatoes cook more quickly than white.

For crockpot:

1. Wrap each potato in foil to completely cover it. Place in crockpot.
2. Bake on low 8 to 10 hours, or until potatoes are tender.

For microwave:

1. DO NOT WRAP IN FOIL! Never, ever put metal (which includes foil) in a microwave—it can burst into flames and ruin your food and very possibly your microwave. Instead, wrap each potato in a damp paper towel and cook 3 minutes, then flip over and cook another 3 minutes.
2. Let rest a few minutes (they will continue to cook), then check with a fork to see if they're evenly soft all the way through. If not, cook another few minutes, turning over halfway through.

VARIATIONS:

- BREAKFAST – Top a sweet potato with plain Greek yogurt, maple syrup, cinnamon and walnuts.
- BROCCOLI-CHEDDAR – Top with steamed broccoli (or other vegetable) and grated Cheddar cheese.
- CHILI – Top with vegetarian or meat chili (see our recipe for SUPER BOWL CHILI).
- LOADED – Top with a pat of butter, sour cream, bacon bits, and chopped chives (or any combination).

- SALAD-STUFFED – Drizzle about 1/2 tablespoon olive oil into potato and fluff up. Top with salad and your favorite dressing.
- SOUTHWEST – Top with spicy beans, sour cream, grated Monterey Jack cheese, and sliced avocado.

BROCCOLI WITH DIJON GARLIC DRESSING

4 cups   Easy $

If you want something besides butter on your steamed broccoli, whip up this quick sauce. The recipe makes 4 large servings of broccoli—a great way to increase your consumption of vegetables. Chill the leftovers and add to a salad the next day.

Prep and Cook Time: 10 minutes, start to finish

Tools: knife and cutting board, measuring cups and spoons, steamer insert (or colander) with large (4-quart) saucepan, small bowl

4 cups broccoli florets

Dressing:

1 garlic clove

1 tablespoon lemon juice

1 teaspoon Dijon mustard

3 tablespoons oil (extra virgin olive oil recommended)

1/8 teaspoon salt

Pinch ground black pepper

1. Cut broccoli into bite-size florets. Place a steamer insert (or colander) in saucepan with about 1/2 inch of water in it. Add broccoli, cover with lid, and bring water to a boil over medium-high heat. Once water starts to boil, turn to low and steam until crisp-tender, about 3 to 4 minutes.

2. While broccoli cooks, mince garlic. Combine with lemon juice and Dijon mustard in a small bowl (or liquid measuring cup). Slowly add oil as you beat with a whisk (or fork). Season with salt and pepper, to taste.

3. **Toss*** dressing with steamed broccoli and serve right away.

> ***Toss** – to mix ingredients together by gently lifting and turning, using one or two utensils, or hands.

VARIATIONS:

- Chop 1/2 red bell pepper and add to mixture.
- Roast broccoli instead of steaming.
- Use dressing on steamed or roasted Brussels sprouts, cauliflower, or green beans.
- Add white beans or chickpeas and serve with brown rice for a vegetarian main meal.

CHINESE CABBAGE STIR-FRY

6 cups   Easy $

Start with Chinese (also called Napa) cabbage or bok choy and add just about any other vegetable you want. We've chosen mushrooms and bean sprouts. Most of the ingredients are inexpensive unless you use an exotic mushroom like shitake. Crimini, baby portobello, and plain white mushrooms are more economical. Frozen mushrooms also work. We like to serve this mixture with a whole, steamed fish (which symbolizes abundance and prosperity) for the Chinese New Year.

Prep Time: 10 minutes   **Cook Time:** 6 to 8 minutes
Tools: knife and cutting board, measuring cups and spoons, large (10-inch) skillet

6 cups thinly sliced Chinese (Napa) cabbage, or bok choy

1 cup sliced mushrooms

4 garlic cloves

1 tablespoon high-heat cooking oil

1 cup bean sprouts (optional)

1 to 2 tablespoons soy sauce

1/8 teaspoon red pepper flakes, or hot pepper sauce

1. Slice cabbage (or bok choy), mushrooms, and garlic. Keep items separate.
2. Heat oil over medium heat in a large skillet. Add mushrooms, then cook and stir 2 to 3 minutes to soften.
3. Stir in cabbage, garlic, and bean sprouts (if using), and continue cooking another few minutes.
4. Add 2 tablespoons soy sauce (only 1 tablespoon if omitting sprouts) and red pepper flakes.
5. Cover skillet and steam 1 to 2 minutes.

SERVING SUGGESTIONS:
- Serve with ASIAN MARINATED CHICKEN, BAKED GINGER SALMON, or POACHED SALMON.

TIP
Adding a small amount of liquid to stir-fries (or any sautéed food) lowers the heat and protects the fatty acids in oil. It also helps steam the vegetables. Water is fine, but broth adds a little extra flavor.

COCONUT SPINACH

5 cups   Easy $

"I love to collect recipes, especially from other countries. This is a typical dish from Guam. As I researched it, I learned that Guamanians and the native people (called Chamorros) love hot sauce—Tabasco in particular (my favorite as well). On average, each Guamanian goes through two (2-ounce) bottles of Tabasco a year. That may not sound like much, but believe me, a little goes a long way! Add hot sauce to taste, then serve more on the side for those who want the true Guamanian experience." BOBBI

Prep and Cook Time: 15 minutes, start to finish

Tools: knife and cutting board, large (4-quart) saucepan, measuring cups

1 small onion

1 tablespoon high-heat cooking oil

4 large garlic cloves

1/2 tablespoon minced fresh ginger (optional)

1 teaspoon salt

1 teaspoon curry powder

1/2 teaspoon ground black pepper

1 (13.5-ounce) can coconut milk (full fat)

16 ounces fresh baby spinach

Hot pepper sauce, to taste (Tabasco recommended)

Juice from 1/2 lime (about 1 tablespoon)

1. Chop onion. Heat oil in a large saucepan over medium-low heat and add onion. Cook and stir while you continue.
2. Mince garlic and fresh ginger. Add to onion and continue cooking 1 minute.
3. Stir in salt, curry powder, and pepper.
4. Add coconut milk and bring to a simmer.
5. Stir in about half of the spinach and cook until reduced enough to add the remaining half.
6. Stir in desired amount of hot sauce and cook another 3 to 5 minutes.
7. Remove from heat and stir in lime juice.

SERVING SUGGESTION:

- Serve in a bowl as a soupy dish with bread for dipping.
- Pour over brown rice or quinoa and serve as a main dish, or as a side to fish or poultry.

CORN ON THE COB

Easy $

Far too often, corn on the cob ends up mushy. The kernels stick to your teeth and suddenly no one wants to smile. So, we went on a quest to determine the proper way to cook corn on the cob, whether you boil, grill, or microwave it. Here's what we found.

BOILED CORN ON THE COB

If you're using a 4-quart saucepan, you might need to shuck the corn and break the ears in half so they'll fit. If you have a larger saucepan, definitely use it. You can cook the corn in the husk or with the husk removed, whichever you prefer. It's less messy to shuck the corn before you boil it, but more nutrients will be preserved if you leave it in the husk. An added benefit of the latter is that the corn will stay nice and warm in its husk until ready to serve.

Prep Time: 2 to 5 minutes
Passive Time: 5 to 10 minutes for water to boil
Cook Time: 3 minutes
Tools: large saucepan

Fresh corn on the cob
Water (for cooking)

TIP
Do not add anything to the water. Salt causes the corn to dry out. Sugar does nothing and is unnecessary.

1. Fill a large saucepan about half full with **water.*** Cover and bring to a boil over high heat (takes about 5 to 10 minutes).
2. While waiting for water to boil, **shuck*** corn if desired.
   • To shuck, remove **husk*** and silk. Cut off stalk and any bad spots.
   • To leave in husk, peel it back just a few inches and remove as much of the corn silk as possible. Smooth husks back into place.
3. Once the water comes to a **rolling*** boil, place corn into pan. Cover and immediately set timer for 3 minutes, turning the heat down to keep at a gentle boil. If cooking more than 4 ears of corn, add 1 minute to cooking time.

***Boil** – to heat a liquid to the point where it bubbles and vaporizes.
Rolling Boil – a vigorous boil.

***Shuck** – as a noun, the outer covering of a grain, like corn on the cob, nuts, and even shellfish.

***Husk** is another term used for the outer covering of vegetables and fruits, and can also be used. Both nouns can be used as a verb meaning to remove the shucks or husks.

4. As soon as the timer goes off, remove corn from the water. It will be crisp and ready to eat. If unshucked, cool a few minutes before removing the husk and silk. (It will continue to cook somewhat as it stands.)

MICROWAVED CORN ON THE COB

This has to be the quickest and easiest way to cook corn, and it usually turns out very well. Be sure to turn the corn halfway through, as indicated in the instructions, and allow it to stand a few minutes (or longer).

Prep Time: 1 minute   **Passive Time:** 2 minutes, or longer   **Cook Time:** 4 minutes

Fresh corn on the cob, in the husk

1. Place corn in the microwave, still in the husk. If preparing more than one ear, do a maximum of two at a time, and make sure there's plenty of room between the cobs to ensure that they will cook evenly.
2. Microwave on high 2 minutes. Turn over and cook another 2 minutes. Let stand a few minutes then carefully peel back the top few inches of the husk to check for doneness.
3. Be sure to cool before shucking or you'll burn yourself!

GRILLED CORN ON THE COB

If we're having a cookout, we like to grill our corn on the cob. There are numerous techniques, but this is how we do it.

Prep Time: 5 minutes   **Cook Time:** 15 minutes
Tools: grill, pastry brush (optional)
Special Supplies: kitchen twine

Fresh corn on the cob, in the husk
Butter (melted or softened)

Salt and pepper
Fresh herbs (optional)

1. Heat grill to medium-high, or according to your meat recipe if cooking both at the same time.
2. Peel back the husks, but leave attached at the base. Remove corn silk.
3. Brush or rub corn with butter, then sprinkle with salt and pepper. Add sprigs of herbs if desired. Good choices include rosemary, oregano, thyme, chives, tarragon, and sage.
4. Bring husks back to the original position and tie the end and middle with kitchen twine.
5. Place on the upper rack of your grill if possible and cook about 15 minutes, turning over halfway through. (The husks will get brown.)
6. Cool slightly before peeling back the husks.

OVEN-ROASTED CORN ON THE COB

If you don't have access to a grill, you can get a similar look and flavor by roasting corn on the cob in the oven. You can also create a crunchy corn on the cob snack.

Prep Time: 2 to 5 minutes   **Cook Time:** 20 to 60 minutes

Fresh corn on the cob

Preheat oven to 450°F.

1. Shuck corn if desired.
   - To shuck, remove husk and silk. Cut off stalk and any bad spots. Wrap in aluminum foil.
   - To leave in husk, peel it back just a few inches and remove as much of the corn silk as possible. Smooth husks back into place. Tie the end with some kitchen twine if desired.
2. Place corn directly onto an oven rack positioned in the center of the oven, and roast 20 minutes for crisp-tender corn. If unshucked, cool a few minutes before shucking. If desired, pull back the husks but leave them attached (like a tail) for a fun presentation. Otherwise, remove husk completely.

VARIATION:

- For a crunchy corn snack, unwrap foil after the first 20 minutes of cooking, and roast an additional 20 to 40 minutes, to taste.

SERVING SUGGESTIONS FOR ALL VERSIONS:

- Eat plain, or simply roll in butter.
- Soften some butter, then stir in your favorite herbs or spices. Try rosemary, chives, tarragon, basil, nutmeg, chili powder, or smoked paprika. Chill and serve on the side, or place a dollop on the corn.
- Squeeze lime juice over the corn and sprinkle with salt and pepper. Add smoked paprika or chili powder if desired.

GARLICKY GREEN BEANS

3 to 4 cups   Easy $

This simple but tasty side vegetable is a family favorite for Thanksgiving and other holiday dinners. When served to guests, we cut the beans in half on the diagonal for a more attractive look.

Prep Time: 5 minutes   **Cook Time:** 7 to 8 minutes

Tools: colander, knife and cutting board, large (10-inch) skillet with lid (or foil) to cover, measuring cups and spoons

1/2 pound green beans (3 to 4 cups)

3 large garlic cloves

1 tablespoon high-heat cooking oil, or butter

1 teaspoon water (optional)

1/2 lemon

Salt and pepper, to taste

1. Rinse green beans in a colander, then trim ends and snap in half.

2. **Peel*** and slice garlic cloves. Heat oil (or butter) in a large skillet over medium-low heat, and add garlic. Cook and stir 1 minute, or until fragrant but not brown.

3. Add green beans and water, if needed. Cover and steam on medium-low or low until crisp-tender, about 6 to 7 minutes.

4. Drain if necessary, then squeeze juice from half a lemon over beans.

5. Season with salt and pepper.

---

*TIP

To **peel** a clove of garlic, cut off the tip of one end. Lay the flat side of the knife over the garlic clove and hit it with the heel of your hand. This crushes the garlic, releasing the flavor and loosening the papery peel. Remove peel, then mince or slice the garlic as indicated in your recipe.

GREEK GREEN BEANS

8 cups   Easy $

In Greece, this is called Fassolakia Yiahni, or Green Bean Stew. Yiahni, the Greek word for stew (or ragout), is cooked in a tomato and olive oil base. The more olive oil you use, the more authentic, so add more if you want. Eat this as a stew or a side dish.

Prep Time: 15 minutes   **Cook time:** 30 to 40 minutes

Tools: colander, knife and cutting board, large (4-quart) saucepan, measuring cups and spoons

1 small onion

3 tablespoons olive oil (extra virgin recommended)

4 garlic cloves

2 medium red potatoes (about 2/3 pound)

3/4 pound green beans

1 (14.5-ounce) can crushed tomatoes

2 tablespoons tomato paste

1-1/4 cups water

1 teaspoon salt

1/8 teaspoon ground black pepper

1/8 teaspoon red pepper flakes

Garnish: (optional)
Grated Parmesan cheese

1. Chop onion and mince garlic. Heat oil in a large saucepan over medium-low heat, then add onion, but set garlic aside. Cook and stir while you continue.

2. Wash and trim potatoes, but do not peel. Cut into large chunks.

3. Rinse green beans in a colander, then trim ends and snap in half (or into smaller pieces if desired).

4. Add garlic to onions and cook another minute.

5. Add crushed tomatoes, tomato paste, water, salt, pepper, and red pepper. Bring to a simmer and cook 2 minutes (uncovered).

6. Stir in green beans and potatoes. Cover and simmer about 10 minutes. Uncover and cook another 20 to 30 minutes, or until vegetables are soft and part of the liquid has cooked off. Remove from heat.

7. Stir in (or garnish with) Parmesan if desired.

SERVING SUGGESTIONS:

- Spoon about 2 cups into a bowl. Top with a slice of feta cheese (in place of Parmesan) and serve with a thick piece of crusty bread.

- Serve on a pasta plate or in a shallow bowl, with a piece of grilled or sautéed fish on top. Cod is a good choice.

VARIATION:

- Drain and rinse 1 (15-ounce) can white beans, and add to dish in the last 5 minutes of cooking to turn this into a complete vegetarian meal.

GREENS AND CARROTS

4 cups   Moderate $

We love this super healthy and tasty way to eat our greens! The recipe calls for kale, but any type of chopped frozen greens will do. Cruciferous vegetables (like kale and collards) are great cancer fighters, as are carrots, which also support vision and heart health. Fresh ginger gives this dish a kick, but you can leave it out if you're not a fan.

Prep and Cook Time: 20 minutes, start to finish

Tools: knife and cutting board, large (10-inch) skillet, measuring cups and spoons

1 small onion
1 tablespoon high-heat cooking oil
2 large garlic cloves
1 teaspoon fresh minced ginger (optional)
1 medium carrot
1/4 cup broth, or water
1 teaspoon curry powder
1/2 teaspoon salt
1/4 teaspoon ground cumin
Pinch red pepper flakes
4 cups chopped frozen **kale***
1/2 lemon

*TIP
To use **fresh kale**, remove leaves from stem and chop. Transfer to a large bowl. Sprinkle oil and juice from the lemon half over greens. Toss and massage a bit with your hands. Let stand while you continue. (The greens should soften and wilt somewhat.) Follow all other recipe instructions.

1. Chop onion. Heat oil in a large skillet over medium-low heat, then add onion. Cook and stir about 3 to 5 minutes, or until very soft and transparent.

2. While onion cooks, mince garlic and optional fresh ginger. Add to onion.

3. Grate or **dice*** carrot, then stir into onion mixture along with broth (or water), curry powder, salt, and red pepper flakes. Cook an additional minute.

3. Stir in kale. Cover and cook 5 to 8 minutes, stirring occasionally. Add more broth if needed.

4. Squeeze lemon juice over vegetables before serving.

*What's the different between dice and cube?
Dice – to cut into very small pieces that are somewhat uniform, about 1/4-inch.
Cube – to cut into uniform sizes. First, cut food into strips, and then cut crosswise into cubes. The recipe will usually indicate the size of the cubes desired.

- Serve with black-eyed peas and NANA'S THIN CORNBREAD for a vegetarian New Year's Day meal, or as a side to TEXAS-STYLE OVEN-BAKED BRISKET, PORK LOIN ROAST, or SMOKED PAPRIKA CHICKEN.

VARIATIONS:

- Use fresh spinach or chard. Chop and add in place of frozen greens.
- Add 1/2 to 1 cup frozen butter (lima) beans or edamame, along with carrot.

ROASTED VEGETABLES WITH COMBINATIONS AND SOLOS

4 cups   Easy $

Roasting vegetables brings out their natural sweetness, making them more palatable to most people. Follow this example for ratios, but adjust to make the number of servings desired. Remember that raw vegetables will cook down to about half the original quantity. Adjust roasting time based on the vegetable, or until all vegetables in a mixture are tender. See our seasonal and recommended combinations below.

Prep Time: 5 to 10 minutes   **Cook Time:** varies
Tools: baking sheet, knife and cutting board, measuring cups and spoons, large bowl
Special Supplies: aluminum foil (optional)

8 cups vegetables	Herbs and spices (optional)
2 tablespoons high-heat cooking oil	1 tablespoon balsamic vinegar (optional)
Salt and pepper, to taste	

Preheat oven to 425°F. Spray or rub oil onto a baking sheet (or line with foil or parchment paper).

1. Cut vegetables into pieces of similar size, usually 1 to 2 inches. *Note:* Most vegetables will reduce in size by about half.
2. Place vegetable pieces in a large bowl and toss with oil, seasonings, herbs, and spices.
3. Spread out on baking sheet in one layer.
4. *Optional step for potatoes, squash, and root vegetables:* Cover with foil and cook 20 minutes. (This steams and cooks the inside.) Remove foil, stir, and continue cooking (uncovered) to brown.
5. *For all other vegetables:* Roast for the shortest amount of time listed in table, then check with a fork. Continue cooking until tender. If possible, stir halfway through cooking time.
6. Remove from oven and toss with vinegar and additional fresh herbs if desired.

CHART OF APPROXIMATE TIMES FOR ROASTING VEGETABLES	
(DEPENDS ON THE VEGETABLE, SIZE OF PIECES, AND AMOUNT)	
30 to 60 minutes	Root vegetables (carrots, parsnips, potatoes, rutabagas, turnips) whole head of cauliflower, winter/fall squash
20 to 30 minutes	Beets, broccoli florets, Brussels sprouts, cabbage wedges, cauliflower florets, eggplant chunks, fennel, onions
10 to 20 minutes	Asparagus, peppers, tomatoes, yellow squash, zucchini

COMBINATIONS

FALL ROOT VEGETABLE MIX

Beets (**golden*** recommended)

Carrots

Onion slices

Parsnips

Potatoes (white, sweet, or a combination)

Turnips and/or Rutabagas

High-heat cooking oil

Salt and pepper, to taste

Rosemary leaves (fresh or dried)

Vinegar (balsamic, apple cider, or red wine vinegar recommended)

*TIP
Red beets tend to bleed onto the other vegetables, turning everything a shade of red. You can avoid this problem by cooking them separately and combining at the end, or by using **golden beets**.

1. Follow basic instructions, leaving out vinegar and rosemary until later. Cover with foil and roast 20 minutes.

2. Stir in balsamic vinegar and rosemary, making sure vegetables get turned over, then uncover and continue cooking another 20 minutes, or until tender.

WINTER BROCCOLI MIX

Broccoli florets

Brussels sprouts, halved or quartered

Cauliflower florets

Garlic cloves

Mushrooms, cut in half

Red onion, cut in chunks or half-rounds

High-heat cooking oil

Thyme leaves (fresh or dried)

Salt and pepper, to taste

1. Follow basic instructions. Roast 30 to 35 minutes, turning once halfway through.

SPRING ARTICHOKE ASPARAGUS MIX

Artichoke hearts cut in quarters (use water-packed)

Asparagus (cut on the diagonal in 3-inch-long pieces)

Cherry tomatoes

Dill leaves (fresh or dried)

High-heat cooking oil

Salt and pepper, to taste

Freshly grated Parmesan cheese

1. Follow basic instructions, leaving out Parmesan. Roast 20 minutes, turning once halfway through.
2. When everything is tender, remove from oven and sprinkle cheese on top. Toss if desired.

SUMMER SQUASH MIX

Yellow squash

Zucchini

Cherry tomatoes (whole)

Eggplant (optional)

Onion (cut in small chunks)

High-heat cooking oil

Oregano leaves (fresh or dried)

Salt and pepper, to taste

1. If using eggplant, cut into 1-inch cubes and **degorge*** first. Rinse, pat dry, then combine with all other vegetables except cherry tomatoes. Toss with oil, oregano and seasonings.
2. Roast 10 minutes, then add tomatoes and stir. Cook another 10 minutes, or until everything is tender.

GREAT SOLOS

- Roasted Brussels Sprouts with Garlic and Balsamic Vinegar
- Roasted Cauliflower with Cumin and Lime Juice
- Roasted Parsnips with Rosemary
- Roasted Onion with Balsamic Vinegar and Thyme
- Roasted Beets with Oregano and Grated Orange Zest (stirred in at end)
- Roasted Carrots with Pesto or Thyme
- Roast the vegetables in our recipes for ASPARAGUS WITH EGGS MIMOSA and BROCCOLI WITH DIJON GARLIC DRESSING.
- See more roasted vegetable recipes below

*Degorge – to sprinkle salt on a vegetable to remove excess water, pull out bitter compounds, and improve the texture. (Also refers to the process of soaking fish, poultry, meats, and some vegetables in water with added acid like lemon or vinegar, to remove impurities.) Cube, slice, or grate the vegetable, then sprinkle generously with salt. Let rest about 30 minutes, then rinse and pat dry or squeeze dry, according to the recipe directions. Examples: Used primarily for eggplant, summer squash, cabbage, and cucumbers.

ROASTED BUTTERNUT SQUASH SLICES

4 cups   Easy $

This makes a great side dish or appetizer. They can be as spicy as you like—it's a very nice contrast to the sweetness of the squash.

Prep Time: 15 minutes   **Cook Time:** 50 minutes

Tools: baking sheet, knife and cutting board, large and small bowls, measuring spoons

1 (2- to 3-pound) butternut squash
   (4 to 5 cups sliced)

2 tablespoons high-heat cooking oil

Hot pepper sauce, to taste

1 tablespoon flour (any type)

2 teaspoons curry powder

1/2 teaspoon salt

1/4 teaspoon ground black pepper

1 lemon (optional)

Preheat oven to 425°F. Spray or rub oil on a baking sheet.

1. Trim ends off squash, cut in half lengthwise, and scoop out seeds. Peel, then slice across to make 1/2-inch-thick slices. Place in a **large bowl*** then add oil and hot sauce. Toss to coat well.

2. Mix together flour, curry powder, salt, and pepper in a small bowl. Sprinkle over squash slices and toss again.

3. Place slices on the greased baking sheet in one layer. Cover with foil and bake 20 minutes. Remove foil and bake another 15 minutes. Use a food turner to turn the slices over and bake another 15 minutes, for a total of 50 minutes.

4. If desired, squeeze some lemon juice over the slices right before serving, or serve with a wedge of lemon so each person can do their own.

SERVING SUGGESTIONS:

- Serve with PORK CHOPS WITH HONEY MUSTARD, ROAST CHICKEN, or CURRIED LENTILS.

VARIATION:

- Cut squash into 1-inch cubes instead.
- Use 1 large or 2 small Delicata squash. Cut in half lengthwise and scoop out seeds, but don't peel (it's edible). Slice across each piece to form 1/2-inch-thick slices. Roast per recipe, or about 5 minutes less.

---

*TIP

Alternatively, place squash slices in a **large bowl** with a lid and shake to coat well.

ROASTED CABBAGE WEDGES

4 servings   Easy $

You can use green or red cabbage or even Savoy or Napa. This is so easy, and surprisingly delicious, which is why it's one of our favorite fall and winter recipes!

Prep Time: 5 minutes   **Cook Time:** 25 minutes
Tools: baking sheet, knife and cutting board, measuring spoon (optional)

1 head cabbage (red or green)
2 tablespoons high-heat cooking oil, or spray oil

Salt and pepper, to taste
1 lemon

Preheat oven to 450°F. Spray or rub oil onto a baking sheet.

1. Cut a head of cabbage in quarters, removing any outer discolored leaves. Place on the baking sheet, cut sides up.

2. Drizzle about 1/2 tablespoon oil over each quarter and spread with a brush or fingers to cover all sides. (Alternatively, spray oil generously to cover all sides.)

3. Season liberally with salt and pepper.

4. Place on baking sheet with a flat (cut) side down and roast for 15 minutes, then turn over so other cut side is down. Cook another 10 minutes.

5. Remove from oven and squeeze lemon juice over the cabbage wedges. Serve immediately.

SERVING SUGGESTIONS:

- Serve with a protein that does not require use of the oven, like PAN-SEARED or POACHED SALMON.
- Chop up cold leftovers and add to a salad.

VARIATIONS:

- Drizzle your favorite vinegar (or vinaigrette) over the cooked wedges, instead of lemon juice.
- Sprinkle grated Parmesan, Gorgonzola, or goat cheese crumbles over the roasted wedges. (Alternatively, do this when you turn the cabbage, with 10 minutes left.) Drizzle balsamic vinegar over them after removing from oven.

ZUCCHINI TOMATO MEDLEY

6 to 9 servings   Easy $

Don't let the simplicity of this dish fool you. It may be simple, but the taste is thoroughly delicious. And, there's an added bonus of very little clean up! It will be easier to toss everything in a bowl first, but sometimes we place it all directly into the baking dish and toss there. See Variations below for turning this into a complete, vegetarian meal.

Prep Time: 10 to 15 minutes   **Cook Time:** 35 minutes
Tools: knife and cutting board, large bowl (optional), measuring cups and spoons, 8×8-inch baking dish

1 small onion
4 large garlic cloves
1 bell pepper (any color)
1 large tomato (about 1 cup chopped)
2 medium zucchini (about 1 pound)
2 tablespoons vinegar
1 tablespoon high-heat cooking oil

1 teaspoon dried thyme leaves
1 teaspoon dried oregano leaves
1/2 teaspoon salt
1/4 teaspoon ground black pepper
2/3 cup grated Parmesan cheese, divided in half

Preheat oven to 425°F.

1. Cut onion in half and slice into half rounds, about 1/4-inch thick. Slice garlic cloves. Coarsely chop bell pepper. Chop tomato or use canned, diced tomatoes. Place everything in a large bowl as you finish cutting each one.

2. To chop zucchini, slice in quarters lengthwise. Slice each spear into 1/2-inch-thick pieces. Add to other vegetables, along with your choice of vinegar. (We prefer balsamic or red wine vinegar in this recipe, but any will do.) Toss to coat well.

3. Add oil, thyme, oregano, salt, pepper, and half (1/3 cup) of the Parmesan. Toss again and transfer to baking dish. Top with remaining Parmesan.

4. Bake (uncovered) 35 minutes, or until vegetables are soft and browned on top.

SERVING SUGGESTION:

- Serve as a side dish to ROAST CHICKEN, or any grilled fish or meat.

VARIATIONS:

- WITH POLENTA – Spray or rub oil into baking dish. Mix vegetables in a bowl. Slice one roll of precooked polenta in 1/2-inch slices. Place 9 slices on the bottom of the dish and pour vegetable/cheese mixture on top. Bake per recipe.

- WITH QUINOA – Spray or rub oil into baking dish. Mix vegetables in a bowl. Spread 2 cups cooked quinoa in the bottom of baking dish and pour vegetable/cheese mixture on top. Bake per recipe.

- Substitute 1 cup feta for Parmesan.

DESSERTS

Although it's best to limit the intake of sugar, an occasional sweet doesn't have to be completely off-limits. We've adjusted old favorites and created new recipes, all using less sugar and more whole grains whenever possible. Most of the recipes do not require an electric mixer, so anyone should have the tools to make them. Some of our desserts are naturally gluten-free (GF), but almost all of them can easily be converted to a gluten-free version, as indicated in each recipe.

ALMOND, FIG, AND OLIVE OIL CAKE (GF)

9 servings Moderate $$$

We're not going to lie—almond meal (sometimes called almond flour) is expensive, but worth it! Almond meal produces a moist and tender cake that is more nutritious than any made with wheat flour, and it's gluten-free to boot. The aroma of this cake fresh out of the oven is intoxicating, and although it's delicious served warm, it's even better the next day (if there's any left).

Prep Time: 10 minutes   **Passive Time:** 10 minutes   **Cook Time:** 35 to 40 minutes

Tools: 8×8-inch baking dish, measuring cups and spoons, knife and cutting board, small, medium, and large bowls

Figs:
8 small black mission figs (dried)

1/2 cup water

1 tablespoon almond meal

Dry ingredients:
2-1/4 cups almond meal (fine ground)   1 teaspoon cardamom

1 teaspoon baking soda   1/2 teaspoon nutmeg

1 teaspoon baking powder   1/2 teaspoon salt

Wet ingredients:
3/4 cup granulated sugar   3 eggs

1/4 cup olive oil (extra virgin recommended) 1/2 cup plain Greek yogurt

1 teaspoon vanilla

Garnish: (optional)
2 tablespoons sliced or slivered almonds

Preheat oven to 350°F. Spray or rub oil into an 8×8-inch baking dish.

1. Measure water in a glass measuring cup, and heat in the microwave for 1 minute. Remove stems from figs then cut each one into four pieces. Add to water and soak while you continue.

2. Combine dry ingredients in a medium bowl. Stir.

3. Combine sugar and oil in a large bowl, and beat with a whisk (or large kitchen spoon).

4. Add vanilla and eggs to the sugar mixture, then beat just until blended.

5. Stir in yogurt until smooth.

6. Drain figs and pat dry with a paper towel. Chop, then place in a small bowl and toss with 1 tablespoon almond meal mixture. Set aside.

7. Add dry ingredients to the wet mixture, stirring just until well blended.

8. **Fold*** in figs. Pour batter into the baking dish. Sprinkle sliced almonds on top if desired.

9. Bake 35 to 40 minutes, or until done. Test by sticking a wooden toothpick in the center. It should come out clean with a few crumbs stuck to it. (Alternatively, press down lightly in the center. It should pop back up, leaving no indentation.)

10. Cool at least 10 minutes before cutting.

*Fold – to gently combine light ingredients into heavier ingredients, with minimal stirring. Use a whisk, spatula, fork, or spoon and slowly go from top to bottom in a circular movement to carry some of the lighter mixture down and the heavier mixture up (and vice versa), until all is blended. This keeps air in the batter for a fluffier texture.

ALMOND GINGERSNAPS

20 cookies   Easy $$

"My dad (aka Papaw) says these are his new favorite cookies, and he doesn't even care that they're packed with protein, iron, and calcium. You can easily make them gluten-free, as noted in the recipe, and you don't even need an electric mixer. The dough will be sticky so make sure you refrigerate it at least 1 hour before baking. Cook 10 minutes for a chewy cookie or 12 minutes for a crisp one." BOBBI

Prep Time: 15 minutes   **Passive Time:** 1 hour to chill   **Cook Time:** 10 to 12 minutes per batch

Tools: large (4-quart) saucepan, measuring cups and spoons, medium mixing bowl, baking sheet

Dry ingredients:

1-2/3 cup almond meal (finely ground)

1/4 cup whole wheat pastry flour, or gluten-free flour

1 tablespoon ground ginger

1 teaspoon ground cinnamon

1 teaspoon **baking soda***

1/4 teaspoon salt

Wet ingredients:

1/4 cup (1/2 stick) butter

2/3 cup granulated sugar

1/4 cup molasses

1 teaspoon vanilla (optional)

1 egg

1. Combine dry ingredients in a medium bowl. Stir to blend and break up lumps. Set aside.
2. Melt butter, sugar, and **molasses*** in a large saucepan over medium-low heat, stirring until smooth. Remove from heat to cool to lukewarm.
3. Stir in vanilla, then quickly stir in egg until smooth. (If butter is too hot, the egg will cook slightly.)
4. Stir in dry ingredients until incorporated. The dough will be very moist and sticky. Refrigerate at least 1 hour, or until firm.

To bake:

1. Preheat oven to 350°F. Spray or rub oil onto a baking sheet.
2. Scoop out a spoonful of dough for each cookie and form loosely into about 1-inch balls. Place on baking sheet, leaving plenty of room around them since they'll flatten and spread into very thin cookies.
3. Bake 10 to 12 minutes. Remove from oven and cool slightly. Use a food turner to transfer the cookies from the baking sheet to a cooling rack or piece of wax (or parchment) paper. Cool completely, then store in an airtight container.

APPLE PECAN CRISP

9 servings   Moderate $

Nothing beats the aroma of apples and pecans baking in the oven, especially on a chilly fall day! We recommend choosing crisp apples that will remain firm, like Granny Smith, Honeycrisp, or Fuji.

Prep Time: 20 minutes   **Passive Time:** 10 minutes   **Cook Time:** 50 minutes

Tools: 8×8-inch baking dish, knife and cutting board, measuring cups and spoons, large bowl

Filling:

7 to 8 cups chopped apples (about 5 large apples)

1/4 cup brown sugar (**firmly packed***)

1 teaspoon ground cinnamon

Topping:

6 tablespoons butter

2/3 cup old-fashioned rolled oats

1/2 cup whole wheat flour, or any gluten-free flour

1/2 cup chopped pecans (optional)

1/3 cup brown sugar (firmly packed)

1 teaspoon ground ginger

1 teaspoon ground cinnamon

1/4 teaspoon ground nutmeg

1/4 teaspoon salt

*To firmly pack brown sugar, fill a measuring cup about half full of brown sugar. Press the sugar down with the back of the spoon. Add more sugar, pressing down and repeating until level with top edge.

For filling:

1. Peel apples, cut in quarters and remove core. Cut into chunks by slicing each quarter lengthwise into two or three pieces, then cutting across in half. Place in a large bowl.
2. Add sugar and cinnamon, then stir to coat.
3. Spray or rub oil into an 8×8-inch baking dish. Pour apples into the baking dish and spread out evenly.
4. Begin to preheat oven to 350°F.

For topping:

1. Cut butter into small pieces and place in the bowl you used for the apples. (No need to clean it.)
2. Add remaining topping ingredients. Stir and use your fingers to combine until crumbly.
3. Sprinkle topping evenly over the apple mixture.
4. Bake 50 minutes, or until apples are soft and mixture is bubbling.
5. Cool at least 10 minutes before serving.
6. Serve with ice cream or whipped cream if desired.

BLACK BEAN BROWNIES (GF)

9 servings   Easy $$

These gluten-free brownies are surprisingly moist, rich, and delicious—really! Black beans (instead of flour) serve as the starch, and they provide high levels of fiber, protein, vitamins, and minerals. Using plain refried beans is what makes this dessert very easy to mix, without the need for an electric mixer or food processor. Molasses and vinegar deepen the chocolate flavor and help the brownies rise. (So don't leave them out!) Finally, prepare your baking dish ahead of time, as indicated. These are very fragile and somewhat difficult to remove if that step is skipped.

Prep Time: 15 minutes   **Passive Time:** 30 minutes to cool   **Cook Time:** 40 minutes

Tools: 8×8-inch baking dish, large (4-quart) saucepan, measuring cups and spoons, knife and cutting board (if chopping nuts)

Special Supplies: parchment or wax paper

1/4 cup (1/2 stick) unsalted butter

1/2 cup unsweetened cocoa powder, or raw cacao powder

3/4 cup brown sugar (firmly packed)

1 tablespoon molasses

1 teaspoon vinegar (balsamic recommended)

1 teaspoon vanilla

1 (15-ounce) can **plain refried black beans***

2 eggs

1/2 teaspoon baking powder

1/2 teaspoon baking soda

1/2 cup chocolate chips (dark or semi-sweet recommended)

1/2 cup chopped nuts (optional)

Preheat oven to 350°F. Spray or rub oil into baking dish.

1. Line dish with one or two pieces of parchment or wax paper, leaving about two inches extra on the sides, so the brownies can be lifted out when done. Spray paper with oil.

2. Melt butter in a large saucepan over low heat.

3. While butter is melting, chop nuts.

---

*TIP

Refried beans are simply mashed beans and can be found in the Mexican food section or with other beans. Make sure you use **refried** beans, not whole beans. Also, read the ingredients carefully and choose one that contains **only** black beans, water, and possibly salt, although no salt is better. **Avoid** those with garlic, peppers, etc.

---

4. Add cocoa (or cacao) powder, stirring continually for about 30 seconds. (This intensifies the cocoa flavor.) Watch carefully and do not burn.

5. Remove from heat and stir in brown sugar, molasses, vinegar, and vanilla.

6. Add refried beans and stir until smooth.

7. Beat in eggs, one at a time.

8. Stir in baking powder and baking soda.

9. Fold in chocolate chips and nuts.

10. Pour batter into the parchment-lined baking dish. Bake 40 minutes, or until the center feels slightly firm (but still soft) to the touch.

11. Cool at least 30 minutes before lifting out and cutting.

VARIATIONS:

- Use white chocolate drops and chopped macadamia nuts.
- Use peanut butter drops and unsalted, roasted peanuts.

CHAI GINGERBREAD

9 servings   Moderate $

Filled with rich molasses and chai flavors, this gingerbread will warm you up from the inside out. Substitute plain black tea if you don't have chai tea.

Prep Time: 15 to 20 minutes   **Passive Time:** 10 minutes   **Cook Time:** 30 to 40 minutes

Tools: 8×8-inch baking dish, measuring cups and spoons, large (4-quart) saucepan, medium bowl

Wet ingredients:

3/4 cup water

2 chai tea bags

1/2 cup (1 stick) butter

2/3 cup granulated sugar

2/3 cup molasses

1 teaspoon vanilla

2 eggs

1/2 tablespoon minced fresh or candied ginger (optional)

Dry ingredients:

1 cup all-purpose white flour

3/4 cup whole wheat flour (pastry flour recommended)

1 tablespoon ground ginger

1 teaspoon ground cinnamon

1 teaspoon ground cardamom

1 teaspoon baking soda

1/2 teaspoon baking powder

1/4 teaspoon salt

Preheat oven to 350°F. Spray or rub oil into an 8×8-inch baking dish.

1. Add water to a microwave-safe liquid measuring cup (or small bowl) and heat about 2 minutes in the microwave on high to bring to a boil. (Alternatively, bring water to a boil in a teakettle or saucepan on the stovetop, then pour boiling water into the measuring cup.) Add tea bags and steep while you continue, or at least 2 minutes.

2. Melt butter in a large saucepan. Remove from heat and stir in brown sugar and molasses.

3. Squeeze excess liquid from tea bags and discard them. If tea is no longer **warm,*** reheat in the microwave about 30 seconds. Add to butter mixture and stir until well blended and sugar has dissolved. Let mixture cool while you continue.

4. Mince ginger if using. Set aside.

5. Combine dry ingredients in a medium bowl. **Stir*** to blend.

6. When butter mixture has cooled to lukewarm, add one egg at a time, **beating*** lightly with a whisk after each one.

7. Stir in optional minced ginger.

8. Add dry ingredients and mix just until flour is incorporated.

9. Pour batter into greased baking dish and bake 35 to 40 minutes, or until done. Test by sticking a wooden toothpick in the center. It should come out clean, or with a few crumbs attached to it.

10. Cool at least 10 minutes before cutting.

---

*What's the difference between stirring and beating?

- **Stir** – to gently mix ingredients together, using a spoon, fork, or whisk.

- **Beat** – to mix ingredients together vigorously either by hand or with an electric beater. Incorporates more air than stirring.

---

*TIP
Warm or hot tea will help dissolve molasses and sugar, which is important for the texture. Also, adding cold liquids to the melted butter mixture will harden the butter and form clumps. If this happens, warm up mixture on the stovetop, then cool to lukewarm again before adding eggs. Do not add eggs to hot mixture because the eggs will start to coagulate (solidify).

SERVING SUGGESTIONS:

- Serve warm, with a dollop of butter on top.

- Cool, then top with whipped cream that is flavored with some sugar and cardamom.

- Top with vanilla, ginger, or green tea ice cream.

VARIATIONS:

- HONEY ORANGE GINGERBREAD – Warm up 3/4 cup orange juice (in the microwave for 30 seconds) and substitute for tea. Use 1/2 cup honey in place of molasses. Add zest from 1 orange.

- Muffins – Bake in muffin tins 20 minutes. Makes 12 large muffins.

CHOCOLATE ICEBOX CAKE WITH BERRIES

9 servings   Easy $$

This is the about the easiest "cake" you could make. The original icebox cake contained a certain popular brand of chocolate wafers made with ingredients we try to avoid, like trans fats and high fructose corn syrup. So, we decided to use Mi-del Chocolate Snaps, which contain more wholesome ingredients. Our version turned out to be a winner for both family and friends, and since then, we've made it with Mi-del Lemon and Mi-del Ginger Snaps, too. If you don't like to bake, you will LOVE this cake!

Prep Time: 10 minutes   **Passive Time:** 24 hours to chill
Tools: large bowl, electric mixer (or whisk), 8×8-inch baking dish, knife and cutting board, medium bowl, measuring spoon

1 pint heavy cream (2 cups)
1 (10-ounce) package Mi-del Chocolate Snaps, or similar

Topping:
2 cups (1 pint) fresh strawberries, or raspberries
1 to 2 tablespoons sugar

1. **Whip*** cream in a large bowl with an electric mixer, or by hand with a whisk, until soft peaks begin to form.

2. Spread a thin layer of whipped cream on the bottom of the baking dish, so the cookies will have something to stick to. Arrange cookies side by side, to form a single layer but not overlapping (there will be gaps). Spread about a third of the whipped cream over them. Make sure there are no air pockets.

*Whip – to beat vigorously with a whisk or electric mixer, in order to incorporate air into the food, rendering it light and fluffy. Examples: cream and egg whites.

TIP

For best results, do not whip cream in a plastic bowl—use a glass or metal bowl. Chefs recommend chilling the metal bowl and beaters (or whisk) before whipping, but we have to admit that we've never done so. However, the colder everything is, including the cream, the fluffier it will be. It will also hold air longer and not separate as quickly.

3. Make another layer of cookies, pressing down a bit, then another layer of cream, leaving half of it for the final topping. Add the last layer of cookies (which should finish the package, but if not, pop the remainder in your mouth before anyone looks). Top with the remaining cream, spreading out evenly, leaving a smooth finish. Check again for air pockets.

4. Cover and refrigerate overnight. (You can serve it after 12 hours, but 24 hours is best.)

5. Slice strawberries. Place in a medium bowl, and toss with 1 to 2 tablespoons sugar. Let stand to soften and bring out juices (macerate).

6. Right before serving, garnish the whole dessert (or each serving) with berries. Alternatively, leave out the berries and dust with cocoa powder.

VARIATIONS:

- LEMON RASPBERRY ICEBOX CAKE – Use Mi-del Lemon Snaps and zest one lemon. Sprinkle equal amounts of zest on top of each layer of whipped cream. Serve with raspberries.

- GINGER ICEBOX CAKE – Use Mi-del Ginger Snaps. Top dessert with about 1 tablespoon finely chopped candied ginger and chopped nuts if desired.

LEMON CARDAMOM RICOTTA CAKE

9 servings   Moderate $$

We follow our easy Finite Foodie technique of melting the butter first, then using the saucepan as the mixing bowl. For a fluffier version, see our Variation using an electric mixer, if you have one. This moist, delicate cake is a favorite in our family, and it can easily be made gluten-free by using 1-to-1 gluten-free baking flour in place of the wheat flour. (Almond meal is naturally gluten-free.) This cake is best while still warm, but it also keeps well for days.

Prep Time: 15 minutes   **Passive Time:** 10 minutes   **Cook Time:** 40 minutes

Tools: 8×8-inch baking dish, large (4-quart) saucepan, grater, measuring cups and spoons, medium bowl

Wet ingredients:

5 tablespoons butter

2/3 cup sugar

1 large lemon

3/4 cup ricotta cheese

1 egg yolk

3 large eggs

Dry ingredients:

2-1/4 cups almond meal (fine ground)

1/4 cup flour (gluten-free, white, or whole wheat pastry)

1/2 tablespoon ground cardamom

1 teaspoon baking powder

1 teaspoon baking soda

1/4 teaspoon salt

Preheat oven to 350°F. Spray or rub oil into an 8×8-inch baking dish.

1. Melt butter and sugar together in a large saucepan, stirring to dissolve most of the sugar. Remove from heat to cool.

2. While butter melts, combine dry ingredients in a medium bowl and stir.

3. Grate the yellow layer of the lemon peel (**zest***) using the small or medium holes to yield about 1 tablespoon. Cut zested lemon in half, and squeeze the juice to yield 3 tablespoons juice. Alternatively use 3 tablespoons bottled lemon juice and no zest—but the lemon flavor will be less intense.

> ***Zest** – the colored part of a citrus fruit peel. Also used as a verb meaning to grate off the zest. Avoid white pith under the colored part, as it can be bitter. Examples: lemons, limes, and oranges. (Grapefruits are not normally zested.)

4. Stir lemon juice, lemon zest, and ricotta into the butter mixture with a whisk (or kitchen spoon) until mostly smooth.

5. **Separate*** one egg, then add yolk to batter. Mix in with a whisk (or kitchen spoon) just until blended. Stir in about one third of the dry ingredients, then another egg. Continue alternating dry ingredients and egg until everything has been blended in, but don't overmix.

6. Pour batter into prepared baking dish. Bake 35 to 40 minutes, or until done. Test with a toothpick by inserting into the center. It should come out clean, with just a few crumbs attached. Alternatively, press down in the center. It should spring back, leaving no indentation.

7. Cool at least 10 minutes before cutting. Serve plain or with fresh berries and whipped cream.

*TIP

To **separate** eggs, gently crack the egg and open slightly over a bowl, allowing the white to drop into it as you transfer the yolk from one half of the shell to the other several times. Place the remaining yolk in a separate bowl (or directly into the batter in this instance). When a recipe calls for more than 1 egg white (for whipping), use three bowls. Always separate the white of each egg into an empty bowl then add that egg white to the other whites, as long as no yolk has accidentally gone into it. If a yolk breaks and drips into the white, transfer that egg to another dish to use in scrambled eggs. A little yolk can prevent egg whites from whipping properly.

VARIATIONS:

- LEMON POPPY SEED CAKE – Add 3 tablespoons poppy seeds to dry ingredients.

- USE AN ELECTRIC MIXER – If you have an electric mixer, take butter out of the refrigerator just long enough to soften a little, but remain cool. Beat (or **cream***) butter and sugar together in a large mixing bowl until fluffy, then beat in remaining wet ingredients. Stir in dry ingredients. (Cakes rise better when the butter and sugar have been creamed).

*Cream – to beat a fat (like butter) with sugar until they are thoroughly blended and look light and fluffy. Do not overcream to the point of looking shiny and wet.

OATMEAL MOLASSES COOKIES

24 cookies   Easy $$

"Richard (aka Dad) always loved his mom's oatmeal cookies, but I rarely made them myself . . . until I decided to come up with a more healthful version. Now everyone in the family is happy. These cookies are packed with whole grains, nuts, and dried fruit, but have a reduced amount of sugar. This recipe is designed to use as few dishes as possible (for easy cleanup), and it does not even require an electric mixer!" BOBBI

Prep Time: 15 minutes   **Cook Time:** 10 minutes per batch

Tools: baking sheet, large (4-quart) saucepan, measuring cups and spoons, medium bowl, knife and cutting board

Wet ingredients:

1 cup butter (2 sticks)

3/4 cup brown sugar (firmly packed)

2 tablespoons molasses

1 egg

1 teaspoon vanilla

TIP

To make your own brown sugar for this recipe, add 1-1/2 tablespoons molasses to 3/4 cup granulated sugar.

Dry ingredients:

1 cup whole wheat flour

1 teaspoon ground cinnamon

1 teaspoon baking powder

1/2 teaspoon baking soda

1/2 teaspoon ground nutmeg (optional)

1/4 teaspoon salt

Add-ins:

2 cups rolled oats

3/4 cup chopped nuts

1/2 cup currants (or raisins)

Preheat oven to 375°F. Lightly spray or rub oil onto baking sheet.

1. Melt butter in a large saucepan. Remove from heat to cool for a few minutes while you continue.

2. Combine dry ingredients in a medium bowl and stir.

3. Chop nuts.

4. Return to slightly cooled butter and add brown sugar and molasses. (There's no need to transfer to a bowl. This cuts down on clean up.) Stir with a whisk (or kitchen spoon).

5. Add egg and beat lightly, until smooth. Stir in vanilla.

6. Add flour mixture to the saucepan and stir just until flour is incorporated.

7. Mix in oats, nuts, and currants (or raisins).

How to use the displacement method for measuring –

Most butter comes in a stick with indicator lines for tablespoons, 1/4 cup, and 1/2 cup (the whole stick). However, when you need to measure from a block of unmarked butter or a tub of coconut oil, use the displacement method. To measure 1/2 cup butter for example, place 1-1/2 cups cold water into a 2-cup measuring cup. Add pieces of butter until the water level reaches the 2-cup mark. Pour off the water and you'll have the proper amount of butter, with no mess.

8. Scoop up a heaping tablespoon of dough, about 1-1/2 inches in diameter, and drop onto the baking sheet, or form into a ball before placing on the baking sheet. Leave as-is, or press down to flatten a bit. (They will not spread much when cooked.)

9. Bake 10 minutes. *Note:* Use your timer so you don't forget about them! Keep in mind that they will continue to cook somewhat after being removed from the oven, so don't overcook them if you want chewy cookies.

10. Remove from oven and cool slightly. Use a food turner to transfer the cookies from the baking sheet to a cooling rack or piece of wax (or parchment) paper. Cool completely, then store in an airtight container.

VARIATIONS:

- CRANBERRY COCONUT CASHEW COOKIES – Substitute maple syrup for molasses, 2 teaspoons ground ginger for cinnamon and nutmeg, cranberries for currants, and use cashews. Substitute 1/2 cup shredded coconut for 1/2 cup of the oats.

- Add 3/4 cup chocolate chips and/or 1/2 cup chopped dates (or other dried fruit like cranberries, cherries, apricots, apples) in place of, or in addition to, currants.

- Substitute 1/2 cup applesauce for 1 stick of butter, adding with sugar. This lowers the fat and calorie count, but changes the texture and taste slightly.

- USE AN ELECTRIC MIXER – Soften butter by leaving it on the counter 15 to 30 minutes. Beat butter and sugar with a mixer until fluffy. Beat in molasses and vanilla, then the egg. Continue with the recipe directions.

PEACH GINGER BATTER COBBLER

9 servings   Moderate $

"This was inspired by a batter cobbler recipe I ran across in Cook's Illustrated. It gave me a great idea for simplifying my Mom-ma's famous peach cobbler. She was a pro at making the lightest, flakiest pastry dough. This version uses a batter instead, which is much simpler. The hardest part is peeling and chopping the peaches, which is why we rate it "Moderate" for difficulty. However, you can simplify it by using frozen (thawed) sliced peaches. We usually make this dessert during the peak of the summer peach season with fresh, freestone peaches, which release easily from the pit. Using frozen peaches allows it to be a year-round treat. Ginger and honey give this recipe an updated twist or see our Variation for a more traditional version." BOBBI

Prep Time: 20 Minutes   **Passive Time:** 30 minutes   **Cook Time:** 50 to 60 minutes
Tools: knife and cutting board, large and medium bowls, measuring cups and spoons, 8×8-inch baking dish

Filling:

3 cups chopped or sliced peaches (about
   1-1/2 pounds, or 3 to 4 peaches)

1 teaspoon minced fresh ginger, or ground
   ginger

2 tablespoons honey, or 3 tablespoons
   sugar

TIP

Be sure to mince or grate fresh
ginger into very tiny pieces, as it
can be unpleasantly spicy if you
bite into a large piece.

Batter:

1/4 cup (1/2 stick) butter

1/2 cup all-purpose white flour

1/3 cup whole wheat flour (pastry flour
   recommended)

1/2 cup granulated sugar

1-1/2 teaspoons ground ginger

1-1/2 teaspoons baking powder

1/4 teaspoon salt

3/4 cup milk

Garnish:

2 tablespoons granulated sugar

Preheat oven to 350°F.

1. Peel peaches if desired and slice or chop
   into large chunks. Place in a large bowl.
   Mince ginger and stir into peaches.
   Do not add honey yet (it will cause the
   peaches to **macerate,** * which you don't
   want here).

   ***Macerate** – to soften by soaking in
   juices. Example: Adding sugar to fruit
   pulls out the juices and softens the
   fruit. It also forms a sweet syrup.

2. When oven has reached the proper temperature, put butter in baking dish and place
   in oven to melt.

3. While butter melts, combine all remaining ingredients for the batter, except the
   milk, in a medium bowl, and mix. Measure out the milk, but do not add it yet.

4. When the butter has melted and is bubbling, but not burned, remove the dish from
   the oven. Immediately stir milk into the dry ingredients with a whisk (or fork). Don't
   overmix. Pour batter directly into the center of the baking dish with the melted butter in it, but do not stir.

5. Toss peaches with honey, then pour on top of the batter. Arrange evenly throughout,
   pushing them down into the batter, but not stirring.

6. Sprinkle sugar over the mixture, and bake 50 to 60 minutes, or until bubbling and
   browned on top.

7. Cool at least 30 minutes to set.

8. Top with ice cream or whipped cream if desired.

VARIATION:

- TRADITIONAL TASTE - Substitute 1 teaspoon cinnamon and 1/2 teaspoon nutmeg for
  the ginger. Use sugar instead of honey in the peaches.

PEANUT BUTTER COOKIES

20 to 24 cookies   Easy $

Who doesn't love peanut butter cookies? This recipe is super easy, but you'll need to chill the dough at least an hour before baking. We recommend all-natural peanut butter for the best peanut flavor, but be aware that the oil separates over time and might need to be stirred in before using.

Prep Time: 15 minutes   **Passive Time:** 1 hour to chill   **Cook Time:** 7 to 8 minutes per batch

Tools: large (4-quart) saucepan, medium bowl, measuring cups and spoons, baking sheet

Dry ingredients:

1 cup whole wheat flour

1 teaspoon baking powder

1 teaspoon cinnamon

1/2 teaspoon allspice

1/4 teaspoon salt (if using unsalted peanut butter)

Wet ingredients:

1/2 cup (1 stick) butter

1/2 cup brown sugar (firmly packed)

1/2 cup all-natural peanut butter (creamy or chunky)

1 egg

1 teaspoon vanilla

Garnish:

2 tablespoons sugar

1. Combine dry ingredients in a medium bowl and stir. Set aside.

2. Melt butter in a large saucepan. Remove from heat.

3. Add brown sugar and peanut butter directly into the saucepan, stirring well after each addition.

4. When butter mixture has cooled somewhat, mix in egg and vanilla until smooth and creamy. (If added too early, the eggs might begin to cook in the hot butter.)

5. Add dry ingredients and stir until flour is incorporated.

6. The dough will be very soft, so you must refrigerate it 1 hour or longer before baking.

TIP

To refrigerate dough overnight or for a few days, form into a ball or cylinder, wrap in wax paper, then place in a plastic baggie. If chilling for only an hour, simply place the whole saucepan with dough in the refrigerator if you have room.

To bake:

1. Preheat oven to 375°F. Spray oil or rub a little oil onto a baking sheet, unless it's non-stick.

2. Pour granulated sugar into a small, shallow bowl or plate.

3. Form into 1-inch balls and roll in the sugar. Use a fork and press each ball of dough in one direction, then the other. This flattens the cookie and leaves the classic peanut butter cookie imprints.

4. Bake 7 to 8 minutes.

5. Remove from oven and cool slightly. Use a food turner to transfer the cookies from the baking sheet to a cooling rack or piece of wax (or parchment) paper. Cool completely, then store in an airtight container.

VARIATIONS:

- CHRISTMAS KISS COOKIES – Do not press cookie with fork. Instead, unwrap a chocolate kiss and press it down into the center.
- Add 2 tablespoons ground flaxseed, or 1/4 cup chopped roasted peanuts to dough.
- GLUTEN-FREE – Substitute Bob's Red Mill Gluten-Free 1 to 1 Baking Flour, (or similar) for wheat flour.
- VEGAN – Substitute coconut oil for butter and 1/4 cup applesauce for egg. Use regular or gluten-free flour.

PUMPKIN PIE BARS

9 servings   Easy $$

This filling is creamy, lightly sweetened, and rich with warming spices that bring out the pumpkin flavor. We pour it over a simple graham cracker crust pressed into an 8×8-inch baking dish. If you don't have a rolling pin, use a wine bottle or canned item to crush crackers, or buy graham cracker crumbs. This is an easy way to make "pumpkin pie," especially if you don't own a pie pan. There's no need to wait until Thanksgiving to make this delicious and relatively healthful dessert!

Prep Time: 20 minutes   **Passive Time:** 30 minutes to cool   **Cook Time:** 55 to 60 minutes
Tools: microwave-safe 8×8-inch baking dish, rolling pin (or similar shape), measuring cups and spoons, small and large bowls

Crust:

6 tablespoons butter, or coconut oil

1 (8-ounce) package graham crackers, or 1-3/4 cups graham cracker crumbs

Filling:

3 eggs

1/4 cup brown sugar (firmly packed)

1/4 cup maple syrup, or honey

1 (15-ounce) can pumpkin purée

1/2 tablespoon ground cinnamon

1/2 tablespoon ground ginger

1/2 teaspoon ground cardamom

1/4 teaspoon ground nutmeg

1/4 teaspoon ground allspice

1/4 teaspoon salt

1/8 teaspoon ground cloves

1 cup heavy cream (8-ounce carton)

Preheat oven to 450°F. Spray or rub oil into a microwave-safe 8×8-inch baking dish.

For crust:

1. Place butter (or coconut oil) in the greased baking dish, and heat in microwave 1 to 2 minutes, or until butter has melted.

2. To make graham crackers crumbs, place one layer of crackers on a sheet of wax paper. Cover with another sheet. Use a rolling pin or other cylindrical object (like a wine bottle) to roll over and crush them.

3. Add crumbs to melted butter in baking dish and stir gently to moisten thoroughly. Press down into a level layer in the bottom.

For filling:

1. Lightly beat eggs with a whisk (or fork) in a large bowl.

2. Add sugar and syrup (or honey) and stir well.

3. Mix in pumpkin and spices, then stir in cream.

4. Pour into prepared graham cracker crust. Bake in preheated oven 10 minutes. Turn heat down to 325°F and continue baking another 45 to 50 minutes, or until done. The center should be somewhat firm, but just a little jiggly. (It will continue to cook after being removed from oven.)

5. Cool at least 30 minutes before cutting. Do not refrigerate until completely cool.

SERVING SUGGESTION:

- Serve plain, or top with whipped cream and chopped pecans.

TIP

If you don't have a measuring spoon for 1/2 tablespoon, remember that 1 tablespoon equals 3 teaspoons. So, 1/2 tablespoon equals 1-1/2 teaspoons. See Measurements and Equivalents (p. 255) for more details.

SNICKERDOODLES

20 cookies   Easy $

"When I was in elementary school, I saved up my pennies and ordered "My First Cook-book" from Imperial Sugar for 25 cents. I've forgotten most of the recipes, but I saved my favorite—Snickerdoodles. I used to make these frequently as a young girl, but eventually forgot about them. Many years later I had my own kids, so I pulled out that old recipe and introduced them to my childhood treat. We've made a few updates for our cookbook, including using whole wheat flour and less sugar, as well as our Finite Foodie technique for making cookies without an electric mixer." BOBBI

Prep Time: 10 to 15 minutes   **Passive Time:** 1 hour to chill

Cook Time: 8 minutes per batch

Tools: measuring cups and spoons, large (4-quart) saucepan, medium bowl, small bowl, baking sheet

Wet ingredients:

1/2 cup (1 stick) butter

2/3 cup granulated sugar

2 teaspoons lemon juice (optional)

1 teaspoon vanilla

1 egg

Dry ingredients:

1-1/3 cups whole wheat pastry flour

1 teaspoon baking powder

1/4 teaspoon salt

Sugar and spice mixture:

2 tablespoons sugar

1/2 tablespoon cinnamon

1. Melt butter and sugar in a large sauce-pan over low heat, stirring frequently. Remove from heat to cool slightly.

2. Combine dry ingredients in a medium bowl, then stir and set aside.

3. Once butter has cooled somewhat, mix in vanilla and egg, until smooth and creamy.

4. Add dry ingredients and stir until flour is incorporated.

5. The dough will be very soft, so you must refrigerate it at least 1 hour before baking.

TIP

When baking with 100% whole wheat flour, your end product will be a little drier than the same recipe made with 100% white flour. However, we like the additional nutrition that whole wheat flour provides, so we've written the recipe to work with 100% whole wheat pastry flour. You can use half whole wheat and half white flour if you want a lighter cookie.

To bake:

1. Preheat oven to 350°F.

2. Place the sugar and cinnamon in a small shallow bowl or plate. Form dough into 1-1/2 inch balls and roll them in the sugar-cinnamon mixture. Place on an ungreased baking sheet.

3. Bake 8 minutes, or until lightly browned but still soft.

4. Remove from oven and cool slightly. Use a food turner to transfer the cookies from the baking sheet to a cooling rack or piece of wax (or parchment) paper. Cool completely, then store in an airtight container.

VARIATIONS:

- GLUTEN-FREE – Substitute Bob's Red Mill Gluten-Free 1 to 1 Baking Flour, (or similar) for wheat flour.
- Combine 1-1/2 tablespoons sugar, 1 teaspoon cinnamon, 1/4 teaspoon nutmeg, 1/4 teaspoon cardamom, and 1/8 teaspoon ground cloves for the sugar and spice mixture.

MISCELLANEOUS

For all those recipes that don't quite fit anywhere else!

CILANTRO-LIME SOUR CREAM

1 cup   Easy $

We use this topping for quesadillas and just about any Mexican dish. It's also good with TEXAS-STYLE PINTO BEANS, CHIPOTLE BLACK BEAN SOUP, BAKED POTATOES, *or on top of an* OMELET. *Keeps up to one week.*

Prep Time: 5 minutes
Tools: grater (optional), knife and cutting board, small bowl, measuring cups

1 large lime, or 2 tablespoons lime juice
1/2 cup lightly packed cilantro
1 cup sour cream

1. *Optional step:* If using a fresh lime, grate lime zest (green layer of peel) using small holes of grater. This addition will give it a bolder lime flavor.
2. Juice the lime into a small bowl (or use bottled lime juice).
3. Chop cilantro and combine with lime juice.
4. Stir in sour cream and lime zest.

CUCUMBER RAITA

2 cups   Easy $

Raita is very popular in India, and you can find many versions using carrots, onions and even fruit. Cucumber raita (called tzatziki in Greece) is the most common type and is a springboard for other variations.

Prep Time: 5 minutes
Tools: medium bowl, measuring cups and spoons, knife and cutting board

1 to 2 tablespoons lemon juice
1 teaspoon honey
1/2 teaspoon salt
Pinch ground black pepper

2 dashes hot pepper sauce (optional)
1 cup chopped cucumber
1/4 cup chopped cilantro
1 cup plain Greek yogurt

Garnish: (optional)
Cilantro **sprigs***
Cucumber slices

***Sprig** – refers to a small (about 1- to 2-inch) piece of herb cut from the tip end of the plant. It is comprised of the stem with leaves attached. Used to garnish dishes or drinks.

1. In a medium bowl, combine lemon juice, honey, salt, pepper, and hot pepper sauce. Beat with a whisk (or fork).

2. Chop cucumbers (peeled or not) and cilantro, then add to bowl. Toss.

3. Stir in yogurt. Adjust seasonings, to taste.

4. Garnish with a few cucumber slices and a sprig of cilantro if desired.

SERVING SUGGESTIONS:

- Serve with a plate of pita bread or crackers as an appetizer.
- Serve as a side to Indian food, chicken, or meat dishes.

VARIATION:

- CARROT RAITA – Substitute grated carrot for cucumber and mint for cilantro.

GARAM MASALA SPICE BLEND

5 tablespoons   Easy $$

Garam masala is a special Indian blend of spices, but it can vary from family to family and brand to brand. Although it's typically made by toasting whole spices then grinding them fresh, we have developed a quick version using our Finite Foodie spices. We rate the cost as moderate because spices aren't cheap. However, you should already have these in your pantry, so it might cost nothing extra to make. And, a little goes a long way.

Prep Time: 5 minutes
Tools: measuring spoons, small bowl
Special Supplies: airtight container

1 tablespoon ground cumin

1 tablespoon ground coriander

1 tablespoon ground cardamom

1 tablespoon ground cinnamon

1/2 tablespoon ground black pepper

1 teaspoon ground nutmeg

3/4 teaspoon ground cloves

1/2 teaspoon red pepper flakes

1. Combine all ingredients in a small bowl and stir to mix well.

2. Transfer to an airtight container and use within one year for best flavor.

TIP
Save empty spice jars. Remove the labels, wash, and use them for mixes like this.

MICROWAVED ICED TEA

2 cups   Easy $

"My cousin Cindy is an avid iced tea fan who insists on making it fresh every day. This is her neat trick that's so easy you may never go back to your tea kettle. You will need a microwave-safe container like a Pyrex® 2-cup liquid measuring cup. We combine teas, including black, green, white, flavored, and herbal." BOBBI

Prep Time: 1 minute   **Passive Time:** 2 to 10 minutes   **Cook Time:** 3 minutes
Tools: 2-cup microwave-safe measuring cup (or other glass container)

2 cups water
2 to 3 tea bags

1. Pour water into a microwave-safe, 2-cup liquid measuring cup.
2. Heat in the microwave on high for 1 minute, then add tea bags. (Make sure they are submerged in the water.)
3. Heat again on high for 2 minutes. The water will be very hot, so leave it in the microwave to steep 2 to 10 minutes, depending on the type of tea and your taste preference.
4. Remove tea bags. Add 2 or 3 ice cubes to cool the tea more quickly if desired.
5. Transfer to a glass jar or pitcher, then add more water to dilute, to taste.
6. Store tea in refrigerator, and drink within 24 to 48 hours for best flavor.

SERVING SUGGESTION:
• Pour over ice and garnish with a slice of citrus fruit and/or a sprig of mint.

VARIATIONS:
• SWEET TEA – Add desired amount of sweetener to the tea after removing tea bags and while still warm. Stir until dissolved.
• WITHOUT A MICROWAVE – Boil 2 cups water in a small saucepan, then remove from heat and add tea bags, or pour boiling water over tea in a teapot.

TIP
Never pour boiling water into a glass container, unless it is made of tempered, shatterproof glass (like Pyrex). Allow the liquid to cool first if using a regular glass pitcher (or jar).

NANA'S THIN CORNBREAD

6 servings   Easy $

"Our family always ate crunchy, thin cornbread, not the sweet, cake-like cornbread many people know. We would crumble it up on a plate and scoop pinto beans on top, or crumble it into a glass and pour milk over it." BOBBI

Prep Time: 10 minutes   **Cook Time:** 20 to 25 minutes

Tools: 15×10-inch rimmed baking sheet, measuring cups and spoons, medium and large bowls

Dry ingredients:

1-1/2 cups cornmeal

2/3 cup whole wheat flour, or all-purpose white flour

1 tablespoon sugar

1 tablespoon baking powder

1/2 teaspoon salt

Wet ingredients:

2 eggs

1-1/2 cups milk

2 tablespoons butter

1 tablespoon oil

Preheat oven to 425°F.

1. Combine dry ingredients in a medium bowl and stir. Set aside.

2. Lightly beat 2 eggs with a whisk (or fork) in a large bowl, then stir in milk.

3. Place butter and oil in the rimmed baking dish and set in preheated oven for 1 to 2 minutes to heat up. Watch carefully and remove before the oil begins to smoke. Tilt to coat entire surface with the fat.

4. Remove baking sheet and turn oven down to 375°F.

5. Stir dry ingredients into wet ingredients with a whisk (or fork) just until blended. Don't over mix. Add a little extra milk if the batter is too thick (it should pour like pancake batter).

6. Pour excess fat from the baking sheet into batter and stir.

7. Pour batter into baking sheet. Bake 20 to 25 minutes. Cool slightly, then cut into 5-inch squares.

PEANUT (OR CASHEW) SAUCE

1/2 cup   Easy $

Make this small amount of sauce for 2 to 4 cups of steamed vegetables. We much prefer roasting nuts when we need them, or just enough to eat within a week. Studies indicate that roasting at 300°F or below for 10 to 15 minutes results in the least amount of nutritional loss.

Prep Time: 5 minutes   **Cook Time:** 10 to 15 minutes

Tools: baking sheet, measuring cups and spoons, small bowl, knife and cutting board (optional)

1/2 cup raw peanuts, or cashews

1 tablespoon lemon juice

1 tablespoon soy sauce

1/2 teaspoon ground ginger, or fresh (minced)

1 tablespoon oil (extra virgin olive oil recommended)

Hot pepper sauce, to taste (sriracha recommended)

For nuts (if not yet roasted):

1. Preheat oven to 275°F.

2. Spread peanuts (or cashews) in a single layer on an ungreased baking sheet. Roast 10 to 15 minutes, or until fragrant and just beginning to turn golden brown.

For sauce: (make while roasting nuts)

1. Mix lemon juice, soy sauce, and ginger in a small bowl.

2. Slowly add oil, beating with a whisk (or fork) until well blended.

3. Stir in hot sauce, then add nuts.

SERVING SUGGESTIONS:

- Serve on steamed broccoli, bok choy, Napa cabbage, Brussels sprouts, green beans, or mixed vegetables.

- Serve over your favorite grain.

RED PEPPER SAUCE

3 cups   Easy $

"One year I hosted a foreign exchange student from Denmark. She shared this family recipe with us and served it over poached salmon. Now it's one of our favorites too. If you have a hand-held stick blender you can blend this directly in the saucepan. Otherwise, purée small batches at a time in your blender. If you don't have a blender, just chop the vegetables more finely and serve a chunky sauce." BOBBI

Prep Time: 5 minutes   **Cook Time:** 35 minutes

Tools: knife and cutting board, measuring cups and spoons, large (4-quart) saucepan, blender

1 small onion

2 tablespoons high-heat cooking oil

3 garlic cloves

4 medium red bell peppers

1-1/2 cups broth

1-1/2 teaspoons salt

1/4 teaspoon ground black pepper

1/4 teaspoon red pepper flakes

2 teaspoons dried dill

1/2 lemon

1. Chop onion. Heat oil in a large saucepan over medium-low heat, then add onion. Cook and stir occasionally while you continue.

2. Chop garlic and bell peppers. Add to onions as you finish each one. Cook and stir occasionally, 3 to 5 minutes. Turn heat to low if needed.

3. Add broth, salt, pepper, and red pepper flakes. Simmer (uncovered) until reduced by half, about 30 minutes.

4. Purée in a blender or with a stick blender placed directly in the saucepan. Stir in dill and juice from half a lemon.

SERVING SUGGESTION:

- Pour about 1/3 cup sauce over POACHED or PAN-SEARED SALMON, grilled fish, boiled potatoes, or pasta.

TIP

While sauce simmers, prepare the item you plan to serve it with. The sauce can be made up to three days in advance, or frozen until ready to use.

SWEET BALSAMIC REDUCTION

1/4 cup   Easy $

Balsamic reduction adds a substantial flavor punch, so you don't need much. We reduce the balsamic with honey or maple syrup for extra sweetness, making it a perfect complement for salads that contain fruit. It's also tasty over ROASTED VEGETABLES.

Prep Time: 1 minute   **Cook Time:** 15 minutes   **Passive Time:** 5 minutes
Tools: measuring cup and spoon, small (1-quart) saucepan

1/2 cup balsamic vinegar
1 tablespoon maple syrup, or honey

1. Bring vinegar to a gentle boil in a small saucepan over medium heat. Immediately turn heat down to keep at a simmer (uncovered) until reduced by half, about 10 minutes.
2. Remove from heat for a moment while you stir in maple syrup (or honey).
3. Return to heat and simmer another few minutes, until thickened to desired consistency (like chocolate syrup).
4. Cool about 5 minutes if desired. (It will continue to thicken as it cools.)
5. Drizzle over fruit, salad, or vegetables right before serving.

SERVING SUGGESTIONS:
- Serve with WATERMELON FETA KABOBS, CANTALOUPE BERRY SALAD, or ROASTED VEGETABLES.
- Drizzle over grilled peaches or fresh strawberries.
- Use as a salad dressing on a green salad (with or without fruit).

TAHINI LEMON DIP/DRESSING

1 cup   Easy $$

*"This has been one of my favorite dips/dressings for decades, so I'm not surprised at its recent surge in popularity. Made with tahini (sesame paste), this dressing has a unique flavor that is delicious on Greek salads, or as a dip for **crudité*** and pita chips. It's usually served with gyro meat (spiced lamb), too. Be sure to keep tahini refrigerated once open, where it should stay fresh for about a year on average. If it begins to taste bitter or rancid, discard and replace."* BOBBI

Prep Time: 5 to 10 minutes

Tools: knife and cutting board, measuring cups and spoons, blender

*Crudité – French word for raw vegetables, usually served with dip, as an appetizer.

1 garlic clove

1/2 cup tahini

1/2 cup water

1/4 cup lemon juice (about 2 lemons)

1 teaspoon ground cumin

1/2 teaspoon salt

2 to 3 dashes hot pepper sauce

1. Peel garlic clove. *Note:* We add the whole clove to our Vitamix blender, but if your blender is not very strong, mince garlic first.

2. Combine everything in a blender and process until smooth. Add more water as needed for desired consistency, or if using as a dressing rather than a dip. (Keep in mind that it thickens once refrigerated.)

3. Adjust seasonings, to taste. Will keep in the refrigerator 5 to 7 days.

VINAIGRETTES

1/4 cup   Easy $

Once you see how easy and delicious homemade vinaigrette is, you'll never buy it at the store again! Use whatever vinegar, oil, and herbs you want, as long as they're a high quality—a vinaigrette is only as good as the ingredients in it. If the taste is too tart for you, adjust the ratio of oil to vinegar, or add a pinch of sugar. Our recipe makes a small amount, because we believe it's best when fresh. If you want more, just double the recipe. Keep in the refrigerator up to 2 weeks.

Prep Time: 2 to 5 minutes

Tools: small bowl (or **mason jar***), measuring spoons, knife and cutting board (optional)

1 tablespoon vinegar

1/2 teaspoon **mayonnaise*** (optional)

1/2 teaspoon dried herbs, or 1 to 2 teaspoons fresh

1/8 teaspoon salt

Pinch ground black pepper

2 to 3 tablespoons oil (extra virgin olive oil recommended)

1. Place vinegar, optional mayonnaise, dried herbs, salt, and pepper in a small bowl. (If using fresh herbs, add right before serving.) Stir to blend well.

2. Drizzle in the oil as you beat it with a whisk (or fork), or add 1 tablespoon at a time and whisk well after each addition to **emulsify*** the liquids (so the dressing becomes thick and creamy).

*Another way to mix vinaigrette is to put everything in a **mason jar** and shake until blended. It will not emulsify quite as well, but will save time.

TIP

Mayonnaise is a natural emulsifier that keeps the vinaigrette from separating.

VARIATIONS:

- FRENCH VINAIGRETTE – The French use sherry vinegar, but white wine, red wine, champagne, or apple cider vinegars also work. Combine 1 tablespoon minced shallot with vinegar and let stand 5 to 10 minutes to allow flavors to develop. Substitute 1/2 teaspoon Dijon mustard for mayonnaise. Use mild herbs like chives, chervil, tarragon, parsley, or dill.

- HEALTHY MEDITERRANEAN DRESSING – Substitute lemon juice for vinegar. Mince 1 garlic clove and combine with lemon juice. Let stand 5 to 10 minutes to allow flavors to develop. Substitute 1/2 teaspoon Dijon mustard for mayonnaise and use oregano or thyme. This is very good on steamed vegetables.

*Emulsify – to mix two substances together that typically don't combine well, in a way that they will become one and not separate. To achieve, beat oil and vinegar forcefully with a whisk until creamy. This produces a temporary emulsion. Adding an emulsifier like egg yolk, mustard, mayonnaise, or honey will keep vinaigrettes creamy longer, without separating.

ACKNOWLEDGMENTS

First and foremost, I want to acknowledge my children and co-authors, Rebecca Huron and Greg Ellson, as well as Rebecca's husband, Nicholas Huron. They provided continual input from a young-adult perspective in the midst of graduate school, new jobs, cross-country moves, and other major life events. Our cookbook is a direct result of their experiences, questions, and discoveries. My husband, Richard, provided much-needed support—financially, emotionally, and by bravely sampling many culinary experiments sometimes at the cost of his waistline.

My extended family and a number of close friends also helped out. Some read through early versions, while others prepared many of the recipes. Their honest yet compassionate suggestions were most valuable, and I'd like to thank each one: Bettye Mullins (my mom), Elizabeth Mullins (my niece), Pat Bortz, Nancy Burkley, Hannah Davis, Jeanette Gordon, Sonja Graf-Schlund, Cynthia Hood, Dene Hurley, Jessica Li, Toni O'Connor, Shelly Poulton, and Evelyn Viana. Thanks to the countless others who shared social media posts and words of encouragement.

I'd like to give a shout-out to Josiah Davis of JD Book Services for editing, proofing, and providing worthwhile feedback. I owe the lovely design and layout to Julie Allred of BW&A Books, Inc.

I can't end without thanking God for sustaining me, and blessing the work of my hands during this process. I am filled with gratitude (and relief)!

Bobbi Mullins

APPENDIX

COMMON USES OF HERBS AND SPICES

HERB OR SPICE	PAIRS WELL WITH
Allspice*	meat, poached fish, sweets
Basil (fresh)	cheese, eggs, salad, sauces, tomatoes, vegetables
Bay leaves*	legumes, sauces, soups, stews
Black pepper*	almost everything, to enhance flavor and add heat
Cardamom*	rice, sauces, sweets
Cayenne pepper	almost everything, to add heat
Chili powder*	barbecue sauce, chili, legumes, meat
Chinese 5-spice*	chicken, meat, soups, stews, stir-fry
Chives, leaves and flowers (fresh)	eggs, cheese, fish, potatoes, tomatoes, soups, salads
Cilantro (fresh)	eggs, chicken, fish, lamb, salads, salsa
Cinnamon*	fruit, ham, meat, stews, sweets
Cloves*	marinades, sauces, sweets
Cumin*	chili, legumes, meat, rice, soups
Curry powder*	meat, poultry, sauces, soups, stews, vegetables
Dill* (fresh or dried)	carrots, cheese, dips, eggs, fish, potatoes, sauces, soups
Ginger* (fresh or dried)	beverages, meat, sauces, smoothies, soups, sweets
Lavender (fresh or dried)	beverages, fruit, poultry, preserves, sauces, sweets
Marjoram (fresh or dried)	eggs, fish, legumes, meat, mushrooms, soups
Mint (fresh)	beverages, fruit, lamb, peas, potatoes, salads
Nutmeg*	custard, eggs, meat, potatoes, sauces, soups, sweets
Oregano* (fresh or dried)	chicken, meat, pasta, soups, tomatoes

Paprika,* regular, smoked, or Hungarian	casseroles, garnish, meat, sauces, soups
Parsley (fresh)	garnish, salads, salsas, sauces
Red pepper flakes*	almost everything, to add heat
Rosemary* (fresh or dried)	chicken, fish, grains, meat, mushrooms, potatoes, stews
Sage (fresh or dried)	cheese, meat, poultry, sauces, soups, stuffing, vegetables
Savory, winter or summer (fresh or dried)	corn, green beans, legumes, potatoes, stuffing
Salt*	almost everything, to enhance flavor
Tarragon (fresh)	asparagus, butter, carrots, cream sauces, eggs, fish, green beans, peas, salads, vinaigrette
Thyme* (fresh or dried)	clam chowder, eggs, fish, meat, mushrooms, potatoes, poultry, soups, stews, vegetables

* Part of the recommended top 20 for your kitchen (p. 8).
Herbs followed by (fresh) are best used fresh, not dried.
Herbs followed by (fresh or dried) retain their flavor either way.

INDEX

MEASUREMENTS AND EQUIVALENTS

MEASUREMENT	EQUIVALENT
1 pound dried beans	2 to 2-1/2 cups, or 5-1/2 to 6 cups cooked
1 cup dried beans	2 to 3 cups cooked
1 cup dried lentils	3 cups cooked
1 cup dried split peas	2-1/2 cups cooked
1 (14 to 15-ounce) can beans	1-1/2 to 1-3/4 cups (drained)
1 cup grain (rice, quinoa, or millet)	3 to 3-1/2 cups cooked
1 pound shelled nuts	3-1/2 to 4 cups
1 egg yolk	About 1 tablespoon (based on large egg)
1 egg white	About 2 tablespoons (based on large egg)
1 (4-ounce) stick butter	1/2 cup, or 8 tablespoons

HOW TO CUT DOWN A RECIPE		
ORIGINAL	HALF THE AMOUNT	ONE THIRD THE AMOUNT
1 cup	1/2 cup	1/3 cup
3/4 cup	6 tablespoons, or 1/4 cup + 2 tablespoons	1/4 cup
2/3 cup	1/3 cup	3-1/2 tablespoons
1/2 cup	1/4 cup	2 tablespoons + 2 teaspoons
1/3 cup	2 tablespoons + 2 teaspoons	5 teaspoons + 1/3* teaspoon
1/4 cup	2 tablespoons, or 1/8 cup	1 tablespoon + 1 teaspoon
1 tablespoon	1-1/2 teaspoons	1 teaspoon
1 teaspoon	1/2 teaspoon	1/3 teaspoon*
1/2 teaspoon	1/4 teaspoon	1/8 teaspoon

* You will not a have measuring spoon for 1/3 teaspoon, so just eyeball it with a heaping 1/4 teaspoon or a scant 1/2 teaspoon.

MEASUREMENT	EQUIVALENT	ALTERNATE/NOTES
Pinch	1/16 teaspoon	Amount you can "pinch" and hold between your thumb and index finger
Dash	1/8 teaspoon	Amount that comes out of a small bottle like hot sauce, when you turn in upside down and give it a shake or squeeze
1/3 tablespoon	1 teaspoon	5 milliliters
1/2 tablespoon	1 and 1/2 teaspoons	Usually written as 1-1/2, or 1 1/2
1 tablespoon	3 teaspoons	15 milliliters
1/8 cup	2 tablespoons	1 ounce (liquid)
1/4 cup	4 tablespoons	2 ounces (liquid)
1/3 cup	16 teaspoons (5 tablespoons + 1 teaspoon)	2.6 ounces (liquid)
1/2 cup	8 tablespoons	4 ounces (liquid)
1 cup	16 tablespoons	8 ounces (liquid)
2 cups	1 pint	16 ounces (liquid)
2 pints	1 quart	32 ounces (liquid)
4 quarts	1 gallon	128 ounces
16 ounces	1 pound	Dry ingredient or liquid
1 ounce	30 milliliters	
750 milliliters	About 25 ounces	Amount in wine bottle
1 liter	About 34 ounces	
1 gram	100 milligrams	

Grams and ounces are measurements for weight, so the physical amount varies unless it's a liquid. If your recipe calls for a dry ingredient by weight, use a scale (or do an online search for approximate conversions). Our website, finitefoodie.com, can convert recipes to metric.

TERM	ABBREVIATIONS
Teaspoon(s)	tsp., t.
Tablespoon(s)	Tbs., Tbsp., tbsp., T.
Cup(s)	c.
Ounce(s)	oz.

Pound(s)	lb. (casual plural is lbs.)
Liter(s)	l.
Milliliter(s)	ml.
Gram(s)	g.
Milligram(s)	mg.